International and Development Education

The *International and Development Education Series* focuses on the complementary areas of comparative, international, and development education. These books emphasize a number of topics ranging from key international education issues, trends, and reforms to examinations of national education systems, social theories, and development education initiatives. Local, national, regional, and global volumes (single authored and edited collections) constitute the breadth of the series and offer potential contributors a great deal of latitude based on their interests and cutting-edge research. The series is supported by a strong network of international scholars and development professionals who serve on the International and Development Education Advisory Board and participate in the selection and review process for manuscript development.

SERIES EDITORS
John N. Hawkins
Professor Emeritus, University of California, Los Angeles
Senior consultant, IFE 2020 East West Center

W. James Jacob
Assistant professor, University of Pittsburgh
Director, Institute for International Studies in Education

PRODUCTION EDITOR
Heejin Park
Project associate, Institute for International Studies in Education

INTERNATIONAL EDITORIAL ADVISORY BOARD
Clementina Acedo, *UNESCO's International Bureau of Education, Switzerland*
Philip G. Altbach, *Boston University, USA*
Carlos E. Blanco, *Universidad Central de Venezuela*
Sheng Yao Cheng, *National Chung Cheng University, Taiwan*
Ruth Hayhoe, *University of Toronto, Canada*
Wanhua Ma, *Peking University, China*
Ka-Ho Mok, *University of Hong Kong, China*
Christine Musselin, *Sciences Po, France*
Yusuf K. Nsubuga, *Ministry of Education and Sports, Uganda*
Namgi Park, *Gwangju National University of Education, Republic of Korea*
Val D. Rust, *University of California, Los Angeles, USA*
Suparno, *State University of Malang, Indonesia*
John C. Weidman, *University of Pittsburgh, USA*
Husam Zaman, *Taibah University, Saudi Arabia*

Institute for International Studies in Education
School of Education, University of Pittsburgh
5714 Wesley W. Posvar Hall, Pittsburgh, PA 15260 USA

Center for International and Development Education
Graduate School of Education & Information Studies, University of California, Los Angeles
Box 951521, Moore Hall, Los Angeles, CA 90095 USA

Titles:

Higher Education in Asia/Pacific: Quality and the Public Good
Edited by Terance W. Bigalke and Deane E. Neubauer

Affirmative Action in China and the U.S.: A Dialogue on Inequality and Minority Education
Edited by Minglang Zhou and Ann Maxwell Hill

Critical Approaches to Comparative Education: Vertical Case Studies from Africa, Europe, the Middle East, and the Americas
Edited by Frances Vavrus and Lesley Bartlett

Curriculum Studies in South Africa: Intellectual Histories & Present Circumstances
Edited by William F. Pinar

Higher Education, Policy, and the Global Competition Phenomenon
Edited by Laura M. Portnoi, Val D. Rust, and Sylvia S. Bagley

The Search for New Governance of Higher Education in Asia
Edited by Ka-Ho Mok

International Students and Global Mobility in Higher Education: National Trends and New Directions
Edited by Rajika Bhandari and Peggy Blumenthal

Curriculum Studies in Brazil: Intellectual Histories, Present Circumstances
Edited by William F. Pinar

Access, Equity, and Capacity in Asia Pacific Higher Education
Edited by Deane Neubauer and Yoshiro Tanaka

Policy Debates in Comparative, International, and Development Education
Edited by John N. Hawkins and W. James Jacob

Increasing Effectiveness of the Community College Financial Model: A Global Perspective for the Global Economy
Edited by Stewart E. Sutin, Daniel Derrico, Rosalind Latiner Raby, and Edward J. Valeau

Curriculum Studies in Mexico: Intellectual Histories, Present Circumstances
William F. Pinar

Internationalization of East Asian Higher Education: Globalization's Impact
John D. Palmer

Taiwan Education at the Crossroad: When Globalization Meets Localization
Chuing Prudence Chou and Gregory Ching

Mobility and Migration in Asian Pacific Higher Education
Edited by Deane E. Neubauer and Kazuo Kuroda

Forthcoming titles:

University Governance and Reform: Policy, Fads, and Experience in International Perspective
Edited by Hans G. Schuetze, William Bruneau, and Garnet Grosjean

Post-Secondary Education and Technology: A Global Perspective on Opportunities and Obstacles to Development
Edited by Rebecca A. Clothey, Stacy Austin-Li, and John C. Weidman

TAIWAN EDUCATION AT THE CROSSROAD

WHEN GLOBALIZATION MEETS LOCALIZATION

AUTHORS

CHUING PRUDENCE CHOU 周祝瑛
GREGORY CHING 莊俊儒

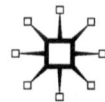

TAIWAN EDUCATION AT THE CROSSROAD.
Copyright © Chuing Prudence Chou, Gregory Ching, 2012.
All rights reserved.
First published in 2012 by
PALGRAVE MACMILLAN®
in the United States—a division of St. Martin's Press LLC,
175 Fifth Avenue, New York, NY 10010.

Where this book is distributed in the UK, Europe and the rest of the world, this is by Palgrave Macmillan, a division of Macmillan Publishers Limited, registered in England, company number 785998, of Houndmills, Basingstoke, Hampshire RG21 6XS.

Palgrave Macmillan is the global academic imprint of the above companies and has companies and representatives throughout the world.

Palgrave® and Macmillan® are registered trademarks in the United States, the United Kingdom, Europe and other countries.

ISBN: 978–0–230–11089–2

Library of Congress Cataloging-in-Publication Data is available from the Library of Congress.

A catalogue record of the book is available from the British Library.

Design by Newgen Imaging Systems (P) Ltd., Chennai, India.

First edition: July 2012

Contents

List of Figures and Tables	vii
Preface	ix
Series Editors' Introduction	xvii
Acknowledgments	xix
List of Acronyms and Abbreviations	xxi

1	Globalization Versus Localization: Notion or Reality in Taiwan?	1
2	Taiwan's Country Profile	11
3	Historical Overview of Education in Taiwan	21
4	East Asian and Taiwan Education in the Context of Worldwide Education Reform	47
5	The Taiwan Education System	67
6	Course, Curriculum, and Textbooks	89
7	Budget Allocation Features	99
8	Structure of Preschool, Primary, and Secondary Education	115
9	Higher Education	163
10	New University Funding, Flexible Salaries, and a Quality Assurance Scheme	183
11	World-Class Research University Project	195
12	Internationalization Efforts of Taiwan's Higher Education Institutions	205

13	Globalization and the Issue of Academic Publishing (the SSCI and the SCI)	221
14	Influx of International Students into Taiwan	243
15	Reform Schemes for Students in Need	257
16	Cross-Strait Relationships between Taiwan and China	263
17	Conclusion	275

Index   289

Figures and Tables

Figures

3.1	The Framework for Education Reform 1996	41
5.1	The Current School System in Taiwan	74
17.1	Blueprint of Future Education Development	282

Tables

7.1	Educational Expenditure per Student in Taiwan	102
8.1	A Sample Grade 6 Class Schedule in Primary School	128
8.2	A Sample Grade 7 Class Schedule in Junior High School	133
8.3	The Typical Senior High School Course and Credit Distribution Outline	147
8.4	A Sample Grade 10 Class Schedule in Senior High School	149
8.5	A Weekly After-School Schedule of an Average High School Student	151
8.6	Regional Discrepancies in High School Students' Performance on PISA	157
9.1	Higher Education Expansion in Taiwan	175
14.1	Reasons for Choosing Taiwan as a Destination (N=648)	248

Preface

The Era of Globalization

We, as human beings, are at the crossroad of development. The trend of globalization has brought us limitless possibilities in terms of communication and information, and yet globalization has also brought devastating consequences to humans and nature that at times seem to be out of control. Wth the arrival of the information era, along with the arrival of the Internet and many more new technologies, such as the cloud network and iPads, our education content and teachers are often strained at the crossroad, confronting the unexpected challenges and struggles that our students face and also present to us.

What choices and options do we have? What direction should we choose in order to cope with this overwhelming global phenomenon? Perhaps we can learn from an ancient Confucian saying: Singing and having fun with your friends will foster "social trust," and consequently, this will lead to social harmony (Bell 2008). But does this belief still hold true in this highly competitive global era? How can education continue to make a difference when people are encountering this world of uncertainty?

The intent of this book is to examine the processes of schooling in Taiwan amid the social, cultural, economic, and political conflicts resulting from local and global dilemmas and issues. The book opens with an introductory chapter detailing recent worldwide phenomena in education, i.e., globalization and localization, followed by chapters that showcase the different perspectives on Taiwan's unique education system. The book's underlying thesis is that the mechanisms of both localization and globalization have led to the issues and dilemmas that Taiwan's educational system now faces. These phenomena also relate to governance, financing, the provision of mass education, issues of equitable educational opportunities, and outcomes for differently situated social groups. They are also defined as common dilemmas endemic to school environments everywhere, and represent global challenges of the twenty-first century that have in one way or another transformed the lives of almost everyone.

The education system in Taiwan, similar to other education systems in East Asia, has undergone an enormous transformation over the last two decades. Education has become interconnected with trends of globalization and internationalization, the development of information communications technology, and a set of political, sociological, economic, and managerial changes. These shifts together have produced multifaceted influences that have an impact on the education system in Taiwan. In particular, the forces of globalization and localization in recent decades have acted as the driving policy agendas in Taiwan. The notion of globalization encompasses a plethora of meanings. According to Mok and Lee (2000, 362), globalization is "the processes that are not only confined to an ever-growing interconnectedness and interdependency among different countries in the economic sphere but also to tighter interactions and interconnections in social, political and cultural realms." Governments in Taiwan have endeavored to follow the trend of globalization, especially in education.

Nations' moves towards globalization and internationalization have caused a striking transformation in the character and function of education not only in East Asian countries but also throughout the world (Burbules and Torres 2000; Mok and Welch 2003; Mok 2006). In addition, globalization processes have increased the broad and steady circulation of individual goods and services, and also of people(s) and their cultural norms and values (Hershock et al. 2007). Similarly, changes in the nation-state's international relations coupled with advancements in information technology, the expansion of business and commerce, and increasing mobility in the workplace are undoubtedly placing greater demands on higher education (Neubauer 2007). In the last decade, these events have become even more critical, requiring higher education to respond in an intentional and comprehensive way (Siaya and Hayward 2003).

Globalization and Internationalization

Since the early 2000s, the term "globalization" has grown in popularity not only in Europe and North America but in East Asia as well (Teichler 2004). Friedman (2005) mentioned that globalization in our age started with the fall of the Berlin Wall and the launch of the Worldwide Web in 1989. Many people have discussed the impact of globalization on the economic, social, political, and cultural fronts for the past two decades (Giddens 1990, 1999; Robertson 1995; Sklair 1995). In fact, there is no generally agreed upon definition of globalization (Mok 2000). It is, rather, viewed more as a paradigm shift—a move from separation to integration, from heterogeneity to homogeneity (Robertson 1995; Friedman 2000).

Globalization is a multidimensional term (Levin 1999). Commonly, globalization is defined as the closer integration of the countries and peoples of the world, brought about by the enormous reduction in costs of transportation and communications, and the breaking down of artificial barriers to the flows of goods, services, capital, knowledge, and people across borders (Stiglitz 2002). It also refers to the process and consequences of instantaneous communication and advanced technology, which have generated tremendous growth in the quantity of information and the degree integration (Grunzweig and Rinehart 2002). While academic systems and institutions may accommodate these trends in different ways, the overall impact on the educational sector is unavoidable. Globalization, as it applies to higher education, involves information technology and the use of a common language for scientific communication (Altbach 2005; Mok and Welch 2003).

Globalization also includes the broad, largely inevitable economic, technological, political, cultural, and scientific trends that directly affect higher education (Altbach 2005). Consequently, this trend has had a strong impact on higher education, because it influences what universities must teach in order to prepare students for their professional lives (Currie and Newson 1998; Currie et al. 2003). In effect, the rapidly changing world requires students to possess broad international knowledge and strong intercultural and social skills, in addition to the more traditional disciplinary knowledge from a university education (Paige 2005).

Along with the process of globalization, internationalization has also become an important concern in the development of higher education. Kerr (1990) mentioned that internationalization is perceived as one of the laws of motion propelling higher-education institutions (HEIs). In fact, internationalization has been a major issue of the past half century (Altbach 2000). It is also one of the most important trends in higher education of the last decade (Teichler 1999), and it will definitely be one of the major themes for the next decade (Davies 1997). In essence, internationalization is part of the fundamentals of HEIs as universities encounter the era of globalization (Scott 1998).

Typically, internationalization is defined as the creation of an environment that is international in character, whether in teaching or in research. It also includes the exposure of students to the cultures and languages of different countries (Paige 2005). In addition, it should also include the policies and programs adopted by governments, and by academic systems as well as departments to cope with or to exploit globalization, thus allowing institutions significant autonomy, initiative, and creativity in dealing with the new milieu (Altbach 2005).

Internationalization at the national, sector, and institutional levels is defined as the process of integrating an international, intercultural, or global dimension into the purpose, functions, or delivery of higher education (Knight 2004). Expanding the definition further, Ellingboe (1998) added that internationalization is the ongoing process of integrating an international perspective into HEIs. It should encompass a multidimensional, interdisciplinary, and future-oriented leadership vision, which involves the many stakeholders of an institution, in order to respond and adapt appropriately to the increasingly diverse and global environment. Hence, the many definitions and dimensions of internationalization is further evidence for its continual discussion in the literature and to the complexity of agreeing upon any single definition.

Comparatively speaking, globalization and internationalization are similar in two respects. Both issues tend to drive the traditional closed system of higher education towards a more open and complex system and to pose a challenge for higher education to change its context and structure (Knight 1997; van der Wende 2001; Teichler 2004). Yet these two forces contrast with respect to their implications. Globalization tends to trigger the blurring or even the disappearance of national borders and economic systems (Ohmae 1990), while internationalization tends to address increased (physical) cross-border activities within national systems of higher education (Teichler 2004; Mok 2006).

Responding to Globalization

In the context of Taiwan, neither higher education nor primary and secondary education can avoid the impact of globalization. Currently, there are around seventeen international schools in Taiwan, which include not only schools that serve primarily foreign expatriates' children but also Catholic and Protestant schools, which mostly offer curricula for primary and secondary education. Bilingual schools and classes, mostly for local students, also represent new trends in fulfilling the needs of global mobility.

In higher education, a sudden influx of international students into Taiwan's HEIs has been clearly evident. For example, in 2011, the total number of students from abroad enrolled at Taiwan universities and technical colleges studying for degrees, learning Mandarin, or participating in exchange programs was approximately forty-five thousand, according to the Ministry of Higher Education (MOE) (Taiwan Today 2011a). The majority of international students study business, Chinese literature, history, or social science, and less than one-fifth study engineering (MOE 2010–2011).

In order to attract more degree-seeking students from abroad, Taiwan launched a four-year NT$5.68 billion (US$196 million) plan in May 2011, in the hope of increasing education-sector competitiveness, improving the learning environment for international students, and promoting Taiwan's higher-education credentials (Taiwan Today 2011b). The rationale behind this policy, in addition to the motive of enhancing university internationalization, is also due to the drastically declining birthrate in Taiwan, whose annual enrollment rate of university students will drop from 320,000 per year to around 270,000 by 2016. The MOE anticipates that international students will comprise 10 percent of the total higher education population (from 130,000 to 140,000 students) by 2020 (Taiwan Today 2011a).

The Cross-Strait Paradigm: Beyond Globalization and Localization

Related to the trends of cooperation between China and Taiwan within the last decade, an official treaty of Economic Cooperation Framework Agreement (ECFA) has recently been signed for Taiwan to reach out to the international community in the light of China (Sharma 2010). The treaty also works as a threshold to the ongoing cross-strait relations for the further development and ripening of regional exchanges, in terms of diplomatic relations, economic expansion, technology enhancement and, last but not least, education between China and Taiwan.

It is worth noting that the authors here attempt to present a unique notion of the *cross-straitization* of education along with a discussion of globalization and localization. Like many other states that have experienced political and social conflicts, Taiwan was faced with issues of identity during the Japanese colonization period (1895–1945), which was followed by re-Sinicization after World War II, and the de-Sinicization era under the Lee and Chen regimes (1988–2008). The constant struggle of Taiwan for a national identity goes beyond the conflicts encountered between globalization and localization due to troublesome cross-strait relations. Nevertheless, unlike other countries in conflict such as the former East and West Germany, North and South Korea, Israel and the Arab world, and even the United States and the Soviet Union, Taiwan and China through the *cross-strait paradigm*, have, quite uniquely, developed ongoing cultural and educational exchanges, in particular as a result of increasing economic cooperation since the 1990s. In this process, through interaction with traditional Chinese culture, the country as a whole and its intellectuals shaped a national identity that is not only multifaceted and dynamic, but is also emerging with some uncertainty in Taiwan. It will be worthwhile to see how education in general affects the shaping of the national identity while encountering multifaceted forces from globalization and localization (Wilde 2005).

In conclusion, contemporary efforts in Taiwan education are seen as an exemplar for the shifting of ideas about globalization and localization. In retrospect, all reform programs adopted in Taiwan's education system have led to major changes inside and outside the academic arena. The question still exists whether academia and the public will be able to embrace such changes and adapt, or whether they will resist and fight back. Such issues remain for all of us to see, as the educational paradox of the twenty-first century continues to elude everyone. It is also interesting to see whether or not the ongoing relationships between Taiwan and China will go beyond the existing framework of globalization and localization and develop into their own unique model as "cross-straitization," which prioritizes cultural and educational exchanges and then creates more acceptable ways of communication based on mutual respect and understanding. Many answers are yet to be realized, but, hopefully, with this book, readers may find some inspiration out of these questions.

References

Altbach, Philip G. 2000. "What Higher Education Does Right." *International Higher Education* 18 (Winter): 2–3.

———. 2005. "Globalization and the University: Myths and Realities in an Unequal World." In *The NEA 2005 Almanac of Higher Education*. Washington, DC: National Education Association 63–74.

Bell, Daniel A. 2008. *China's New Confucianism: Politics and Everyday Life in a Changing Society*. Princeton, NJ: Princeton University Press.

Burbules, Nicholas C., and Carlos A. Torres, eds. 2000. *Globalization and Education: Critical Perspectives*. London: Routledge.

Currie, J., R. DeAngelis, H. de Boer, J. Huisman, and C. Lacotte. 2003. *Globalizing Practices and University Responses: European and Anglo-American Differences*. Westport, CT: Praeger.

Currie, Janice K., and Janice Newson, eds. 1998. *Universities and Globalization: Critical Perspectives*. Thousand Oaks, CA: Sage.

Davies, John L. 1997. "A European Agenda for Change for Higher Education in the XXIst Century: Comparative Analysis of Twenty Institutional Case Studies." *CRE-Action* 111: 47–92.

Ellingboe, Brenda J. 1998. "Divisional Strategies to Internationalize a Campus Portrait: Results, Resistance, and Recommendations from a Case Study at a U.S. University." In *Reforming the Higher Education Curriculum: Internationalizing the Campus*, edited by J. A. Mestenhauser and B. J. Ellingboe, 198–228. Washington, DC: American Council on Education.

Friedman, Thomas. 2000. *The Lexus and the Olive Tree*. New York: Farrar, Straus & Giroux.

———. 2005. *The World Is Flat: A Brief History of the Twenty-First Century*. New York: Farrar, Straus & Giroux.

Giddens, Anthony. 1990. *The Consequences of Modernity*. Cambridge, UK: Polity Press.

———. 1999. *Runaway World*. London: Profile Books Limited.

Grunzweig, W., and N. Rinehart, eds. 2002. *Rocking in Red Square: Critical Approaches to International Education in the Age of Cyberculture*. Berlin: LIT Verlag.

Hershock, Peter D., Mark Mason, and John N. Hawkins, eds. 2007. *Changing Education—Leadership Innovation and Development in a Globalizing Asia Pacific*. Hong Kong: Comparative Education Research Centre-Springer.

Kerr, Clark. 1990. "The Internationalisation of Learning and the Nationalisation of the Purposes of Higher Education: Two 'Laws of Motion' in Conflict?" *European Journal of Education* 25: 5–22.

Knight, Jane. 1997. "Internationalisation of Higher Education: A Conceptual Framework." In *Internationalisation of Higher Education in Asia Pacific Countries*, edited by Jane Knight and Hans de Wit. Amsterdam: European Association of International Education.

———. 2004. "Internationalization Remodeled: Definition, Approaches, and Rationales." *Journal of Studies in International Education* 8 (1): 5–31.

Levin, John S. 1999. "Missions and Structures: Bringing Clarity to Perceptions about Globalization and Higher Education in Canada." *Higher Education* 37: 377–399.

Ministry of Education (MOE). 2010–2011. Education in Taiwan. Taipei: MOE. Availale online at: http://www.gio.gov.tw.

Mok, Ka Ho. 2000. "Reflecting Globalization Effects on Local Policy: Higher Education Reform in Taiwan." *Journal of Education Policy* 15 (6): 637–660.

———. 2006. "Questing for Internationalization of Universities in East Asia: Critical Reflections." Paper prepented at the International Symposium, Osaka, Japan, January 13–14.

Mok, Ka Ho, and Hiu-Hong Lee. 2000. "Globalization or Re-Colonization: Higher Education Reforms in Hong Kong." *Higher Education Policy* 13: 361–377.

Mok, Ka Ho, and Anthony Welch, eds. 2003. *Globalization and Educational Restructuring in the Asia Pacific Region*. Basingstoke, UK: Palgrave Macmillan.

Neubauer, Deane. 2007. "Globalization and Education—Characteristics, Dynamics, Implications." In *Changing Education—Leadership Innovation and Development in a Globalizing Asia Pacific*, edited by Peter D. Hershock, Mark Mason and John N. Hawkins, 29–62. Hong Kong: Comparative Education Research Centre; Springer.

Ohmae, Kenichi. 1990. *The Borderless World: Power and Strategy in the Interlinked World Economy*. New York: Harper Business.
Paige, Michael R. 2005. "Internationalization of Higher Education: Performance Assessment and Indicators." *Nagoya Journal of Higher Education* 5: 99–122.
Robertson, Roland. 1995. "Globalization: Time-Space and Homogeneity-Heterogeneity." In *Global Modernities*, edited by M. Featherstone, S. Lash, and R. Robertson, 25–44. London: Sage Publications.
Scott, Peter. 1998. "Massification, Internationalization and Globalization." In *The Globalization of Higher Education*, edited by P. Scott, 42–55. Buckingham, UK: SRHE and Open University Press.
Sharma, Shalendra D. 2010. "Taiwan Takes On China...and Wins." *Global Asia* 5(4). Available online at: http://www.globalasia.org.
Siaya, Laura, and Fred M. Hayward. 2003. *Mapping Internationalization on U.S. Campuses*. Washington, DC: American Council on Education.
Sklair, Leslie. 1995. *Sociology of the Global System*. Baltimore, MD: John Hopkins University Press.
Stiglitz, Joseph E. 2002. *Globalization and Its Discontents*. New York: W. W. Norton.
Taiwan Today. 2011a. *MOE Recruitment Drive Lands Overseas Students*. Taipei: Government Information Office. December 6. Available online at: http://www.taiwantoday.tw.
Taiwan Today. 2011b. *Taiwan's Cabinet OKs Higher Education Development Plan*. Taipei: Government Information Office. December 6. Available online at: http://www.taiwantoday.tw.
Teichler, Ulrich. 1999. "Internationalisation as a Challenge for Higher Education in Europe." *Tertiary Education and Management* 5: 5–23.
———. 2004. "The Changing Debate on Internationalisation of Higher Education." *Higher Education* 48: 5–26.
van der Wende, Marijk C. 2001. "Internationalisation Policies: About New Trends and Contrasting Paradigms." *Higher Education Policy* 14 (3): 249–259.
Wilde, Stephanie. 2005. *Political and Citizenship Education*. Oxford, UK: Symposium Books.

Series Editors' Introduction

Taiwan's economic achievements have been impressive over the past few globalization decades, and this is true of its educational system as well. It is a complex and complicated story and one told well by Chuing Prudence Chou and Gregory Ching. We are pleased to be able to welcome their study into our series on comparative and development education. The authors trace the history of these achievements in the context of globalization and localization in a way that sets Taiwan in the context of the broader economic and educational development of East Asia. The historical context occupies a significant portion of the study, and rightly so, as it is this history that defines Taiwan's place among its more powerful and larger neighbors. Once the discussion turns to the nuts and bolts of the education system, the treatment is detailed and analytical. The statistical and curricular background is discussed along with specifics of teacher education, the "shadow" educational system (*buxiban*), and the various levels of schooling. Much attention is paid to Taiwan's impressive growth in higher education and quest for world-class university status. Throughout this discussion the interplay between global forces and factors and local needs is apparent and skillfully woven into the discussion. Not all is as it seems, especially with respect to capacity and access issues. Some may not know that Taiwan seems to be in the enviable position of being able to offer a seat in a postsecondary institution to any student who might want one; in other words, higher education enrollment and capacity for enrollment is near 100 percent. Yet, there is great diversity and differentiation in the system, and the quality of many of the institutions has recently been called into question. Quality assurance, accreditation, and accountability are all issues that are very much in the forefront of the higher education discussion in Taiwan, at both the ministry level and institutional levels. Difficult decisions will have to be made on both levels if Taiwan is to proceed into the twenty-first century in a competitive and distinctive fashion. Critical to all of this will be cross-strait relations with China. This too the authors discuss, thus rounding out a well-conceived book that will be useful for students and scholars of Taiwan as well as the East Asia region as a whole.

JOHN N. HAWKINS
University of California, Los Angeles

W. JAMES JACOB
University of Pittsburgh

Acknowledgments

For centuries, Taiwan was referred to, especially in the West, as Formosa. It has been renowned for its breathtaking natural scenery, and its miraculous economic development earned it the title of one of only four Asian Tigers. In the mid-sixteenth century, when their ships passed through the Taiwan Straits, the Portuguese were astounded at the forested island, and said, "Ilha Formosa," which means "Beautiful Island." And this was the first encounter of many between the Western world and Taiwan.

After 1949, Taiwan became one of the main shelters for the mainland Chinese who left to escape the communist occupation. More than 1.2 million Chinese civilians, government officials, and military troops relocated from mainland China to Taiwan. Over the next five decades (1949–2000), the ruling authorities gradually democratized and incorporated the local Taiwanese within the governing structure that existed at the time. In 2000 and 2008, Taiwan underwent its two peaceful transfers of power between the Nationalists and the Democratic Progressive Party (DPP). The island has prospered and become one of East Asia's economic "Little Tigers" since the 1970s. The dominant political issues across the island remain the question of eventual unification with mainland China, or whether to try to maintain a "live-and-let-live" status (or the status quo) regardless of differences. Moreover, as a result of more and more interaction as well cooperation that has been taking place among all societal sectors, the education system in Taiwan, similar to other education systems in East Asia, has undergone an enormous transformation over the last two decades. Education has become interwoven with the trends of globalization and localization, along with the development of information and communications technology, after a series of social changes.

These changes altogether have produced multifaceted influences on education in Taiwan. In particular, the trends of globalization and localization represent not only one of the driving policy agendas in Taiwan but also the origin of education reforms over the last two decades on the island. Even more importantly, these shifts have generated a "cross-strait" relationship between Taiwan-China, which will eventually drive education reforms to levels yet to be attained. It is also worth noting that Taiwan's overall education development coincides with the great transformation that many countries have experienced due to this globalization/localization convergence, coupled with the impact of neoliberal principles worldwide since the 1980s. This is the reason why the authors here tend to share a common approach to presenting Taiwan's education system to the world as an ideal testimony to how an educational restructuring process can take place in response to the nature of market economy competition. They also demonstrate how Taiwan is setting an example for its counterparts, which have also undergone and therefore struggled with the bewildering forces of globalization and localization in the twenty-first century. Alongside the cross-strait trends mentioned above, there exist several parallel and in contrasting scenarios with the competing forces between the two Chinas, similar to what was once found in the former West and East Germany and as can currently be found between and North and South Korea.

I would like to give special thanks to Professor John Hawkins, who not only initiated this book project but also has played a role as a lifelong mentor to me in the field of China Studies and Comparative Education, and Professor W. James Jacob, who contributed his time and advice on editing throughout the whole process. The continuing support and input of my coauthor, Dr. Gregory Ching, helped me break through the obstacle of putting ideas into words. Also, colleagues from the Ministry of Education, such as former Minister Dr. Ching-ji Wu, and Deputy Minister Dr.Yi-hsing Chen, as well as Professor Yueh-Luen Hu and many more from the NCCU Department of Education have provided me with generous information and support in the course of writing. I am also indebted to my assistants, Iris Lai, Candy Lu, and Mauricio A. Molina, who have assisted tirelessly to make this book possible from scratch over the last three years. My beloved family, Dr. Ying-yu Ian, Hao and Ying Chen, and Chou Won gave me their unconditional support in my pursuit of academic curiosity as I unraveled issues, as Professor Ruth Hayhoe effectively illustrates in her paper entitled "A Chinese Puzzle," over the last two decades. I am also grateful to the National Science Council in Taiwan for its financial support.

CHUING PRUDENCE CHOU (周祝瑛)
Xin-dien, New Taipei City, Taiwan
February 1, 2012 (Year of the Dragon)

Dedicated to my father, J. T. Hu (胡金台, 1932–2005), and father-in-law, Y. S. Chen (陳宇樹, 1923–2003), who went through and witnessed the transformation of Taiwan's education over their lifetimes.

Acronyms and Abbreviations

A&HCI	Arts & Humanities Citation Index
ACE	American Council for Education
AFTA	Association of Southeast Asian Nations [ASEAN] Free Trade Area
APEC	Asia-Pacific Economic Cooperation
ARF	Asian Regional Fund
ASEM	Asia European Meeting
ATU Plan	Aiming for the Top University and Elite Research Center Development Plan
AUCC	Association of Universities and Colleges of Canada
BCTEST	Basic Competence Test for Junior High School Students
CES	Civic Education Study
CYCU	Chung Yuan Christian University
DGBAS	Nation's Chief Statisticians and Accountants
DPP	Democratic Progressive Party
ECFA	Economic Cooperation Framework Agreement
EI	Engineering Index
ESI	Essential Science Indicators
ESL	English As the Second Language
ESP	English for Specific Purposes
FY	Fiscal Year
GATS	General Agreement on Trade in Services
GDP	Gross Domestic Product
GEPT	General English Proficiency Test
GSAT	General Scholastic Ability Test
HEEACT	Higher Education Evaluation and Accreditation Council of Taiwan
HEI/HEIs	Higher Education Institution / Higher Education Institutions
IAU	International Association of Universities
IEA	International Association for the Evaluation of Educational Achievement
IMF	International Monetary Fund

ISI	International Statistical Institute
ISI WOS	ISI Web of Science
JUEE	Joint University Entrance Examination
KMT	Kuomingtang
MOE	Ministry of Education
MOFA	Ministry of Foreign Affairs
MSCHE	American Middle States Commission on Higher Education
NAPCU	National Association for the Promotion of Community Universities
NCCU	National Cheng-Chi University
NCKU	National Cheng Kung University
NCTU	National Chiao Tung University
NGOs	Nongovernmental Organizations
NICT	National Institute for Compilation and Translation
NSC	National Science Council
NSF	National Science Foundation
NTA	National Teachers' Association ROC
NTHU	National Tsing Hua University
NTNU	National Taiwan Normal University
NTU	National Taiwan University
OECD	Organisation for Economic Co-operation and Development
PDCA	Plan-Do-Check-Act
PDFURC	Plan to Develop First-class Universities and Top-level Research Centers
PISA	Programme for International Student Assessment
PPAE	Program for Promoting Academic Excellence in Universities
PPP	Purchasing Power Parity
PRC	People's Republic of China
PTA	Parent-Teacher Association
R&D	Research and Development
RCI	Relative Citation Index
SCI	Science Citation Index
SJTU	Shanghai Jiao Tong University
SSCI	Social Science Citation Index
STEM	Science, Technology, Engineering and Mathematics
SWOT	Strengths, Weaknesses, Opportunities, and Threats
TCSL	Teaching Chinese as Second/Foreign Language
TCTE	Testing Center for Technological and Vocational Education
TEPS	Taiwan Education Panel Survey
TIMSS	The Trends in International Mathematics and Science Study
TOEIC	Test of English for International Communication
TSSCI	Taiwan Social Sciences Citation Index

TVE	Technological and Vocational Education
TWAEA	Taiwan Assessment and Evaluation Association
UDRT	University Department Required Test
UNICEF	United Nations Children's Fund
UNESCO	United Nations Educational, Scientific and Cultural Organization
WB	World Bank
WTO	World Trade Organization

Chapter 1

Globalization Versus Localization: Notion or Reality in Taiwan?

Though it is often seen as "global Westernization" and a continuation of Western imperialism, globalization's contribution to the world is unquestionable and the term does not have to imply dominance by the West (Sen 2002). The West has been much influenced by other parts of the world as well, such as the importation of exotic goods and the emerging popularity of second language learning in schools. Under the tremendous impact of globalization, the idea of localization sprouted to protect each country's workforce and traditions, which is achieved by promoting local goods and traditional activities, not to mention endorsing a national spirit through various kinds of campaigns, major celebrations, and educational activities. After all, differences among cultures exist without question. The world is becoming smaller, and the processes of economic and social changes throughout the world, facilitated by the West, are separating people from their longstanding local identities (Huntington 1993); therefore, it is only natural for cultures around the world to enhance their own identity, which makes them stand out from others.

Globalization is a trend that has been rapidly making its presence felt throughout the world for the last few decades. It is especially marked by the emergence of corporate giants, global partnerships, and the exchange of ideas and products around the world. Globalization has also made an enormous impact on the culture and economy of different countries, such as in the exchange of food and plants, international trade, academic exchanges, and language learning. Not only has it drastically influenced the economy of many countries by expanding the labor market and increasing the sources of raw materials and products, it has also changed the form of education by introducing new courses such as foreign languages, and programs such as academic exchanges that seem so familiar to us today.

According to Hermans and Dimaggio (2007), globalization is a trend that promotes boundary crossing and leads to international and intercultural connectedness and exchange, while localization, in contrast, consists of the sets of customs or practices emerging from particular places, regions, or countries. Rather than being two conflicting concepts, these forces coexist and fuel each other. Taiwan is no exception to this phenomenon, and the process of globalization and localization can be easily observed in its education system today, because it not only actively reaches out in the foreign language and exchange context but also deals with many cultural features that are local in nature.

As the world transforms into a knowledge-based economy, together with the unprecedented forces of globalization, the education system of each country has become one of the national imperatives for international competitiveness. However, the impact of globalization on education has generated mixed results. On the one hand, the Internet and scientific communities have created a new world full of easily accessible and transparent knowledge, while on the other hand, the increasing worldwide inequality in educational resources and university expansion in the name of the massification of higher education present challenges to many developing societies (Altbach 2004). It is also argued that globalization has transformed public universities from public entities into private commodities and consequently increased the number of private higher education institutions (HEIs). Moreover, in order to meet new global challenges, schools and universities are mandated to respond by restructuring their format, operation, management, and even the mission of learning (Chou 2008a). Policy makers across the world also have started to reexamine universities' funding schemes, especially those of public institutions, with the hope of identifying universities based on efficiency and accountability. In essence, academic systems and institutions are already making different accommodations for these trends, which are quite important and cannot be ignored.

Localization and Taiwan

Taiwan has also had to strive to localize as well as globalize since the 1990s. As Giddens (1990) acknowledged, globalization is connected to localization. The two concepts can be viewed as two sides of the same coin that jointly shape the identity of self and the nation. In addition to facing issues of globalization, Taiwan has also been confronted with the demand for education localization within the country. This phenomenon can be dated back to 1945, when Taiwan was under Japanese rule. Under Japanese administration (1895–1945), the purpose of Taiwanese education was to assimilate the local people into Japanese culture. After the restoration of Taiwan to China in 1945, the urgent mission of the Taiwan authorities was to abolish the effect of Japanese colonialism on Taiwan by setting up a new education system to help advance the Chinese national identity (Yang 2001). A process emphasizing Chinese-oriented education aimed to preserve the Chinese culture and the national language, Mandarin. The American "six-three-three-four" system was adopted in Taiwan after World War II. Therefore, in the latter half of the twentieth century, Taiwanese education went through a series of nationalism campaigns that drew heavily on Chinese culture and economic rationalism, while at the same time striving for Western efficiency and effectiveness.

For Taiwan, localization also consisted of the conflict between pursuing the country's independence versus its political unification. In practice, the use of school textbooks relevant to Chinese subject matter was reduced to a great extent starting in 1987, when President Lee, the first local Taiwanese leader in the country's history, assumed the presidency. Local dialect and indigenous languages were introduced to the primary schools and became required courses along with Chinese and English. History and Chinese courses were tailored more to Taiwanese, instead of Chinese, issues. Education in Taiwan has focused extensively on local issues and the Taiwanese identity, such as calls for the country to be known as Taiwan rather than the Republic of China, the shift of textbook content in elementary and secondary schools from Chinese to Taiwanese issues, and an increasing Taiwanization of the national civil service examination questions.

A study examined two sets of social studies textbooks for grade four, published from 1978 to 1995 (the first set between 1978 and 1989, the second between 1989 and 1995), to determine whether or not they reinforced the dominance of traditional Chinese cultural identity and neglected the diverse representation of different gender, cultural, ethnic groups, and so forth. Also, the textbooks were analyzed to determine whether their ideology had changed or not owing to the political and socioeconomic pressures Taiwan experienced after the democratization process in the late 1980s. The research findings indicated that not only the historical interpretation but also the ideology of a unified Chinese national identity were emphasized in both series of social studies textbooks before 1995. These two series often legitimated the notion that Taiwanese ancestors had migrated from mainland China, a notion that the Kuomingtang (KMT, 國民黨)

ruling party used in school textbooks as a means of asserting political legitimacy to convey special values, assumptions, and principles that reflected the interests of the political authority (Apple 2004). In line with this approach, many politically and culturally sensitive and controversial issues were removed from textbooks (Apple and Christian-Smith 1991). For example, both sets of textbooks contrasted the different ways of life between the period of Dutch/Japanese political and economic oppression and the prosperity of the Chinese ruling period without portraying in detail the integration and prosperity of the Japanese colony between the years 1895 and 1945.

Ideological Representations of Taiwanese History

Localization in Taiwan is a phenomenon whose roots were planted over a long period that reaches back to the Japanese occupation. In order to form her own national and cultural identity, Taiwan has tried in every possible way to rid itself of the Japanese colonial influence and escape from China-oriented nationalism. These notions have led to an influx of teaching materials that focus on local history and geography as well as local arts in the curriculum reform at every level of the education system, hence shaping the localization of Taiwanese education.

Recently, tensions between the forces of globalization and localization seem to be arising in the field of education reform. However, globalization should not be confined to the understanding of other cultures and the exchanging of values and knowledge in the international arena. In essence, the localization of Taiwanese education will make its people better aware of their own cultural roots so as to give them a point of reference that will enable them to determine their place in the world. Such a clear cultural self-identity is the starting point of a process that moves toward understanding and respect for the cultures and spiritual values of various civilizations. The final ideal of education reform in Taiwan should therefore lie in a harmonious integration of localization and globalization that leads to helping people have a better understanding of themselves and the world overall (Chou 2008b).

More specifically, education in Taiwan has come to be one of the most influential avenues for nation building and economic development. Drawing on the influences of Japanese educational practices and ideals during the colonization period, Chinese culture, and Confucian traditions from mainland China, Taiwanese schools have experienced dramatic increases in enrollments.

Contextualization of Social Change and Education Reform

In considering Taiwan's efforts to globalize its education system while preserving its cultural heritage with a local identity, the following section discusses policies and laws in response to issues of globalization since the late 1980s. This section also focuses on issues surrounding the impact of neoliberal ideology on Taiwanese higher education since the late 1980s, addressing specific questions, such as: What initiated change? What exactly has changed? And what is going to happen in the future for Taiwanese higher education and the education system in general as a result of the introduction of neoliberal economies?

Until the lifting of martial law, higher education had long been administered by the Taiwanese government due to the political tension that existed between Taiwan and China since 1949. Since then, higher education has come into a period of dramatic transformation alongside the introduction of market mechanisms into the education system in the early 1990s. First, the 1994 University Law was passed to reduce the power of the central government by granting more academic freedom, institutional flexibility, and autonomy to universities (MOE 2010). Meanwhile, Taiwan also experienced an unprecedented expansion in the number of universities and student enrollment as a result of this political openness and economic deregulation. Following this period of growth, private higher-education institutions came to outnumber public institutions. In Taiwan, public universities traditionally have enjoyed more resources and higher status. Yet with the global influence of neoliberalism, which focuses on privatization and privileges a market economy, universities are increasingly considered to be fee-charging, public institutions, and they are suffering from a loss of public funds, as a result of the expansion of higher education and increased public funding for private universities. The consequences of neoliberalism's influence have been mixed; the results of this philosophy may provide some valuable lessons to those attempting to introduce market economies to their higher-education systems.

The growth of higher education throughout the world has been a topic of discussion during the last several decades as an unavoidable fact. In Taiwan, on the other hand, higher education appears to have been expanding at a much faster pace than expected, generating an undervaluation of the university diploma and a large surplus in the supply of college graduates in relation to the needs of the job market. Along with this, admission to the university appears to have lost, to some extent, a certain prestige by placing an emphasis on admissions over selectivity, and it is now less competitive than before. Currently, admission criteria in general have been modified to be more suited to students with less academic preparation and motivation, which is also a result of universities pursuing student recruitment at present. Therefore, due to the drastic expansion of HEIs, the quality of higher education in general has been and still is experiencing a significant decline over the last ten years. The upgraded projections of the quality of higher education in Taiwan appear not to have reached a peak, even though the main objective is to foster the preparation of the younger generations to compete better in this era of globalization.

As governments pursue a neoliberal market ideology, higher education is also experiencing specific changes. Universities have shifted from traditional norms of state control to those of state supervision (Song 2005). The previous government role of initiating rules and regulations for HEIs is now shifting largely to that of specifying funding standards for universities and colleges that then compete based on accountability and performance. Market-oriented higher education is becoming primarily focused on structures and actions tailored to "competition" and "deregulation." In concrete terms, this includes taking such steps as employing performance-based funding schemes, encouraging greater competition for resources, supporting fundraising efforts by universities, establishing more private institutions, deploying external evaluation, and raising tuition fees. Policy makers are convinced that adopting market-oriented mechanisms will encourage universities to share the financial burden of higher education, especially in light of increased student enrollment. This outlook also seeks cost-effective behavior among HEIs, increased efficiency, and eventually better educational quality. The result may not only be improved autonomy within universities, but also lead to increased choice for students, while at the same time enabling them to be conscious of their rights as consumers of an educational product.

This global trend toward establishing market economies has particularly affected many HEIs in Asia and other countries, and especially in Australia, Canada, China, Japan, Korea, New Zealand, and Taiwan. Taiwan is a good example that that has adopted neoliberal principles in its higher-education policy since the late 1980s, when the country was experiencing great political and economic transformation.

What Initiated the Changes in Taiwan's Higher Education?

Since the late 1980s, governments in Taiwan have responded to the worldwide trend of globalization and neoliberalism along with the processes of political democratization and economic transformation (Chou 2008). After the lifting of martial law and the end of an authoritarian regime that had lasted four decades, and the beginning of more Taiwan cross-strait dialogues and interactions between China and Taiwan, higher education in Taiwan entered a new stage of dramatic transformation. It was a time when many advocates demanded greater social change through abolishing media censorship, granting more freedom to the banking establishment, and producing more competent college students to accommodate Taiwan's emerging high technology industry. The traditional school system also came under fire for being unable to cope with the new social demands in this transitional period. Successive governments, priding themselves on being more responsive to local needs and global challenges than the regime that preceded them, introduced market-oriented reforms as a way of relieving government budgetary pressures and giving HEIs more autonomy. Consequently, the Educational Reform Committee (1994–1996), led by a Nobel Laureate, was established to produce five reform papers that served as guidelines for launching a nationwide reform movement in the 1990s (Chou 2003). At the same time, the passing of the new revised University Law (1994) and the shifting of responsibility for administrative funding from the government to public universities (1996) were measures taken to assist in introducing market dynamics to Taiwan during that time.

REFERENCES

Altbach, Philip G. 2004. "Globalization and the University: Myths and Realities in an Unequal World." *Tertiary Education and Management* 10: 3–25.

———. 2005. "Globalization and the University: Myths and Realities in an Unequal World." In *The NEA 2005 Almanac of Higher Education*, 63–74. Washington, DC: National Education Association.

Apple, Michael W. 2004. *Ideology and Curriculum*. New York: Falmer Press.

Apple, Michael W., and Linda Christian-Smith. 1991. *The Politics of the Textbooks*. New York: Routledge, Chapman and Hall.

China Post. 2010. "Gov't Mulls Professor Salary Raise." *The China Post*, January 24. Available online at: http://www.chinapost.com.tw.

Chou, Chuing Prudence. 2003. *The Great Experiment of Taiwanese Education: 1987–2003*. Taipei: Psychology Publishing.

———. 2010. *Expectation of Academicians and Academic Sinica*. Hong Kong: China Review News. http://www.chinareviewnews.com.

———. 2008. "The Impact of Neo-Liberalism on Taiwanese Higher Education." *International Perspectives on Education and Society* 9: 297–311.

———. 2008. *Mr. President: How Are You Going to Deal with Education in Taiwan?* Taipei: Psychology.

Currie, Jan, Richard DeAngelis, Harry de Boer, Jeroen Huisman, and Claude Lacotte. 2003. *Globalizing Practices and University Responses: European and Anglo American Differences*. Westport, CT: Praeger.
Fiske, Edward B. 2004. *The Fiske Guide to Colleges 2003* Naperville, IL: Sourcebooks.
Friedman, Thomas. 2000. *The Lexus and the Olive Tree*. New York: Farrar, Straus & Giroux.
———. 2005. *The World Is Flat: A Brief History of the Twenty-First Century*. New York: Farrar, Straus & Giroux.
Giddens, Anthony. 1990. *The Consequences of Modernity*. Cambridge, UK: Polity Press.
Hermans, Hubert, and Giancarlo Dimaggio. 2007. "Self, Identity, and Globalization in Times of Uncertainty: A Dialogical Analysis." *Review of General Psychology* 11 (1): 31–61.
Hershock, Peter D., Mark Mason, and John N. Hawkins, eds. 2007. *Changing Education: Leadership Innovation and Development in a Globalizing Asia Pacific*. Hong Kong: Comparative Education Research Centre-Springer.
Huntington, Samuel. 1993. "The Clash of Civilizations?" *Foreign Affairs* 72 (3): 22–49.
Levin, John S. 1999. "Missions and Structures: Bringing Clarity to Perceptions about Globalization and Higher Education in Canada." *Higher Education* 37 (4): 377–399.
Ministry of Education (MOE). 2010a. *Increasing Extent of Tuition vs. GDP*. Taipei: MOE. http://www.edu.tw.
———. 2010b. *University Act*. Taipei: MOE.
Mok, Ka Ho. 2000. "Reflecting Globalization Effects on Local Policy: Higher Education Reform in Taiwan." *Journal of Education Policy* 15 (6): 637–660.
Mok, Ka Ho, and Hiu-Hong Lee. 2000. "Globalization or Re-Colonization: Higher Education Reforms in Hong Kong." *Higher Education Policy* 13 (4): 361–377.
Neubauer, Deane. 2007. "Globalization and Education—Characteristics, Dynamics, Implications." In *Changing Education—Leadership Innovation and Development in a Globalizing Asia Pacific*, edited by Peter D. Hershock, Mark Mason, and John N. Hawkins, 1–45. Hong Kong: Comparative Education Research Centre; Springer.
NowNews. 2009. *High Salary in Hong Kong*. Taipei: NowNews Network. Available online at: http://www.nownews.com.
Organization for Economic Co-operation and Development (OECD). 2009. *Education at a Glance*. Paris: OECD.
Paige, Michael R. 2005. "Internationalization of Higher Education: Performance Assessment and Indicators." *Nagoya Journal of Higher Education* 5: 99–122.
Sen, Amartya. 2002. "How to Judge Globalism." *The American Prospect* 13 (1): Supplement A2, 1–8.
Siaya, Laura, and Fred M. Hayward. 2003. *Mapping Internationalization on U.S. Campuses*. Washington, DC: American Council on Education.

Song, Mei-Mei. 2005. "Relationship of Government and High Education within Marketization: Its Implications for the Role and Development of Private Higher Education Institution in China." Paper presented at the Seminar of Transformation in University Management, Tamkang University, Taiwan, June 9.

Stiglitz, Joseph E. 2002. *Globalization and Its Discontents*. New York: W. W. Norton.

Taipei Times. 2010. "Academic Sector Proposes Flexible Salary for Experts." *Taipei Times*, January 1. http://www.taipeitimes.com.

Teichler, Ulrich. 2004. "The Changing Debate on Internationalisation of Higher Education." *Higher Education* 48: 5–26.

Trow, Martin A. 2005. "Reflections on the Transition from Elite to Mass to Universal Access: Forms and Phases of Higher Education in Modern Societies since WWII." In *International Handbook of Higher Education*, edited by P. G. Altbach. New York: Springer, 243–280. http://repositories.cdlib.org/igs/WP2005-4.

Tsai, Ching-Hwa. 1996. *The Deregulation of Higher Education in Taiwan*. Chestnut Hill, MA: Boston College. Available online at: http://www.bc.edu.

Wang, Bao-jin. 2010. "University Evaluation Based on the Whole School Evaluation Approach." *Bimonthly Evaluation*, 23.

Wang, Tsai-Li. 2009. *Salary of Assistant Professor Is Lower Than Those Who Teach in Primary/Junior High School*. Taipei: United Daily News Group. http://mag.udn.com.

Wu, Chris C. 2009. *Higher Education Expansion in Taiwan: The Problems Faced*. Taipei: National Taiwan Normal University. Available online at: http://cve.ntnu.edu.tw.

Yang, Shen-Keng. 2001. "Dilemmas of Education Reform in Taiwan: Internationalization or Localization?" Paper presented at the Annual Meeting of the Comparative and International Education Society, Washington, DC, March 14–17.

Chapter 2

Taiwan's Country Profile

Taiwan is an island located on two straits in East Asia, the Taiwan Strait off the southeastern coast of China, and the Luzon strait, which connects the South China Sea with the Pacific Ocean. Taiwan has a total area of 35,980 square kilometers (U.S. Library of Congress 2005). The eastern two-thirds of Taiwan are mainly mountainous, with a number of mountains topping 3,000 meters. The large majority of the western part of the island is made up of hills that are reduced into plains until the coast is reached. The island of Taiwan is also surrounded by a number of other small islands.

While Taiwan is currently officially known as the Republic of China, in the international arena it was formerly known as Formosa. This name was given to the island by the Portuguese (*Formosa* meaning "beautiful") upon their arrival on the island in 1624. Before the Chinese and the Europeans arrived, the island was already home to Austronesian people, whose first settlements can be dated back to 15,000 years ago (Cheng and Jacob 2002).

According to the Chinese, Taiwan was called Yizhou or Liuqiu in ancient times, and different dynasties set up administrative bodies to exercise jurisdiction over the island beginning in the mid-twelfth century. The Dutch East India Company occupied Peng-Hu (an offshore island of Taiwan) as a trading harbor base for the company's East Asian business dealings in the seventeenth century. In 1622, a war broke out between China's Ming Dynasty government and the Dutch troops. Spain then arrived as the first European nation to establish settlements in Formosa in 1628, but was soon driven out by the Dutch in 1632. As a result, Taiwan was colonized by the Dutch from 1642 to 1662. The Dutch themselves, however, were defeated in 1662 by a Chinese trader and a former Ming government official, Zheng Chenggong.

For more than 20 years (1662–1683), Zheng and his family ruled Taiwan and used it as a military foundation against the Qing government while staying loyal to the emperor of the former Ming Dynasty (1368–1643). Taiwan, during this period, once again underwent social reconstruction and economic development. It was known as the Taiwanese Kingdom or the Kingdom of Formosa by the English East India Company. However, in 1683 when Zheng was defeated by Chi-Lang, a Qing general, the Qing Dynasty (1644–1911) took control of the island, which eventually led to it gaining status as mainland China's Taiwan province in 1885. This was the first time that Taiwan was reclaimed officially by the Chinese government.

In the mid-nineteenth century, the European countries threatened China in the Opium War of 1840, which led to China's loss of Hong Kong until 1997. Although the Qing government took a more positive attitude toward Taiwan's development, the Qing were defeated in the First Sino-Japanese War (1894–1895). In 1895, under the terms of the Treaty of Shimonoseki, Taiwan was yielded to Japan, and for 50 years the island of Taiwan remained a Japanese colony.

The island made for a good strategic outpost with a source of raw materials, and Japan intended to make Taiwan a model colony for its expanding empire. The Japanese introduced compulsory primary education to Taiwan even before it was initiated in Japan itself. While the period of Japanese rule brought Taiwan into the modern age, scholars also see this period as the time when the island began to develop a separate identity from mainland China (U.S. Library of Congress 2005).

When the Japanese were defeated in World War II (1945), the Republic of China under the Kuomintang (KMT) arrived in Taiwan, bringing Chinese political, economic, and cultural influences, which led to friction and clashes with the local population. Nevertheless, following the Chinese communist party takeover of the mainland in 1949, Taiwan became a shelter for Mainlanders who supported the Nationalist KMT leader, Chiang Kai-Shek. Nearly 2 million Chinese civilians, government officials, and military troops relocated from the mainland to Taiwan.

These events led to the island receiving economic and military support from the U.S. government and, combined with heavy investments from the United States and Japan in the island's industry, Taiwan prospered. During the economic boom of the 1960s, Taiwan was the fastest growing economy in the world, and was named as one of the Four Asian Tigers (together with South Korea, Hong Kong, and Singapore).

While economically Taiwan was doing very well, politically it was less successful. During the 1970s, Taiwan withdrew from the United Nations and also temporarily suspended diplomatic relations with the United States, resulting in diplomatic isolation for the island. Domestically, the Taiwanese were living under martial law from 1948 to 1987, but as international pressure increased, national elections were held for the first time in 1996. The reigning KMT won those elections, but lost in the elections that followed in 2000, and again in 2004, to the Democratic Progressive Party (DPP, 民進黨), which promoted the island distancing itself from mainland Chinese influence. The KMT regained control of the government in the elections of 2008. Taiwan at the moment still has a political climate that is very polarized between the two main parties (DPP and KMT).

The current population of Taiwan stands at a little over 23 million, with a population growth rate of 0.23 percent (Government Information Office 2010). The population is split into four general groups: the Fukienese (people who immigrated to Taiwan from the Fukien province in China before 1949), the Hakka (people who immigrated from Guangdong province in China before 1949), the Mainlanders (people who immigrated from China after 1949), and the indigenous Taiwanese (who include the 14 officially recognized indigenous groups). These four groups can be categorized into two larger groups. The majority are: the Han Chinese, consisting of the Fukienese (74 percent); the Mainlanders (14 percent); and the Hakka (10 percent). The other group represents the non-Han Austronesians, the indigenous population, which accounts for the remaining 2 percent of the population (Government Information Office 2010). There are also New Immigrants, who have in the last decade become part of the population through marriage. Each group has its own dialect and cultural perspectives.

Taiwan has heavily populated urban areas that were home to just under 70 percent of the population in 2004 (Government Information Office 2010). These areas are considerably more developed than the rural regions, where the people are generally assumed to have more conservative values than urban residents (Yi et al. 2008). About half of the Taiwanese population are members of a religious association. Among these groups, 42.9 percent are Buddhist, 35.6 percent Taoist, 6.6 percent I-Kuan Tao, 4.7 percent Protestant, 4.1 percent Muslim, and 2.3 percent Roman Catholic (U.S. Library of Congress 2005).

Taiwan, in 2009, had a nominal gross domestic product (GDP) of US$16,442 per capita, which translated into a GDP at Purchasing Power Parity (PPP) of US$31,834 per capita (Government Information Office 2010). That same year, the GDP had a negative growth of 1.9 percent, and the GDP per capita at PPP ranked forty-third in the world (Central Intelligence Agency 2010). Inflation for 2009 was -0.9 percent, and the unemployment rate as of May 2010 stood at 5.22 percent (Sung 2010). Since the 1990s, Taiwan has enjoyed a dynamic capitalist economy with a gradual decrease in government control of investment and foreign trade.

In keeping with this development trend, some large government-owned banks and industrial firms have undergone incorporation and privatization. Generally speaking, exports have provided the primary impetus for Taiwan's development; the trade surplus was substantial up to August 2010. Agriculture currently contributes less than 2 percent to the GDP, in contrast to 32 percent in 1952. Taiwan is also one of the major investors throughout Southeast Asia. In addition, the Chinese mainland has already taken over the position formally held by the United States as Taiwan's largest export market. Growing economic ties with the mainland since the 1990s have led to many of Taiwan's assembly plants for parts and equipment related to the production of exportable goods being successfully moved to developed countries.

Taiwan has for all practical purposes been independent for half a century, but China regards the country as a rebel region that must be reunited with the mainland. China has claimed sovereignty over Taiwan since the end of the Chinese civil war in 1949, when the defeated Nationalist government fled to the island as the Communists, under Mao Zedong, swept to power.

The long-standing tension between Taiwan and the mainland has eased since Taiwan's China-friendly president, Ma Ying-Jeou, took office in March 2008. In July 2009, the leaders of China and Taiwan exchanged direct messages for the first time in more than 60 years, and in June 2010, the two countries signed a historic trade pact that was described by some analysts as the most significant agreement in 60 years of separation (BBC 2011).

Regarding Taiwan's political development in the past five decades (1949–2000), the KMT gradually democratized and incorporated the local Taiwanese within the governing structure. In 2000, Taiwan underwent its first peaceful transfer of power from the Nationalists to the DPP. The dominant political issues across the island remained the question of the eventual unification with mainland China, as well as domestic political and economic reform. The Economic Cooperation Framework Agreement (ECFA), signed by the governments of Taiwan and China on June 2010, was developed to decrease trading barriers between Taiwan and China, but it also created much controversy across the Taiwan Strait.

Politics, Laws, and Education

Taiwan was established as a country with a constitutional system based on the Three Principles of the People that were conceived by her founding father, Sun-Yat Sen, in 1905. The Constitution of the Republic of China (Office of the President 2011) was adopted on December 25, 1946, by the National Assembly. The opening of the document declares: "The Republic of China, founded on the Three Principles of the People, shall be a democratic republic of the people, to be governed by the people and for the people." The Constitution safeguarded the rights and obligations of the people. Yet, due to the war and cross-strait tension, it was replaced by Temporary Provisions Effective during the Period of Communist Rebellion that were in effect until the end of the martial period (1949–1987).

In 1975, President Chiang Ching-kuo succeeded his father, Chiang Kai-shek, after the older man passed away, and began to change Taiwan's political reality. He first allowed the Tangwai group (i.e., the non-KMT group) to form the first opposition party in Taiwan—the DPP—in September 1986 (McBeath 1998), and then announced the lifting of martial law in the following July. With the Constitution of the Republic of China returning to its absolute position, the people of Taiwan were once again protected in their rights as citizens to receive an education and to enjoy freedom of speech in teaching, writing, and publishing, for example. Taiwan, starting in the 1980s, began its journey of democratization under his leadership, and the democratization of Taiwan's electoral systems was completed within only one decade.

Government Structure

As laid out in the National Constitution, Taiwan's political system is divided into three levels, central, provincial, and local (including municipal, county, and city), and those levels have established official governments to supervise specific affairs. The provincial level, however, was suspended in the constitution's fourth revision in 1977 (Office of the President 2011). Therefore, only the central government and the local government remain. (In this version of the constitution, "the requirement [that] minimum funding for education, science and culture...be abolished" became a factor in schools' current operating difficulties, as it not only caused harm to education but also reduced national competitiveness and generated social problems because of the lack of sufficient government coherence and funding.)

As far as the organization of the government is concerned, the central government consists of the Office of the President and five branches (called *Yuan*)—the Executive Yuan, the Legislative Yuan, the Judicial Yuan, the Examination Yuan, and the Control Yuan. The Ministry of Education (MOE), which is under the Executive Yuan, is in charge of national education affairs. Matters that formerly were handled by the provinces are now being supervised by the Executive Yuan.

The Five Yuan and Education

Executive Yuan

As head of the Five Yuan, the Executive Yuan is the highest administrative organization and is responsible for implementing policies for all the issues related to the nation and the people. In particular, the policies of the eight ministries, including Interior, Foreign Affairs, National Defense, Finance, Education, Justice, Economic Affairs, and Transportation and Communications, play an important role in the country's future and its position in the world. Among these public institutions, the MOE and the National Science Council deeply influence national education policy and the direction of technical development. An introduction to the Educational Executive Organizations will be provided in chapter 5.

Legislative Yuan

The Legislative Yuan is the highest lawmaking body of the state, possessing absolute legislative power to decide whether any budgetary bills or important affairs related to the state, such as declarations of war or peace, martial law, amnesties, treaties, and so forth are passed or not. In a word, all (including the field of education, of course) laws, rules, and regulations must be discussed and approved in the Legislative Yuan. There is an Education and Culture Committee, which, according to Article 5(1)(v) of the organic regulation of the Procedure Committee, is responsible for deliberating policies of education and culture, and bills related to the powers of the MOE, the Council for Cultural Affairs, the National Palace Museum, the Government Information Office, the National Youth Commission, the National Council on Physical Fitness and Sports, the Academia Sinica, the National Science Council, and the Atomic Energy Council, the last two of which are part of the Executive Yuan.

Judicial Yuan

The Judicial Yuan is the highest judicial institution of the Republic, and among its seven main functions, interpreting the constitution and unifying the interpretation of laws and orders are of the greatest importance. When citizens feel trapped by the bureaucracy or that they have suffered unjustly, they may file a petition and await a judicial interpretation. For example, in the latest interpretation, no. 684 (Judicial Yuan 2011) (published on January 17, 2011), three students accused the schools of neglect when the students were seeking help. According to the interpretation, based on Article 16 of the constitution (Office of the President 2011), people have the right to present petitions, log complaints, or institute legal proceedings; therefore, the students had the right bring an administrative litigation to their school when they felt they had experienced unfair treatment.

In another ruling, No. 626 (Judicial Yuan 2011) (published on June 8, 2007), according to the honorable justices, although the constitution ensures all citizens of the right to receive an education, considering that the Central Police Academy is responsible for training future police officers and that an officer may need to distinguish colors while on duty, it is reasonable to exclude individuals from enrolling in the academy if they are color blind. As these two examples indicate, the Judicial Yuan makes an interpretation by overall consideration of an issue. In addition, the courts at all levels are supervised in their judgments of illegal or immoral behaviors and crimes, and administrative litigation.

In particular, the Committee on the Discipline of Public Functionaries helps to oversee and reprimand those public officials accused of malfeasance. Also, the Judicial Yuan is in charge of educating citizens in the law and human rights, in order to help establish a concept of how citizens may live peaceably in a society governed by the "rule of law."

Examination Yuan

The Examination Yuan, the highest level examination organization in the country, is responsible for the nation's civil service system. It oversees examinations, qualification screenings, the security of tenure, pecuniary aid in case of death, retirement, and all legal matters related to employment, discharge, performance evaluation, scale of salaries, promotion, transfer, commendation, and the presentation of awards to civil servants. The Examination Yuan promotes personnel through holding national exams, and people who pass the exams successfully are appointed to serve in the government administration.

Control Yuan

The Control Yuan, the highest supervisory organization of the country, exercises the powers of impeachment, censure, and audit. Moreover, it takes corrective measures against government organizations. The power of impeachment thus consists of a whole range of government supervision from central to local, and from the president to new public functionaries, once they are caught either violating laws or failing to fulfill their duties.

We can review the overall operation of the five Yuans based on the following example. "John Doe," after studying hard for a year, passed the exam held by the Examination Yuan and became a public functionary in the Department of Social Education under the MOE. His responsibility was to oversee social education institutions and guide community colleges; therefore, he had plenty of opportunities to have contact with those institutions' representatives. He was, however, soon suspected of taking advantage of his position while implementing a policy established by the MOE, according to a related law passed by the Legislative Yuan. The Control Yuan then brought an impeachment case against him and began to investigate. Finally, the completed investigation was offered to the Judicial Yuan as part of their reference materials when they judged the case. John had to be punished for his crime in the end.

Provincial Government

The former Taiwan provincial government and the Fujian provincial government were downsized in the 1990s, and thereafter they surrendered their governing operations to central government departments. Additionally, after the *Local Government Act* was promulgated in 1999, the provincial governments became subordinate agencies to the Executive Yuan, meaning that they were no longer self-governing bodies.

Local Government

Taiwan's local government can be divided into three levels: special municipalities, counties and provincial municipalities, and townships and county municipalities. Citizens have the right to vote directly for their mayors of cities and their magistrates of counties and townships every four years. They also choose their representatives in cities and counties through popular election.

In April 2009, the legislature passed amendments to the Local Government Act, providing a legal basis for cities and counties to merge or upgrade to special municipalities, and the following December, after the restructuring of Taiwan's local governments, there were now five special municipalities, increased from two, which are the original Taipei city; New Taipei city, from Taipei county; Taichung city, from combining Taichung county and city; Tainan city, from combining Tainan county and city; and Kaohsiung city, from combining Kaohsiung county and city. There are also 18 counties and provincial municipalities. All these 23 local governments set up a bureau of education to deal with affairs of the city or county schools. It is expected that the new restructuring effort will increase the effectiveness and efficiency of the public and educational administration in Taiwan.

Taiwan has undergone many drastic political, social, and economic changes during the past few decades. All of these changes have a direct relationship to its unique historical past with China and Japan. Current political, geographic, social, and economic reforms and reorganizations have helped place Taiwan in a position to better face globalization challenges and remain competitive in areas of education and economic development.

REFERENCES

British Broadcasting Corporation (BBC). 2011. "e 2011." London: BBC. Available online at: http://news.bbc.co.uk.
Central Intelligence Agency. 2010. *The World Factbook*. Washington, DC: CIA. Available online at: www.cia.gov.
Cheng, Sheng Yao, and James W. Jacob. 2002. "Marginality and Aboriginal Education Policy Analysis in the United States and Taiwan." Paper presented at the Annual Meeting of the Comparative and International Education Society, Orlando, Florida.
Government Information Office. 2010. *The Republic of China at a Glance*. Taipei: Government Information Office. Available onlie at: http://www.gio.gov.tw.
Judicial Yuan. 2011. *Interpretation No. 684*. Taipei: Judicial Yuan. Available online at: http://www.judicial.gov.tw.
McBeath, Gerald A. 1998. *Wealth and Freedom: Taiwan's New Political Economy*. London: Ashgate.
Office of the President. 2011. "Constitution." Taipei: Office of the President. Available from http://english.president.gov.tw.
Sung, Chin-Mei. 2010. "Taiwan Unemployment Rate Fell to 17-Month Low in May 2010." *Businessweek*, Hong Kong: Times News. Available online at: http://www.businessweek.com.

U.S. Library of Congress. 2005. "Country Profile: Taiwan 2005." Washington, DC: U.S. Library of Congress. Available online at: http://lcweb2.loc.gov.

Yi, Chin-Chun, Hsiang-Ming Kung, Yu-Hua Chen, and Joujuo Chu. 2008. "The Importance of Social Context in the Formation of the Value of Children for Adolescents: Social Class and Rural Urban Differences in Taiwan." *Journal of Comparative Family Studies* 39 (3): 371–392.

Chapter 3

Historical Overview of Education in Taiwan

Education during Ancient Times (before 1626)

There are records of settlement and agricultural education on the island of Penghu dating back to the early seventeenth century. As far as we know, this may be the earliest example of vocational education in Taiwan (Hsu 1993). Other than the type of education documented in these records, education in Taiwan has been similar to that of China, consisting of private education or self-study that focuses on the *Keju* examinations. Keju (the imperial examination system) is an examination system used in ancient China to test and select government officials. It was first adopted in the Sui Dynasty (581–618) and lasted through the Qing Dynasty (1644–1911). Intellectuals who wanted to become an official were required take these multitier examinations.

Formal imperial examinations consisted of three levels: the provincial, the metropolitan, and the final examination. The provincial examination was held triennially in the provincial city. Those admitted were called *Juren* (elevated men). The metropolitan examination was held in the following spring after the provincial examination at the Ministry of Rites in the capital. Those admitted were called *Gongshi*, and those who received first place on the examination, *Huiyuan*. The final imperial examination was administered under the direct supervision of the emperor of the dynasty. Only Gongshi were qualified to take the exam. The matriculation had three levels of excellence. The first level was granted to three candidates, and it conferred *Jinshi* (China's Ministry of Culture n. d.) on the candidate.

The Keju examination includes questions on classical literature, poetry, and writing. Due to the exam's difficulty and heavy emphasis on memorization, very few of the examinees pass it. However, it is because of the Keju system that academics in China and Taiwan are so respected and are so numerous throughout the two countries. Passing the exam brings great honor and status, so many have chosen to pursue academia for their entire life, rather than enter other fields.

Spanish Occupation (1626–1642)

In the early seventeenth century, Catholic Spain was in competition with Protestant Holland for trade in East Asia. With the establishment of a Dutch colony in the south of Taiwan, the Dutch effectively threatened Spanish trade in the region. As a counter to this threat, the Spanish decided to establish their colony in the north of the island, and remained there for sixteen years before being driven away by the Dutch. In addition to economic reasons, Spain also wanted to exert a religious influence on East Asia.

At first, only soldiers could enter the aboriginal villages in Taiwan; it was not until the arrival of Father Jacinto Esquivel that missionaries gained access to villages. In order to make his missionary work easier, he wrote two books on Taiwanese aboriginal languages and education, *Vocabularino de la lengua de los Indios Tanchui en la Isla Hermosa* (Vocabulary of the Tanchui aborigines' language on the Beautiful Island) and *Doctrina cristiana en la lengua de los Indios Tanchui en la Isla Hermosa* (Christian doctrine of the Tanchui aborigines' language on the Beautiful Island). He also founded a brotherhood in Taiwan (Hermandad de la Santa Misericordia) and planned on establishing a seminary (Davidson 2005). However, the brotherhood did last long due to his sudden death. Because the Spanish only remained in Taiwan for sixteen years and employed missionaries, not trained teachers, as educators, the extent of Spanish education was rather weak (Hsu 1993).

Spain's territory and influence were limited by force to areas now in the northern part of island, such as Keelung City, Danshui Town, and Yilan County. The aboriginals in these areas accepted Catholicism for various reasons besides their belief in Christianity, including for safety concerns, because Spanish soldiers were less likely to harass them if there were missionaries in the villages. Moreover, Spanish missionaries believed that extending their power to China and Japan was more important than controlling the island of Formosa; therefore, they usually did not stay long in Taiwan, so the Spanish influence on education in Taiwan was not significant in comparison to that of the Dutch and Japanese (Chou 2003).

Dutch Occupation (1642–1662)

After Spanish occupation, the Dutch East India Company occupied Penghu (an offshore island of Taiwan) as a trading harbor base for its East Asian business dealings in the seventeenth century. In 1622, an armed conflict broke out between China's Ming Dynasty government (1368–1644) and Dutch troops. As a result of this conflict, Taiwan was colonized by the Dutch from 1642 to 1662.

The conversion of the natives to Christianity was one of the great successes of the Dutch during their colonization of the island. The missionaries were also responsible for setting up schools in the villages under Dutch control, teaching not only the religion of the colonists but also other skills such as reading and writing. Prior to the Dutch arriving, the native inhabitants did not have a system of written language, and the number of Romanization schemes that the Dutch created for various Formosan languages improved the efficiency of communication greatly (Everts 2000). In order to make their missionary work easier, the Dutch established the first school in southern Taiwan on May 26, 1636.

Other than religious content, the curriculum included reading and writing aboriginal languages in Latin (Zhen 2004). The school had three categories of students: children, adult men, and women; only male students were permitted to receive lessons in reading and writing. Lessons were mostly carried out in aboriginal languages in order for the students to understand, but after 1648, other schools started teaching Dutch, along with establishing traditional Dutch timetables and requiring the aboriginals to have Dutch names and clothes. The introduction of Roman letters was also a significant change for Taiwan Aborigines.

The teachers of the Dutch era included missionaries, soldiers, and aboriginals. In 1659, a seminary was established to train aboriginal teachers; there were only 30 openings, and students had to pass an examination to gain entrance.

Japanese Colonization (1895–1945)

Prior to Taiwan's colonization by Japan, there were some forms of primary, secondary, and specialized schools on the island that served different purposes. Under Japanese rule, a formal education system was established in 1919. Prior to that time, the Japanese government implemented the Taiwanese Education Act that divided the education system into four categories: general, vocational, specialized, and normal (teacher) education. At the general education or primary level, there were public schools, upper general schools, and girls' high schools, all of which admitted children between the ages of 7 and 13. Students were to learn knowledge and skills for life and basic needs. However, it was only in 1943 that six-year compulsory education was instituted. By that time, the enrollment rate for the primary school level in Taiwan was 71.3 percent versus 99.6 percent for Japanese children (among the highest in Asia) (Tsurumi 1999).

In 1922, the American "six-three-three-four" system was established in mainland China: six years of elementary school, three of junior high, three of senior high, and four of university. Taiwan's major educational development under Japanese rule can be summed up in the following timeline:

- 1895–1910: In the beginning of the Japanese colonization, education was focused on building Japanese schools and spreading the Japanese language through primary education.
- 1910–1925: In order to decrease fatalities due to epidemic diseases of the subtropics, a medical school was established to train medical assistants, and it became the only institution of higher education in Taiwan.
- 1922: Taipei Junior High School was built, which became the current Taipei Municipal Jian-guo High School, one of the most highly respected and elite senior high schools for boys.
- 1925: Taipei Senior High School was built, which became the current National Taiwan Normal University (NTNU).
- 1928: Taipei Imperial University, which became the current National Taiwan University, was established, with an agricultural department and a politics department.
- 1936: The medical school was integrated into the Imperial University and became the medical department.
- 1941: Since students graduating from Taipei Senior High School were unwilling to enter Taipei Imperial University and insisted on going to other imperial universities in Japan, a preparatory course for Taipei Imperial University was established.

During the Japanese era, senior high schools were considered as preparatory schools for universities, so strictly speaking, there are six years of university (three years of senior high school and three years of university), which is different from the Chinese system that separates the three years of senior high school and four years of university (Duann 2010).

In conclusion, Taiwanese education has undergone many significant changes in the past few centuries. It has experienced the Chinese Keju system, Spanish Catholic teachings, Dutch Protestant education, and the formal Japanese education system. Through its diverse experiences, Taiwanese education has developed to its current state, and it is still striving for reform and transformation. Taiwanese education today, which is somewhat similar to the system during the era of Japanese colonization, is now looking both out to the world and within its own boundaries for an even more diverse education policy and learning environment.

Postwar Education (1945–1994)

Education during Liberation and Postcolonial Education (1945–1987)

After World War II, when Taiwan was returned to China, only the medical and agricultural departments remained at Taipei Imperial University (now National Taiwan University [NTU]). The chief executive of Taiwan at the time, Chen Yi, was against the Imperial University, so the school received no funding at all from 1945 to 1947, causing it to stop functioning as a university until the scholar Fu Si-Nian took over the school. Fu Si-Nian changed the completely practical aspect of the university and established other departments. Moreover, he separated the Imperial University from its Japanese influences by revising the course materials, shifting from the lecture system to the department and credit system, abolishing the university preparatory schools, extending the three-year system to a four-year system, and implementing cross-department courses in the first year of university study. By 1947, Taipei Imperial University operated as a completely Chinese system (Yang 2000).

An act related to compulsory primary education in Taiwan was implemented in 1947. According to the Directorate General of Budget, Accounting and Statistics of Taiwan (2010), by 1968 compulsory education was extended to nine years. By 1984, both the primary and secondary education enrollment rates of Taiwan had reached over 99 percent, outnumbering many of Taiwan's counterparts in Asia.

Since the 1950s, Taiwan had encountered political and military uncertainty across the strait, but between 1957 and 1980, the emphasis in the country shifted to the planning and development of human resources together with the national goal of economic development. Additional challenges for the education system came in response to the forces of economic liberalization and globalization that have transformed Taiwan since the 1980s.

Taiwan has strived for its national identity over the last few centuries. As previously discussed, under the Japanese administration (1895–1945), the purpose of Taiwanese education was to assimilate local people into the Japanese culture. Only after 1949 was the priority changed to the strengthening of Chinese identity as a means of preparing for the reassertion of China's sovereignty over Taiwan. During that period of time, Taiwan Aboriginal cultures and languages were banned in society (including in schools and in public), especially after February 28, 1947 (commonly known as the 228 Incident), a day that involved social conflicts between the local people and Chinese troops that had withdrawn from China, and that turned into the violent suppression of Taiwanese civilians by Kuomintang (KMT) troops. This incident later served as a symbolic root for the Taiwanese call for independence from China. Many years later, since the late 1980s, Taiwanese society has gone through a period of localization involving the renovation of the Chinese identity through the Taiwanese heritage and traditions. These trends of indigenization, or so-called localization, may have stemmed from historical complaints against the Chinese KMT authoritarianism.

Education has been highly valued in Taiwan, and it has been a key item on the policy agenda of the Republic of China (Taiwan) since the Kuomintang government's relocation from the mainland to Taiwan in 1949. The promulgation of educational legislation by the central government laid the foundation for the nation's ongoing educational development and achievement. For example, the nine-year compulsory education initiated in 1968 is a milestone in contemporary Taiwanese education history for its significant impact on the development of the nation's human capital. All levels of education institutions have experienced a dramatic growth in student enrollment and school numbers since the implementation of this nine-year program. This system was, after all, initiated to boost the education level and quality of workers in what at the time was an industry- and export-based economy. Eventually, the Education Basic Law (the Law) came into force in 1999 to fully protect people's right to education, and it entitled the government to extend the period for compulsory education from the current nine years to twelve years (Yang 2001).

Since the 1980s, the economy of Taiwan has grown rapidly, and the country's political stability has provided the government with a safe ground to pursue democratization, pluralism, and liberalization in every sociocultural sphere (Chou 2003). The current education system, moving towards more comprehensiveness, therefore reflects the social, political, and economic status of Taiwan.

The Age of Educational Restructuring (1987–1994)

The education system in Taiwan is not very different from that of its East Asian neighbors, although a great number of changes have taken place in Taiwan's system in the last twenty years. Global trends of change, such as information development, internationalization, globalization, politics, and technology have come to overlap with education, not to mention the economic and management changes that are always a constant in most education environments. For instance, technology plays an active role in classrooms in Taiwan through the Internet, electronic boards and, of course, computers and gadgets, while internationalization has exerted a gradual influence through the delivery of instruction in foreign languages. One of the most relevant changes concerns management, where education policies have led to radical changes such as the banning of physical punishment in classrooms. There are, however, some particular constraints on change that are at the top of the agenda for the Taiwanese education system, such as internationalization and globalization.

Taiwanese universities entered an era of dramatic development after the lifting of martial law in 1987. This event marked the end of four decades of authoritarian leadership and the beginning of cross-strait dialogues between China and Taiwan. Advocates for improved relations supported social changes such as the abolishment of media censorship, autonomy of decision-making processes within banks, and provisions to enable promising college students to concentrate their academic interests within Taiwan's emerging high technology-oriented industries. During this transitional era, Taiwan's school system was criticized for its inability to evolve with the changes taking place in social and academic thought. In response, the national government introduced market-oriented reforms to relieve budgetary pressures and increase the autonomy of Higher Education Institutions (HEIs). During this period, several foundations dedicated to the improvement of education were also established, such as the Zhen Duo Committee, the Humanistic Education Foundation, and the Teachers' Human Rights Association, all of which contributed to reform by pushing for better and more human rights-oriented education (Chou 2003).

The Rise of Educational Reform Groups

Civil education reform groups emerged rapidly after the enactment of the Civil Organizations Law in 1989. Several groups developed into long-term civil education reform organizations and exerted an impact on Taiwan's educational reform movement, especially in the 1990s. The majority of these groups were formally established in 1989, and included the Humanistic Education Foundation; the Homemakers' Union and Foundation (*Ju-fu lian-meng*), which aims to unite women in order to promote harmony between the sexes and improve the quality of life, and is also concerned with improvement of the educational environment; the Jen-duo Association, which promotes the formation of a teachers' organization and the diversification of Taiwan's education system; and the Promotion of University Education Reform Association (*Da-shiue jieu-yu gai-ge tsu-jin huei*), which seeks to reform university education, protect academic freedom, and support students' self-governance as well as democracy on campuses (Chou 2003). The Taiwan Association of University Professors (*Taiwan jieu-shou shie-huei*) was founded in 1990 with the goal of uniting academic professionals to promote academic freedom, political democracy, and social justice. They also advocate the independence of Taiwan's politics (Taiwan Association of University Professors 2006).

These civil education reform groups had different purposes in forming, based on their areas of concern in the field of education. However, they were all dissatisfied with the KMT government's hegemonic control of the education system. The common goals among these groups created opportunities for them to form alliances to work together. They united to organize mass demonstrations or hold large conferences to stand against the KMT government on some educational issues that they felt were incompatible with Taiwan's new social circumstances.

During the political transition period of the 1990s, the former president, Lee Teng Hui, tried to incite a Taiwanese independence movement against China. Since then, education has focused extensively on local issues and Taiwanese identity, such as the calls for the country to be known as Taiwan rather than the Republic of China, the shift of textbook content in elementary and secondary schools from Chinese to Taiwanese issues, and the increased proportion of "Taiwanized" national civil service examination questions. Taiwan's educational system also entered an era of transition and reform as the nation's industrial structure shifted from a labor-intensive to a capital- and technology-intensive base, and as political democratization intensified.

Taiwanese universities have undergone a great transformation as well, as the country has enforced governmental restructuring policies by embracing a global neoliberal ideology since the late 1980s. Until the lifting of martial law in 1987, higher education had long been controlled by the Taiwanese government due to the political tension between Taiwan and China that arose in 1949. Since then, higher education has come into a period of dramatic transformation alongside the introduction of market mechanisms into the education system in the early 1990s.

The adoption of neoliberal, free-market economic policies in the 1980s and the subsequent deregulation of education have had an impact on many systems in Europe, North and South America, and Asia (including New Zealand and Australia) (Olssen 2002). Many countries in these regions have restructured their systems of public education in an attempt to give HEIs relative autonomy and enable them to assume responsibility as independent institutions. As a result of deregulation and liberalization, individual institutions have tended to become more competitive and accountable through the creation of an overall market mechanism within the education system (Giroux 2002). The issuance of educational loans by the International Monetary Fund (IMF) and the World Bank (WB) supports these trends. In general, the IMF and WB serve as a support mechanism for neoliberalism in Latin America, Africa, and Eastern Europe through the promotion of market mechanisms that effect increases in private investment in education and accountability in HEIs (Chou 2003). As governments pursue this ideology, systems of higher education are consequently faced with a series of transformations, shifting from more specific norms of state control to those of state supervision. In brief, policy makers are convinced that HEIs' adoption of market-oriented mechanisms will encourage universities to share the financial burden, especially in light of expanded student enrollment (Chou 2008).

This stance also facilitates the idea of cost-effectiveness among HEIs, in terms of increasing efficiency and improving educational quality. It is assumed that such a positive impact will enhance institutional academic autonomy, as well as increase choice for students and parents as empowered consumers of higher education. As a global trend, the establishment of market economies has particularly had an impact on Asian HEIs, especially in China, Japan, Korea, and Taiwan, where higher education has experienced tremendous growth since the last decade (Altbach 2003). The case of Taiwan serves as an excellent example, given the influence of neoliberal principles in higher education policy since late 1980s when the country was in the process of political and economic transition.

Education Reform Era (after 1994)

Education Reform Appeals for Deregulation and Empowerment

If we look at the development of Taiwan's education system since 1994, it is obvious that, despite pursuing "diversity" and "excellence," educational policy has continually followed two main principles, "deregulation" and "empowerment," as was declared in 1987 during the period of post-martial law. Between 1994 and 1996, in order to offer a blueprint for future education reform, the Education Reform Council worked out five Consultation Reports of Education Reform through numerous discussions. These reports contain the following recommendations:

1. Deregulate Education

It is suggested that the function and organization of the Ministry of Education (MOE) be revised to enlarge the power of local institutions, amend various regulations related to school education and teachers, improve the organization of schools at all levels, and deregulate various types of schools (such as alternative schools, private schools, public schools, chartered schools, and experimental schools) and the legal system as well. It is also recommended that private schools and the alternative education system should be offered more space to develop.

2. Focus on Each Individual Student

There should be efforts in primary and secondary schools to replace a "curriculum" with a "course outline," reinforce the connections between courses and improve the integration of courses, reduce the number of subjects and study hours required, decrease school and class sizes, reduce the inequalities that exist between the country's elite and regular schools, establish assessment standards for school performance, promote basic competency, strengthen education for the disabled, and ensure that every person has access to education.

3. Provide Multiple Ways to Advance Learning

This can be attained by developing comprehensive high schools and implementing multiadmission programs, and by setting up various HEIs to provide opportunities for lifelong learning.

4. Raise Education Quality

There is a need to strengthen teachers' professionalism, education research, and evaluation methods; to establish a higher education deliberation committee that will act as an adviser; to encourage diversification; and to refine technical and vocational education.

5. Establish a Lifelong Learning Society
Emphasize the concept of lifelong learning and integrate lifelong learning systems, and establish a mechanism for continuing education.

Since education reform involves a wide range of actions, the Education Reform Council sorted them according to merit and, for future reference, listed the most important issues that are awaiting reorganization. Moreover, to carry out the suggestions for reform issued by the Education Reform Council, the Executive Yuan requested that all related ministries establish an education reform promotion committee, and it issued a Twelve-Step Plan for Education Reform in May 1998, as recommended by the Education Reform Council. This five-year plan was implemented during 1998–2003, for a total investment of NT$15.77million. The twelve steps mentioned above include:

1. Improve the national education system
2. Provide universal preschool education
3. Improve the teacher education and teacher training systems
4. Encourage the diversification and refinement of technical and vocational education
5. Pursue excellence in higher education
6. Promote lifelong education and information network education
7. Promote family education
8. Strengthen the education of students with disabilities
9. Strengthen and improve the education of aboriginal students
10. Offer multiple avenues to higher education
11. Create a new student counseling system
12. Enrich the education budget and strengthen education research

This cross-century plan can be described as the most comprehensive education reform policy that Taiwan has ever announced as well as invested in financially, and as a result, the Education Reform Committee was established and led by the Executive Yuan. The committee consisted of a vice president as the convener and members who included the ministers of the main ministries and professional scholars and experts. Furthermore, the committee practically put into place the education reform proposals mentioned here, which had a great impact on future educational development.

The MOE held a National Education Reform Review Conference in May 1999, which focused on reviewing whether the 12 critical education reform topics had been addressed, and its conclusion was called the Revision of Education Reform Action Plan. With the first-ever ruling party rotation in the national government occurring the following year, a national Review and Improve Education Reform Conference was held in December to examine the gains and losses in education reform and develop response strategies.

This conference was organized to develop an educational vision that was named "New Thought, New Action and New Vision," and planned as a way to exchange viewpoints thoroughly on five central topics, including preparing the education environment, upgrading the quality of primary and secondary school teachers, improving the education of vulnerable groups, revising educational content, and pursuing excellence in universities. Again, the outcome of this conference was the basic revision of the Education Reform Action Plan. Two years later, tired of facing never-ending complaints and questions from the society—such as concerns about imposing even more pressure on students to study and requiring too many textbooks, and misunderstandings regarding multiple entrance programs, all of which had resulted from the efforts to put in place education reform—the MOE held another conference, the National Education Development Conference, to communicate with the public and also promote its policies.

The conference issued an education vision, which was expressed in the motto "To create a happy learning environment, to inspire educational innovative motivating power, and to nurture dynamic, creative and competitive new citizens of the E-generation," and which included the goals of caring for vulnerable groups to fulfill social justice, returning to the essence of national education and gradually implementing twelve-year compulsory education, and, finally, promoting the efficiency of higher education and enhancing the country's international competitiveness. This time, the Education Promoting Program was set up after the conference. In the following January, 2005, the MOE held a National Education Fair in Taiwan's northern, central, southern, and eastern areas, and took this opportunity to reveal the four principles of education policy, which were to cultivate modern citizens, build a Taiwan-centered concept, expand a global vision, and strengthen social care and awareness.

With the exception of the education policy and budget mentioned above, the orientation of the country's education plan was legally confirmed as well. The Education Basic Law, approved by the Legislative Yuan on June 4, 1999, was accepted as the country's basic principle of education policy. Also called the Quasi-Educational Constitution, it contained 17 articles in total, including the main ideas outlined below:

1. Education is for the people and is intended to build modern citizens with a national consciousness and worldview.
2. Four main principles related to implementing education are:
   a. All people possess the right to education, and education should satisfy the needs of individuals.
   b. There should be equal educational opportunities.
   c. There should be neutrality.
   d. Class size and schools in compulsory education should be small.
3. The source of the educational budget (as regulated by other laws) will be ensured.
4. The responsibilities of both the central government and local educational bureaus (the trend of decentralization) are confirmed.
5. The operation of the local educational administration should be encouraged to adopt the collegiate system and the executive system (e.g., to establish an education commission in municipalities and counties).
6. Private schools should be encouraged (by offering them subsidies and permitting authorized private schools to manage national schools).
7. Teachers' professional autonomy and students' rights to study are ensured.
8. Students should possess indicative norms of identification regarding scholastic aptitude.

Thereafter, the MOE issued various reports and white papers on a wide range of topics, including its vision of education in the twentieth century, education in creative thinking, gender equity, giftedness, information technology, life longevity, moral education, science, and marine education, higher education, technical and vocational education, education for the disabled, the elderly, and indigenous people, and so forth. This can be described as a crucial period in which the government endeavored to put all its energy into planning comprehensively for a brand new century.

At the same time, institutions such as the Republic of China Education Reform Association, the Teacher Association, and the National Parents Union were quickly established to take part in educational reforms and offer suggestions. All these educational groups hoped to combine forces not only with domestic groups but also with support from overseas and to form an irresistible power that would promote common issues related to education reform.

Specific Education Policy Regarding Diversity and Excellence

In using the terms "diversity" and "excellence" to describe this period since 1994, we can say that the Taiwanese government has turned its decision-making model upside down, from having previously been the sole central authority to listening to the voices of the public. Education policy concerns the reform of primary and secondary courses (a nine-year integrated curriculum), teaching materials (textbooks, privatization, more than one optional outline), admission methods (multiple entrance programs for high school and university), transcription evaluation (multiple assessments to replace the traditional examination), teacher training (creating multiple forms of training), the educational system (deliberation of ten- to twelve-year compulsory education), the selection of principals, teachers, and parents associations, the expansion of senior high schools and universities, and so forth.

As for the term "excellence," it means to pursue good quality or an excellent performance (i.e., quality education), which can be achieved by improving the environment, equipment, and teaching activities. Thus, the government promotes policies related to autonomy, corporatization, school funding, academic and teaching excellence, evaluation, and the internationalization of university campuses, and supports the restructuring and upgrading of technical and vocational colleges. The government also plays a role in bringing about the "communalization" of senior high schools and technical and vocational schools, establishing more comprehensive public senior high schools and more complete secondary schools, implementing self-learning classes and skill training classes in junior high schools, reducing the size of schools and classrooms for compulsory education, putting in place the basic aptitude test, and supporting the teaching of the mother language, English, local education (history), and sixth grade Construction of Mathematics in elementary school.

In devising and selecting current reform strategies, the government should place a high priority on deregulation, and should aim to achieve educational "diversity" by revising or establishing laws, regulations, or acts. For example,

1. Deregulation of Education
Initially, the appeal of deregulation was focused on educational liberalization, democratization, and diversity to make an adjustment for the over-regulation by the central government (especially the MOE) in the past and to protect teachers' professional autonomy by empowering local authorities

and schools. The deregulation policy was first reflected in the revision of the University Act (first enacted in 1948 and revised in 1994). According to the articles mentioned (MOE 2007) below, universities are empowered with the rights of autonomy (including the election of the principal) in Article 1, and Article 14 offers a legal basis for governance by the faculty. Moreover, Article 33 clearly calls for students' attendance at meetings related to both academic and student affairs. Beyond these requirements, universities are ultimately free of the central authority's supervision and able to attend to their own business to their best advantage.

- Article 1: Universities shall be guaranteed academic freedom and shall enjoy autonomy within the range of laws and regulations.
- Article 14: Executive posts of different levels in national universities may be held by teaching or research personnel and shall be stipulated in the organizational procedure of the university.
- Article 33: To enhance education, universities shall require that the elected representatives of students attend academic affairs meetings and also meetings relating to their study, living, and the formulating of regulations related to reward and punishment.

Furthermore, universities began to nurture qualified teachers after the passing of the *Teacher Education Law* in 1994. Then a teacher act was enacted to specify teachers' rights and obligations and to safeguard their career and livelihood (Article 1), which has influenced teachers greatly. As to the *Education Basic Law* announced in 1999, it has the status of an educational constitution and plays a role in setting norms to regulate other educational laws, regulations, and acts. In addition, the *Education Basic Law* is expected to promote the participation in education and educational neutrality, and also take care of vulnerable students and promote respect for the rights of teachers, students, and even parents, which is meaningful. Moreover, regarding the deregulation of textbooks that is specified in the *Education Basic Law*, Article 8, restrictions on textbooks have been totally revoked. Furthermore, those experimental programs such as open learning environments (school buildings without interior walls that traditionally separate classes), which were promoted by local government for a short time period to offer students a much more free-thinking atmosphere, and other alternative school models, have led Taiwan's education system to become more open and flexible.

2. Multiple Paths to Advanced Study
Efforts to ease academic pressure by offering multiple ways for students to enroll in a school at a higher level can be approached in various ways. First,

there can be increasing opportunities to enroll in institutions of higher education. For example, there are three educational highways by which students can access higher education. One is an academic educational system that enables students to enter senior high school directly after compulsory education. The second one expands the number of four-year technical colleges, two-year junior colleges, and two-year technical colleges so that students can continue their study after graduating from senior technical and vocational schools and junior colleges. The last one encourages the public to return to the campus of a university or college to study. Citizens have complete freedom to attend any course offered in the curriculum. This type of education helps to generate profits; therefore, almost all universities and colleges have set up a continuing education division to administer such programs.

During this time period the number of students attending secondary education greatly expanded. Qualified junior high schools were enabled to be selected through a public appraisal process and restructured into high schools with six grade levels (Grades 7–12). In this way, junior high schools and senior high schools were merged into one school. Also, regular senior high schools and senior technical or vocational schools were also encouraged to restructure to become to comprehensive high schools with three grade levels (Grades 10–12). Through these measures, the education situation across school districts was improved.

Furthermore, the enrollment system has been reformed and multiple entrance programs have also been implemented already. Previous entrance examinations, inherited from the centuries-old traditional Keju, have already been abolished and replaced by other methods of enrollment, which has returned rights to students and enabled them to choose a suitable entrance mode based on their individual requirements. The entrance modes for admission to a school that are now offered include a proficiency examination, admission by application, voluntary enrollment, and superior recommendations. All modes mentioned above are suitable for students to enter schools at the senior high level. Nevertheless, the Basic Academic Competence Test has been implemented broadly, and "the combination of the examination and enrollment system" has been especially welcomed among technical colleges and universities.

3. Focus on Each Individual Student

The goal of tending to and nurturing every student in a class has great potential to support a student's individual development, and there are plenty of ways for teachers to provide students with inspiration for their various talents. Protecting their educational rights is an example. Due to the emphasis on human-rights education in the international sphere,

Taiwan has also begun to emphasize respect for students' right to be educated and parents' rights to educational options. Both the Declaration on the Rights of Education issued by the Humanistic Education Foundation in 1987 and the declarations of student rights issued by domestic student associations call for the safeguarding of basic human rights, the right of autonomy, and the right of learning.

As for parents' rights, with the exception of fighting for the rights of parents to participate in educational affairs, the regulation also expects to deregulate restrictions on private schools and empower them with autonomy. With the establishment of more private schools, then, parents' rights to educational options for their children can be properly realized. Regarding teachers' rights, these have been even better protected since the establishment of the Teacher Evaluation Committee and various teachers' organizations created through the Teacher Act.

Related to the discussion about the protection of vulnerable groups, the measures listed below have been put in place to help them adapt to society:

a. Strengthen aboriginal education, establish an Indigenous Affairs Commission in the Executive Yuan, enact an Education Act for Indigenous Peoples, and safeguard the education budget for indigenous peoples
b. Establish a gender equity unit in every institution, for example, the Commission on the Promotion of Women's Rights in the Executive Yuan and the Gender Equality Education Committee in the MOE, and apply the norm of gender equality as a criterion when reviewing textbooks
c. Improve the education of students with disabilities, including upgrading the both hardware and software systems
d. Add courses on the mother tongue in primary schools in order to provide students with an opportunity to study their mother tongue and also to help preserve that language's culture
e. Promote local education and add local culture courses to the compulsory education curriculum, in order to enhance students' greater understanding and appreciation of local affairs and encourage the preservation of local culture and regional development

4. Raise Education Quality

The first step toward improving the quality of education is to enhance preservice teacher education work on a broad scale. This goal is aimed at current teachers in schools below the senior high level, to promote in-service training and improve working conditions and professional status.

Moreover, the plan is to push ahead with universities' academic development and to award government grants to universities to undertake projects related to scholarly excellence and also to participate in the project called Five-Year Fifty Billion–Aiming for the Top University and Elite Research Center Development Plan. The education evaluations and teaching excellence projects employed in universities and technical colleges are key points intended to enhance the quality of higher education.

As for the curriculum of primary and secondary schools, since the implementation of the Nine-Year Integrated Curriculum in 2001, ten capabilities that modern citizens should possess have been issued, and the traditional structure of subjects has been broken up and rearranged into seven learning fields, including languages, mathematics, the social sciences, health and sports, the arts and humanities, science and technology, and integrative activities. The integration of courses and the team-based teaching model are emphasized. In addition, English learning is scheduled to start in fifth grade, the study hours for every grade have been reduced, and the development of a school-based curriculum has been encouraged. Moreover, class size has been reduced to less than thirty-five students so that teachers can teaching a smaller number of students. This practice is intended to promote a small class teaching experiment in order to prove its efficiency, reducing the size of Taiwan's classrooms to the Chinese class size of below thirty-five students per class.

The amended *Compulsory Education Law* allowed schools to become a real decision-making body and have the autonomy to be involved in the election of the principal, the school budget, school development plans, textbook selection, students' bonus-penalty provisions, students' grade evaluations, and so forth through discussion in the school faculty. Finally, one of the aims of the national education budget (around NT$400 billion) is to ensure government commitment to education and to enhance and improve the efficiency of its implementation at all levels.

5. Creating a Learning Society

To fulfill the goal of creating a learning society, Taiwan should not only focus on promoting the concept of lifelong learning but also integrate a lifelong learning system into its educational system and set up a mechanism by which individuals can return to school. For example, it is important to create a flexible and diverse school system for adults of all ages. Meanwhile, a consistent system of technical and vocational education is needed, including universities and colleges of technology, vocational schools, and comprehensive senior high schools and junior high schools, which provide practical training classes and require more attention from students. In addition, the MOE has published a White Paper on the

Implementation of Lifelong Education, intended as a guideline for establishing a learning society. It is worth mentioning that, especially since 1998, hundreds of community colleges have already been set up throughout the country. They are taking charge of leading a culture of lifelong learning and offering the public an opportunity to learn something new at any time, which has contributed quite a lot to enhancing the quality of education for all citizens.

In the past sixteen years, from 1994 to 2010, the government has published a series of educational laws: the University Act, the Teacher Education Law, the Teacher Act, the National Education Act, the Education Basic Law, the Faculty and Staff Retirement and Pension Rule, Regulations for Establishing a Parents Association, and so forth. The development of Taiwan's education system since then has moved toward more diversity and excellence. As far as primary and secondary schools are concerned, schools now have the autonomy not only to select their own textbooks but also to choose their own ground rules and principles to follow. As for higher education, except for the deregulation and empowerment mentioned above, the government has also taken steps toward financial reform and structural adjustment, encouraging private donations and the establishment of endowment funds. Moreover, the government has bridged the gap between public and private universities with regard to education costs and tuition fees by shifting funds from public universities' reduced state subsidies to private universities. There are also projects such as the Five-Year Fifty Billion–Aiming for the Top University and Elite Research Center Development Plan and the Teaching Excellent Project that have been implemented to upgrade universities' competitive edge. In particular, the recently announced plan to make uniform the tuition of public and private senior regular and vocational high schools can be said to be in preparation for the future twelve-year compulsory education plan.

The 1994–1996 Educational Reform Master Plan

After the national government's withdrawal from mainland China in 1949, education policy was embedded in a nationalism (or patriotism that opposed Chinese communism and the military threat) that was based on the Chinese culture and Western economic rationalism. Teacher training classes, regarded as a "psychological national defense," were established and monitored exclusively by the government. The central government monopolized and handled all the budget allocations, textbook content and publications, high school and college admissions, student recruitment, and school daily-operation codes. A strong China-oriented cultural nationalism also stood as the core value throughout the curriculum, textbooks, teacher preparation, and daily school practices.

On the other hand, in order to improve Taiwan's economic development by providing more qualified personnel, the country also embraced educational principles based on Western economic capitalism through the influence of American economic foreign aid, labor-intensive industry, and export-oriented trade. Theories of human capital, structural-functionalism, modernization, and behavioral competency-based education were adopted into education policy beginning in the 1960s (Yang 2000).

Up to the 1980s, as a result of the great challenge from the high-tech industry, coupled with continuing protests from political opposition parties as well as the general public in Taiwan, the nearly four-decade-long martial law was at last lifted on July 15, 1987. The demand for political democratization, cultural pluralism, and social liberalization arose all over the country from all walks of life, including the mass media, the banking sector, the elected legislature, and so on. The whole nation was full of zealous expectation and calls for change. One of the major concerns in this social transformation was educational reform: people demanded greater deregulation and a liberation from the central planned economy and political monopoly to allow more civilian participation and parental choice in education.

A series of social demonstrations and movements for education transformation spread throughout the whole island, echoing the worldwide trend of technological, economic, and sociocultural restructuring. As a result, the inability of schools to cope with emerging social problems and the increasing gap between social classes in the field of education were challenged. More and more taxpayers and shareholders were less and less patient about the insensitive way in which existing institutions of public education operated in the 1980s and early 1990s (Berman 1996).

In order to follow the worldwide trend in reconstructing education, Taiwan launched a series of reform proposals starting in the early 1990s, including the establishment of a cabinet-level ad hoc Council on Education Reform (教育改革審議委員會) in September 1994 in response to the societal urge for democratization, pluralism, and liberalization. The council, led by Lee Yuan-Tze, Nobel Laureate in Chemistry (1986), was tasked with building the scaffolding of Taiwan's future educational master plan that would fulfill the new demands for the twenty-first century. After a two-year public survey and research study, the council published five reports, including the concluding General Consultation Report for

Education Reform (教育改革總諮議報告書), released on December 2, 1996. Specifically, the report identified the following education reform goals, which covered preschool to adulthood (see Figure 3.1):

1. Modernizing educational processes and end results
2. Meeting individual as well as social needs
3. Establishing a society of lifelong learning
4. Promoting extensive and penetrative innovation of the educational system

A year later, in January 1997, the Executive Yuan established another interministerial Commission for Promoting Education Reform (教育改革推動委員會) to implement and follow up on the earlier 1996 reform proposals. Twelve Education Reform Mandates (教育改革行動方案) were released in 1998, and allocated special governmental aid totaling NT$150,000,000,000 (equivalent to US$5 Billion) to carry out the

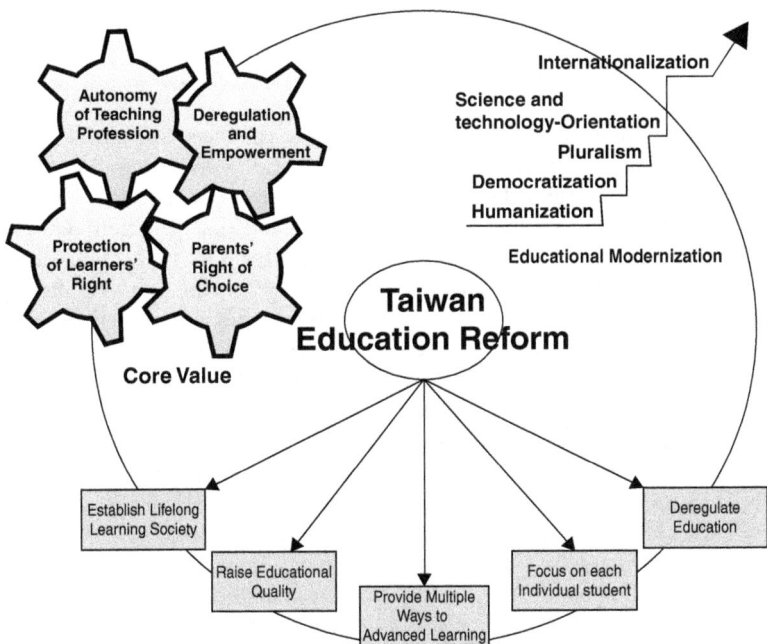

Figure 3.1 The Framework for Education Reform 1996.
Source: Chou (2003).

reform plan in the next five years. These twelve mandates were intended to cultivate Taiwan's outstanding talents, encourage lifelong learning, and enhance Taiwan international competitiveness in an emerging "knowledge-based society" (Chou and Ho 2007). The goals are as follows:

1. Revamping National Education Projects, K-12
2. Fostering Preschool and Kindergarten Education Programs
3. Renovating Teacher Education and In-Service Training Programs
4. Promoting Impeccable Diversified Vocational Education
5. Pursuing Excellence in Higher Education and Its Development
6. Advocating Lifelong Learning Projects
7. Strengthening Educational Programs Designed for the Handicapped
8. Invigorating Educational Programs for the Native Taiwanese (Aboriginals)
9. Expanding Access to Colleges and Universities
10. Creating a New System That Integrates Teaching, Guidance, and Counseling
11. Increasing the Educational Budget for the Enhancement of Educational Research
12. Accelerating the Promotion of Family Values/Ethics through Parental Education

Throughout Taiwan's history, the government has been in charge of controlling and publishing textbooks, and thus spreading its own political and social agenda/ideologies. The issues concerning government-controlled textbooks bloomed during the decades of the '70s and the '80s, alongside the political reform and social protest movements. Textbooks have been criticized in the last few decades for reinforcing the governing party's ability to plant their own point of view without considering various other perspectives, sides, and differences, such as those related to gender, culture, and ethnicity. In order to decentralize the textbook publication system, a new arrangement was introduced in 1996, in parallel with the diversification and liberalization trends being felt in Taiwanese society and its education system. The revised system encompasses the National Institute for Compilation and Translation (NICT) under the MOE, and once textbooks and teaching materials are screened and approved by this institute, private companies are entitled to publish new material (Pan and Yu 1999). This approach implies, however, that the MOE is still in charge of setting the standards for the curriculum and monitoring education quality (Chou and Ho 2007).

In sum, the core of the early 1990s reform plans, interwoven with the General Consultation Report for education reform, included: (1) deregulating governmental control over education (鬆綁), (2) exempting education from unnecessary constraints (放權), (3) protecting children's and students' right to learn, (4) respecting parents' right to choose the education patterns and paths for their children, and (5) guaranteeing teachers' professional autonomy.

Out of all of these steps, the proposal to broaden and diversify channels for admission to higher schools and universities, and to facilitate lifelong learning was expected to have the greatest impact on reducing students' stress that resulted from exams. Along with the master reform plan and other schemes, the MOE and the related education authorities in Taiwan initiated a series of legislative reforms in education. Among these efforts, the revised *University Law* (1994, 1998, and 2005), the new *Teacher Education Act* (1993, 2009), and the new Labor *Union Act* (2010, 6), which allows teachers to organize labor unions, are the major breakthrough in terms of reforming Taiwan's education system.

Above all, the promulgation of the Education Basic Law in 1999 is regarded as the most important piece of educational legislation in recent years in Taiwan. This law paved the way for promoting student rights, education based on individual differences, equal opportunities in education, educational neutrality, class and school downsizing, duty regulation between central and local governance, educational privatization, and so on. In addition, underprivileged students, including those who live in remote areas, have now been given special status in order to ensure that they receive equal opportunities in education. The law also requires educational authorities to remain neutral in dealing with subject matter and instruction. Some fundamental changes in education have occurred since the enactment of the law.

During the 1990s, a series of government policy reports and education laws were released and passed, such as: the *Twenty-First Century Prospects for Education* in the Republic of China (1995), the *Government Report on Equal Education Opportunity for Disadvantaged Children* (1995), the *Government Report on Equal Education Opportunity for Indigenous People* (1997), an *Approach to a Learning Society* (1998), and a *White Paper Report on Creativity Education for Primary and Secondary Schools* (2002). In addition, reports on gifted education, gender equity education, marine science education, vocational education, higher education, science education, and information and technology education were released to provide guidelines for Taiwan's education system in the twenty-first century. It is time for the government to take over education reforms, which attempt to raise the standards for Taiwan's new generation so that they can meet the need for global competitiveness. However, there is still great controversy surrounding ongoing education reform, which deserves further exploration (Hwang 2003).

The "controversial reform stage" (1994 to the present) has been characterized by much negative public opinion against educational reform programs. Chou (2008) and Hwang (2003) identifiy some of the problematic reform areas, including:

1. Seven Ministers of Education between 1987 and 2003, which resulted in discontinuity and conflicts between various reform policies
2. Lack of small-scale pilot or trial studies of reform practices
3. Lack of in-service teacher training
4. Miscommunication and misinformation among schools, parents, and the government
5. Increasing gaps between urban versus rural areas, and rich versus poor have aroused great concern in the country.

Yang (2001) also argues that some of these problems are rooted in ideological conflicts that underlie education reform measures, the imbalance between competition and social justice, and the tussle for power among the private sector, parents, schools, and government. Other problems are connected to the lack of new norms to maintain educational excellence, the shortfall in educational budgets, the crisis in teacher professionalism, and the lack of recognition of the school as a center for change (Pan and Yu 1999).

The focus of the twenty-first century is on global competition and how to best meet the needs of diverse students. "Excellence," "efficiency," and "equity" have become the three main goals of education in Taiwan for the next ten years. Raising global competitiveness, fostering global citizenship, encouraging localization and globalization, and creating a well-rounded education are all current goals of Taiwan's MOE.

In conclusion, education in Taiwan has been employed as one of the most influential avenues for building the nation and for economic development. Due to the country's diverse cultural heritage and the increased access of the masses to the Taiwan education system, which combines Japanese educational practices and ideals from the colonization period, and Chinese culture and Confucian traditions from the mainland, schools in Taiwan have experienced dramatic increases in enrollments. The pressure for earning credentials and passing examinations, also part of the Taiwanese heritage, remained constant throughout the twentieth century, however. Many educational innovations have been launched to deal with the examination systems and curricular contents and instruction, and to reduce the government's ideological control. As a result, teachers will now have more flexibility to self-govern and more autonomy to enhance students' creativity and thinking skills for the twenty-first century. Nevertheless, the increasing discrepancies in income distribution and resources between urban and rural areas, the dilemma of the pursuit of educational quality versus quantity, and the balance between localization and internationalization have created numerous challenges and risks for the people of Taiwan.

REFERENCES

Altbach, Philip G. 2003. "Why the United States Will Not Be a Market for Foreign Higher Education Products: A Case against GATS 2003." *International Higher Education* 31 (Spring): 5–8.
Berman, Morris. 1996. "The Politics of American Education and Struggle for Cultural Dominance." *Melbourne Studies in Education* 37 (1): 21–45.
China's Ministry of Culture. n.d. *Keju (Imperial Examination System)*. Beijing: Ministry of Culture, People's Republic of China. Available online at: http://www1.chinaculture.org.
Chou, Chuing Prudence. 2003. *The Great Experiment of Taiwanese Education: 1987–2003*. Taipei: Psychology Publishing.
———. 2008. "The Impact of Neo-Liberalism on Taiwanese Higher Education." In *The Worldwide Transformation of Higher Education*, eds., David P. Baker and Alexander W. Wiseman, 9: 297–311: Greenwich, CT: JAI Press.
Chou, Chuing Prudence, and Ai-Hsin Ho. 2007. "Schooling in Taiwan." In *Going to School in East Asia*, edited by G. Postiglione and J. Tan, 344–377. New York: Greenwood.
Davidson, James. 2005. *The Island of Formosa, Past and Present*. Taipei: SMC Publishing.
Directorate General of Budget. 2010. *Summary of Country Profile*. Taipei: Directorate General of Budget. Available online at: http://ebas1.ebas.gov.tw.
Duann, Pu. 2010. *Taiwanese Education during the Japanese Era*. Taipei: National Cheng Chi University.
Everts, Natalie. 2000. *Jacob van Lamay van Tayouan: An Indigenous Formosan Who Became an Amsterdam Citizen*. Berkeley: University of California Press.
Giroux, Henry A. 2002. "Neo-Liberalism, Corporate Culture, and the Promise of Higher Education: The University as a Democratic Public Sphere." *Harvard Educational Review* 72 (4): 424–463.
Hsu, Nan-Hao. 1993. *Taiwanese Education History*. Taipei: National Taiwan Normal University.
Hwang, Guang-Guo. 2003. *What's Wrong with Taiwanese Education Reform*. Taipei: Ink Publishing.
Ministry of Education (MOE). 2007, October 1. *Enforcement Results of the University Act*. Taipei: MOE. Available online at: http://edu.law.moe.gov.tw.
Olssen, Mark. 2002. "The Restructuring of Tertiary Education in New Zealand: Governmentality, Neo-liberalism, Democracy." *McGill Journal of Education* 37 (1): 57–88.

Pan, Hui-Ling, and Chien Yu. 1999. "Educational Reforms with Their Impacts on School Effectiveness and School Improvement in Taiwan, R.O.C." *School Effectiveness and School Improvement* 10 (1): 72–85.

Taiwan Association of University Professors. 2006. "Title of Article." Taipei: Taiwan Association of University Professors. Available onlie at: http://taup.yam.org.tw.

Tsurumi, Patricia. 1999. *Japanese Colonial Education in Taiwan: 1895–1945*. Yilan: Young Sun Foundation.

Yang, Shen-Keng. 2000. "Education Reform Facing the New Millenium—Methodological Reflection and International Comparison." *Bulletin of Educational Research* 44: 1–34.

———. 2001. "Dilemmas of Education Reform in Taiwan: Internationalization or Localization?" Paper presented at the Annual Meeting of the Comparative and International Education Society, Washington, DC, March 14–17, 2001.

Zhen, Wei-Zhong. 2004. *Taiwanese Society in the Dutch Era*. Taipei: Avanguard Publishing.

Chapter 4

East Asian and Taiwan Education in the Context of Worldwide Education Reform

Education reforms worldwide in the last half century have been typically associated with major social events that were taking place at the time (Levin 2001). After World War II, around 1950, many countries took the initiative on education reform programs to promote the enhancement of economic growth as a long-term plan, as well as strengthen the national economic system, based on principals such as human capital theories or modernization ideology. Several stages of reform can be described, as follows.

First stage, education reform in the 1950–1960s: many newly independent countries, including Indonesia, India, and Pakistan, which were in an unhealthy economic and social state were in need of revitalizing their channels of growth after facing postwar ruin. Education is regarded as one of the major avenues for independence and modernization. As a result, in many countries, the government made efforts to invest in education in the hope that this would boost the national economy and social development. One of the reform objectives was to transform society through education with the support of the community and taxpayers, to revitalize national strength, spirit, and dignity. Through a variety of public funds, governments increased investment in all sectors related to education. Meanwhile, the unprecedented fertility of the postwar Baby Boomer population reached its peak. Consequently, governments found it necessary to expand the educational scale, and they built more schools to improve the quality of education.

Second stage, education reform of the 1960–1970s: growth in the numbers of university graduates reached a peak, and the unemployment rate as well rose. In other words, although educational opportunities had expanded, the market could not absorb this excess workforce since the demand-supply ratio was uneven, and therefore, economies did not flourish as expected. Up until this time, the birth rate had been gradually slowing down. Education experts as well as policy makers in the past had been full of hope, and they later found themselves unable to counter problems such as poverty, unemployment, and crime. Many emerging countries that invested heavily in education discovered that most of this investment did not automatically result in economic prosperity. Many of them started asking, "Can education investment lead to a country's economic recovery?" This was especially the case when there were two worldwide oil crises as well as heavy spending on defense by the United States and the Soviet Union during the Cold War, right after 1970, which reduced the priority of the education budgets in these two countries. During this time, many states began facing fiscal austerity and budget deficits, and inflation was becoming more and more serious for many governments. Such conditions led, in the long run, to a very unsustainable economic situation. Therefore, these countries became unable to continue their ongoing investment in education.

Third stage, educational reform of the 1970–1980s: governments such as those of British Prime Minister Margaret Thatcher (in office, May 4, 1979–November 28, 1990), and U.S. President Ronald Reagan (in office, January 20, 1981–January 20, 1989) launched a series of public policies limiting government power and authority over the public sectors; allowed for a freer market economy, i.e., a neoliberal ideology in support of "small government and big market" policies; and advocated tax cuts for the rich, the reduction of social welfare, and education expenditures. These reforms helped strengthen the economies of the United Kingdom and the United States, and empowered local communities and school districts in establishing and regulating education reforms.

Fourth stage, education reform in the 1980s: this period is usually called a time of "postmodernism," when the "information society" came to challenge government's role in education, according to Giddens's (1994), Ball's (1998), and others' critiques. As a result of neoliberal ideology, a great deal of public investment has consistently been allocated to the business and market sectors rather than the education sector. As a result, the practice of reducing government's role in so-called political responsibility led to the curbing of people's rights (Dai et al. 2002). Countries such as New Zealand, Australia, and the United States invited more political and business leaders, instead of representatives of the education sector, to participate in conferences on education reform when formulating education policies. At the same time, government gradually took the form of a business, employing strategies that included reducing state intervention by introducing market mechanisms into its policy-making process. In short, following the 1980s, a sharp reduction in public budgets in many countries influenced the educational organization structure, culture, values, resource allocation, management, social relations, and public welfare. Furthermore, in order to increase parents' participation in decision-making and the sharing of funding, the government took the lead in providing additional financial support to parent groups.

In particular, as they felt the impact of globalization in higher education, almost all countries worldwide started urging university reforms, whether in the form of mainland China's 211 project and 985 project, Korea's BK21 program, Taiwan's Five Years Five Top University program, or Japan's National University of Administrative Corporation, all of which are responses to the process of globalization.

The way a country maintains its own cultural traditions in order to respond to the needs of its people has always been the major concern of most citizens. Education is generally the vehicle by which governments establish and maintain this socialization process in society. It is a political issue, however, and sometimes there is instability in the political education arena. In Germany, for example, political parties have hotly debated the issue of the operation of comprehensive schools and grammar schools. The United Kingdom also came under the influence of conservative governance, such as during the government of Prime Minister Margaret Thatcher, who held power for over 18 years, a period of time that saw the thorough implementation of neoliberal concepts that transformed the British education and social welfare system into market-oriented mechanisms. Similar changes took place in New Zealand's, Australia's, and Canada's education systems.

Education reform also occurred in Taiwan, Japan, Korea, and many other countries in Asia as different political parties with various ideologies took office. In addition, the transformation of the traditional educational administration system can be classified as a "centralized" system, a "regional decentralization system," or something "in the middle." The centralized administrative system is usually set up by a unified national education system, namely the Ministry of Education (Department of Science, Education, Employment, or Human Development), which is in charge of regulations, policies, funding, and the administration of national education standards, on behalf of the state, such as in France, the former Soviet Union, China, and so forth. In the regional decentralization system, the local governments of each province, state, or municipality, or local school districts hold their own authority over educational management, which is commonly seen in the United States, Germany, and Australia (Xie 2007).

In recent years, education systems have become increasingly complex. Therefore, in many countries, education administration has gradually turned to one of the above modes of centralization or decentralization, developing in this particular way into a partnership between national and local government, such as the United Kingdom, Japan, and China. Yet as more and more deregulation and competitive pressures reign, the question of how to enhance administrative efficiency and improve teaching and evaluation, in order to achieve "efficiency and effectiveness" is facing an unprecedented challenge (Dale 2001).

Educational administrative departments in many countries are unable to maintain their original framework, and have started to combine education, youth development, vocational training, talent development, and the cultural and creative sectors, in order to strengthen relations with other departments. For example, in the United Kingdom, in June 2007, the original Department for Education and Skills was changed to the Department for Children, Schools and Families and the Department for Innovation, Universities and Skills. In Japan, the Ministry of Education was renamed the Ministry of Education and Science in 2001, and in Korea, the Department of Education Human Resources and the Ministry of Science and Technology was reestablished in 2008.

All of these restructuring efforts were mainly in response to a more precise division of interdisciplinary integration and expansion of the original service sector under the pressure of public demand for national competitiveness and the need to adjust from one political party to another. In the process of such a restructuring movement, the central government has tended to weaken its role in regulating the disparities in and the quality of national education. This has in some cases led to inequalities in education. Issues such as equity and efficiency are always the subject of much attention, especially before and after a reform has promoted the improvement of efficiency and the maintaining of social justice at the same time. As education reforms have progressed in the last twenty years, social-class division has become increasingly obvious in many countries. For example, the societies of Japan, Kenya, and Taiwan in the early 1960s enjoyed a fairer pay structure, the gap between individuals with less schooling and those with more was evident, education tended to be an important mechanism for social mobility, and many poor children were able to achieve upward mobility through education.

After the 1980s, as education reform took place, namely through the decentralization of government, the introduction of market mechanisms, a relaxing of the school curriculum, and the increasing trend towards the commercialization of education, the reinforcement of class distinctions and social inequalities was exacerbated. These reforms seemed to raise issues of inequality and social justice. Issues of fairness and efficiency surfaced especially on topics like the right to education regardless of gender, race, ethnicity, or disadvantaged status.

A Changing East Asia and Taiwan

The Regional Context

East Asia, as a developing area, is undergoing rapid development and far-reaching changes that transcend national borders. There are four trends of special significance (Chen 2001b). First, East Asia has become one of the foci of world attention because of its fast-growing numbers of students and the expansion of quality education services. East Asia has been renowned for its culture of frugality, hardwork, and family values, which has distinguished it from the rest of the world. The region is also in the process of rapid demographic transition, which is reflected in increased life expectancy, the decline in the mortality rate, and at the same time, the drastic decline in the birth rate. Nevertheless, the high literacy rates and massification of higher education in the region are also impressive .

Nevertheless, many Asian economies continue to experience fundamental and tumultuous change in a time of globalization, which has led not only to a drastic social, cultural, and ecological transformation but also the growing gap between rich and poor, and between the urban and rural areas in each society. This is especially the case with respect to the economic crisis of 2008 that resulted in the collapse of the rapid and sustained economic growth that took place in Asia over the last four decades. Despite great cultural and geographical diversity, coupled with huge economic and political differences in Asia, an emerging regional economic cooperation and integration is in progress. While continental economic integration (Asia-Pacific Economic Cooperation [APEC], the Association of Southeast Asian Nations [ASEAN], and the Free Trade Area [AFTA]) is driven by intraregional investment, Taiwan, which long suffered from diplomatic isolation, is expected to promote and strengthen regional collaboration since passing the Economic Cooperation Free-Trade Agreement (ECFA) with China. Asian governments have set up trading blocs aimed at consolidating the markets. With the rebirth of ASEAN and the formation of APEC, the Asian Regional Fund (ARF), AFTA, and the Asia European Meeting (ASEM), corporate power is being further strengthened. Nevertheless, such regional integration and collaboration can also further weaken the ability of each government to promote its own social, economic, and environmental policies that address the needs of its people.

Finally, these trends have also been accompanied by the opening of a democratic movement, resulting in the phenomenal growth of nongovernmental organizations (NGOs), including their emergence in Taiwan, Singapore, and so on. Asian coalitions that focus on human rights, the environment, and sustainable human development have been created, and there is a growing recognition by governments and multilateral bodies of the strategic role these organizations play in building a civil society in the region. This trend has been accelerating since the economic and political rise of China whose literacy rate and educational development at all levels reached its peak over the last decade.

Toward a Civil Society

Asia is a region of countries that have recently started to rediscover national potentialities, renewed energy, and a proper work ethic. It is an area dominated by the economic giant Japan, with newly emerging industrialized countries developing at a rapid rate. Japan's recovery after World War II was sparked by a national determination to excel again in the world through means other than military might and power. The Republic of China (Taiwan) was an extremely poor country when it fought against Japan during World War II, and it was soon divided by the superpowers into two parts across the Taiwan Strait, and later was devastated by its civil war. Nevertheless, Taiwan's traditionally high educational zeal originated from the period of Japanese colonization and Chinese traditions. Coupled with its strong desire for modernization and prosperity, Taiwan has set a reliable example of economic development. All the economically viable countries in this area, including Japan, Korea, Singapore, and Hong Kong, share the common traditions of Confucian educational thought and strong kinship and family ties. These are the foundations of the spirit of industry, peacefulness, and order that contribute to high economic incentive, respect for the elderly and authority, and the harmony of society (Chen 2001a).

The cultural characteristics of East Asian countries that are stressed here—the spiritual realm of man and society—make the pursuit of educational and economic development, coupled with the goal of national growth, a priority. These factors all contribute to a strong ethical framework and are the basis for putting the needs of society before individual needs and rights. Asian countries had a later start than their Western counterparts in regard to guaranteeing their people human rights, equity, privacy, and security, which are the foundation of a civil society. However, people in the Asian region are eager to participate in the global village, regardless of the costs, to achieve better social outcomes.

Family Values and Education Priority

A society with strong social capital is one in which social trust facilitates cooperation and networking for mutual benefit (Coleman 1990). The Asian culture emphasizes family values and a sense of belongingness among clan. Confusion may arise among ethics, law, and the common good in most Asian societies, and family values may conflict with the public interest. It is an Asian value that families are invited into decision-making processes; therefore, the process of forming a social consensus, including any form of educational policies, should take the family into consideration.

In many developed countries, education policy is very much influenced by economic and technological development at the expense of individual rights or traditional values. Thomas Murray (1992), after comparing ten countries (China, Egypt, Indonesia, Pakistan, Papua New Guinea, Soviet Union, Korea, and Zaire), proposed some items that appear to be necessary within the national development network, including moral/social values. Murray indicated that students should be educated adequately with values related to national development and cultural traditions. But here I would like to raise a question. If technology guides a country's values and resource distribution, should "education" still take up the heavy responsibility of passing on traditional values?

When scholars like Kas Mazurek et al. discussed the role of educators, they too realized that teachers' training programs should focus on interdisciplinary ability, including economic, technological, political, and ecological skills, and so on, to cope with the future growth of a society made up of diverse cultures, ethnic groups, and nationalities. Therefore, when discussing the education profession, these responsibilities and aspects should be included, and teachers should be aware of the overall social developmental network, as well as properly trained in the ability to exercise good judgment and think critically (Mazurek et al. 1999). It will be worthwhile to discuss the role of teachers from a global perspective. In regards to the quickly spreading technology in the region, schools are facing unprecedented challenges. The rapid pace of technological development suggests ceaseless curricula renewals. Combining the curricula with technology does not exactly mean to use technology as a teaching medium, but rather to incorporate into instruction the impact on humanity and the ramifications in society that result from technology. Drawing on Henry Giroux's idea, we should integrate technology training in "civic courage" into the present education curriculum. In so doing, we can equip our students with passion, imagination, and wisdom so they can excel regardless of economic, political, or social pressure (Giroux 1985). This is especially timely in conducting research on value clarification in the context of curriculum planning, for what we have at present, at least in East Asia, technology and science is taking over to a great extent in education in the name of social modernization and national development (Elwyn 2000).

Concerning parental domestic tutoring assistance, it is becoming more and more difficult for parents to tutor their children in their homework, as information and knowledge advance so rapidly. New research methods and teaching materials widen the gap between school and family. In areas with scarce resources and for families that lack resources, the gap becomes even wider. This transformation and growing issue exist largely in terms of the distribution of education resources and access to educational opportunities.

The first responsibility of astute teachers is to research what students know, and how they speak, experience, and feel. From this starting point, an empowering curriculum can be developed (Shor 1992). We then begin to form the basic questions: What kind of teaching approach do we need? What have we learned about the ability to make a critical judgment? Other than passing on values and transmitting knowledge, what capacity do we have to help students clarify their intellectual confusion and problem-solving abilities? Do teachers possess what they need in order to deal with the changes in social values? Or are they merely passively accepting values and passing them on (Chen 2001a)?

Social transformation and the interpretation of values deserve more attention as well as constructive criticism. For centuries, it was believed that Asian did not value the cultivation of critical thinking in education as its Western counterparts did. Not until the late 1980s did analytical skills start to be included in the curriculum. Critical thinking is not only a technique and a method but also an attitude that is often regarded as a metaphor for values orientation, and as a conflict between the fixed values that most students will encounter in their daily life. Thus, "critical" implies the combination of an active attitude and ideology (Thomas 1993). If we accept this spirit and viewpoint in order to see new aspects, such as how the recently developed biotech industry has brought many innovations to the world, we might take a more active role in helping students enter a diverse society, make appropriate judgments, and obtain correct and objective information. This would be helpful to the overall raising of citizens' problem-solving ability in the new century, which is the ultimate goal of technological development in East Asia and Taiwan (Chen 2001b).

The Social Context of Taiwan's Education System

Like other East Asian societies, Taiwan's society has been very much influenced by Confucian values, such as political authoritarianism, the family system, academic examination systems, saving habits, local organization, and family networks (Tu 1995). Education has been regarded as a priority in Confucian culture, and study is considered as hard work, effort, persistence, cultivation, and rigidity, whereas playing games is considered idleness (Yao 2000; Zhou, 2000).

Consequently, Taiwanese society places much emphasis on credentials and the practice of taking examinations. The Imperial examination in ancient China (694–1895), which lasted for more than one thousand years, had the functions of diminishing the effect of social and family origin on social mobility and enforcing the social control of the ruling class by identifying intellectuals for the governing class through public examinations. Although the Chinese Imperial examination was abolished in 1905, Taiwan is still influenced by this tradition, in which the examinations are expected to be fair and to pave the way for social upward mobility.

After the central government's relocation to Taiwan in 1949, the American "six-three-three-four" system continued until 1968, at which time a nine-year compulsory education plan was carried out. This plan continued for the next four decades, and now another twelve-year basic education reform program is about to launch in 2014 with the hope that it will alleviate exam pressure on secondary students and increase the potential of Taiwan's human resources.

Since the 1950s, Taiwan has encountered uncertainty and tensions in the political environment due to the military threat from China. Between 1957 and 1980, emphasis shifted to the planning and developing of human resources in coordination with the national goal of economic development. Additional challenges to the educational system have come in response to the forces of economic liberalization and globalization, which have transformed Taiwan since the 1980s. As the nation's industrial structure has shifted from a labor-intensive to a capital- and technology-intensive base, along with her political democratization movement, Taiwan's educational system has entered an era of transition and reform.

In a research project that studied participants from Taiwan, Hong Kong, Singapore, and China, it was found that schools in the Pacific Rim have something in common, i.e., an exam is nothing new in the school system. Credentials are highly regarded in these societies, in which parents highly value their children's academic performance and are actively involved in school affairs. The school curriculum has a high correlation with school exams. Sometimes, in fact, the exam results carry more weight than actual instruction. School accountability is usually judged by the society and parents based on students' exam performance, in fact. Consequently, most secondary schools provide exam preparation programs for children after school. There is a common belief that a student with a higher academic degree will earn a higher income in his or her later career. Although many Asian countries have gone through a series education reforms in the last decade, in the hope of solving the problem of excessive exam competition among schools, the outcome is still unclear. This exam-oriented phenomenon is not merely an education issue. It needs to be dealt with instead as a sophisticated cultural issue of "credentialism" and a belief about education among the general public.

In order to demonstrate the transitional dynamic profile of Taiwan's education, and its response to globalization and localization, four critical issues deserve attention in contrast to other Asian counterparts.

Localization versus Globalization

During the period of Japanese colonization (1895–1945), the purpose of Taiwan's education system was to go beyond local education and also include education in Japanese culture. After Taiwan was restored to China in 1945, an urgent aim of Taiwanese authorities was to abolish the influence of Japanese colonialism on the country by setting up a new education system that would advance the Chinese national identity (Yang 2001). This so-called "patriotization" was actually "Chinization," which emphasized education aimed at preserving the Chinese culture and the national language, Mandarin. The new Chinese school system first established in 1922 from the mainland, as the American six-three-three-four system, was restored in Taiwan after World War II, the end of Japanese colonization. Thus, in the latter half-century, the Taiwanese education system experienced a series of phases of nationalism derived from Chinese culture and economic rationalism, and it has been striving for Western efficiency and effectiveness since 1949.

Since the 1980s, much emphasis has been placed on the high-tech industry as a national priority. It was not until July 15, 1987, with the lifting of martial law, which had long imposed social and legal order in Taiwan, that a new era arrived that helped the country to rise in many aspects. As a result, every part of the social sphere has loudly demanded pluralism and liberalization (Yang 2001). Education reform, consequently, became a target for cultivating the next generation and leading them into a new era of national development.

The trend of "localization" that has been evident in Taiwanese society since the late 1980s aims to replace the Chinese identity with the Taiwanese heritage and traditions. These forces of indigenization, or "localization," stem from historical complaints against the Chinese authoritarian mandate after the takeover of the Kuomintang (KMT) in 1949.

As indicated in chapter 1, after the national government withdrew from mainland China to Taiwan after 1949, the priority was to strengthen the Chinese identity and sovereignty of China over Taiwan. During that period, many parts of the Taiwanese culture as well as languages were banned, especially after the 228 (February 28) incident in 1947, in which disputes arose between Chinese troops and the Taiwanese people. As time went on, this crackdown on the Taiwanese culture and language did not disappear, but instead it was sustained.

After the political transition period during the 1990s, former president Li Deng-Hui tried to provoke a Taiwanese independence movement against China. Since then, education has been very much focused on local issues and the Taiwanese identity, such as the declaration of Taiwan against the Republic of China, the shift in textbook content from matters related China to Taiwanese issues, and the Taiwanization of questions on the national civil service exam.

According to Yang (2001), different periods of Taiwanese education reform seem inevitably to reflect an ideological conflict focused on the hope of regaining Taiwan's own national and cultural identity. The country made a great effort to include a greater proportion of instructional content related to local history and geography along with local events in the recent curriculum reform. In the wake of the movement toward multiculturalism and respect for all the ethnic groups, Taiwan's schools have assumed authority over the curriculum, which prior to the 1990s was dominated by content related to the mainland. The trend toward localization has led to efforts to establish the Taiwanese identity and emphasize national prosperity as part of education reform measures, especially since the transfer of the political regime in 2000.

With a more globalized economy and society, coupled with Taiwan's increasing dependence on China as a trading partner, the Taiwanese education system has acted as a pendulum, swinging between internationalization and localization in the last decade. As a small island, Taiwan cannot avoid participating in the processes of internationalization, in terms of world trade and cultural exchange, occurring between different regions of the world. The localization of education has also made Taiwanese more aware of their own cultural heritage and allowed the younger generation to search for self-identity. Therefore, in education reform, the current idea is to integrate the trends of internationalization and localization in order to create a clear understanding of the world and Taiwan itself (Yang 2001).

The Influence of Examinations and Cultural Heritage

The examination/test systems in Taiwan have overwhelmingly dominated the education system for decades. Studies have shown that approximately 10 percent of the entire family budget in general, in comparison to education expenses in many countries (in terms of funds, time, or resource investment), is spent on children's preparation for the exams, which generates enormous pressure on the general family life.

Examinations are usually divided into two different kinds: the concluding evaluation and the formative evaluation. Formative evaluation in Western culture consists of students' homework, teacher monitoring, and interviews, which can take place anytime during the learning process, whereas the concluding assessment is mainly implemented from time to time, such as monthly exams or final exams, and even final examinations as a whole, and so on. Although these test patterns vary, the origin of the examination system may be attributed to China's Sui Dynasty (589–618), when the system was first designed to select talented people of strong moral character and respectable behavior, and then gradually changed to the use of special written subjects based on Confucius's teaching, consisting of four great classic books, as the major evaluation criteria overall.

The most notable and the greatest difference between China and Western countries is that Western knowledge emphasizes logic and argumentation, debate, and comparison, whereas the Chinese selection system later came to emphasize the memorization of scripture and recital for public services. As a result, innovation is not valued as much by Chinese as by their Western counterparts. In China, the Imperial examination system lasted more than one thousand years and was repealed in 1905. Prior to that, missionaries to Europe introduced this kind of exam system in the seventeenth century.

For example, by the year 1788, Prussia introduced its major classical middle school certificate examination system, (the *Abitur*), which later became a requirement as a university entrance credential. Up to the early nineteenth century, the examination system was formally the basis for selection in Germany. In addition, in the nineteenth century, the British East India Company, under China's influence, also introduced this type of examination system, which functioned as a way to identify personnel as well.

In 1872, the government of the United Kingdom formally introduced the official examination of a project, in which the examination system basically became one of the social selection mechanisms not only for an officer of the Crown but also for medical, legal, and commercial certificates. After the rise of the public school system, the examination system was finally adopted into formal education (Cummings 2003). It is believed that these exam systems established in Europe can be traced back to the impact of the Chinese imperial exam system, which still maintains its influence in the greater Chinese societies and East Asia.

Why then did this examination system not play as crucial a role in this so-called "credentialism" (or diploma disease) in Western countries as it did in Taiwan, China, Japan, and South Korea? The answer has to do with the social and cultural traditions in East Asia. For instance, in the West, more importance is placed on education in school than on an examination itself. In contrast, an examination has always been an important selection mechanism in East Asian society, and "selection" and "talent" have been separated into different orbits. Moreover, the examination in Imperial China used to serve as a crucial "super stable" mechanism for maintaining the authoritarian regime and society throughout the history of China, Japan, and Korea for more than 1,300 years, even after the examination was abolished in 1905. The exam's influence continues to take the lead over daily school teaching, and society at large still values high exam scores over other accomplishments at school, believing higher academic achievement in pen-and-pencil exams will lead to students being admitted to a better high school and university, which will eventually lead to a more successful career path.

Other questions have also been asked. For instance, although the examination culture continues to exert its influence, why has the modern school system in Taiwan or any other country in Asia lost its traditional traits and model? Why have most of the schools in Taiwan changed to the Western system in the twentieth century and lost their cultural heritage?

Although Taiwan's education system achieved much under the KMT regime, there were serious problems that emerged from this system. First of all, many scholars who have had experience in the Taiwanese educational system have noted that the overemphasis on examinations places enormous pressure on a student's life and attitude towards learning. Many young students are affected as a result of such a competitive national examination system throughout K–12. For instance, Lew (1981) points out three disadvantages of Taiwan's national examination system:

1. In order to allow efficient grading by computers, tests must be constructed for objective rather than creative responses.
2. Examination results are the sole yardstick for the selection of students, ignoring entirely the cumulative record in schools at a lower level.
3. The entrance examination is held only once a year; anyone who fails must wait for a whole year in order to try again.

Many studies describe the overwhelming exam pressure on students and teachers at the expense teenagers' healthy body and soul in Taiwan (Cohen,1988; Einhorn, 2005). Consequently, education reform policies over the past decades have targeted the alleviation of the examination pressure by introducing new curricula and instruction to reduce the government's centralized control. It is hoped that under the recent reform policies, teachers will have more flexibility for self-governance and autonomy to stimulate students' creativity and sharpen their critical thinking skills for the twenty-first century. However, the increasing discrepancies between urban and rural areas with regard to income distribution and resources, the conflict between the pursuit of educational quality versus quantity, and the balance between localization/regionalization and globalization have created numerous challenges and foreseeable risks for the people of Taiwan.

Education in Taiwan has become one of the most influential avenues for the building of the nation and for economic development. As previously noted, Taiwanese schools, with their heritage of Japanese education practices, Chinese cultural values, and Confucian traditions from mainland China, have experienced dramatic increases in enrollments. Nevertheless, throughout the entire twentieth century, the constant pressure for credentials based upon examination results remained unchanged.

Dedication to Gender Equity Education

A well-known issue in Asian societies and, of course, Taiwan is the practice of putting males first culturally and socially. Male dominance is a traditional benchmark in Taiwan, where women "without talent" were once regarded as invisible beings, metaphorically speaking. As previously mentioned, girls and women traditionally always came second in a society in which priority was given to boys and men in the inheritance of family names and properties. The practice of couples trying every method in order to have a male child has been criticized, because investment in education for boys is typically greater. Notwithstanding its traditions and cultural history, Taiwanese society has become a more open-minded and industrialized state that values gender equity and the social welfare of the disadvantaged.

In order to promote gender equality in Taiwan, the government has implemented several laws to encourage the development of a modern society. An act initiated in 1997 by the Ministry of Education (MOE) requires that at the primary and secondary school levels all students are to receive a compulsory minimum of four hours of class per semester on the subject of gender equity. This is an effort to enhance the concept of gender equality in the country (Tsai and Shavit 2002).

Another critical law, known as the *Gender Equity Education Act*, approved in 2004, serves as a milestone in promoting gender equity education in Taiwan. The act aims to facilitate gender equity through education resources and provision. All central and local educational authorities are required to establish a "gender equity education committee," whose tasks are to promote more awareness on gender equity education via curricula, instruction, assessments, and teaching training. In addition, sexual assault or harassment on campus, especially between teachers and students, is considered a serious violation and should be reported according to relevant laws (Gender Equity Education, MOE 2012).

As a result, in terms of educational achievement, the number of women enrolled at all levels of education has thus grown over the past few years. Particularly in higher education, the participation of females increased more than fourfold, from 11 percent in 1951 to 49 percent in 2005, and kept growing up to 2010 (MOE 2010). Though women in Taiwan still have a long way to go in the job market and political participation, the first female vice president, Annette Lu, was elected and served her terms between 2000 and 2008 in Taiwan. Another presidential candidate from the Democratic Progressive Party (DDP), Tsai, Ing-wen, though defeated, still yreceived 45.63 percent of the votes in the 2012 presidential election in Taiwan (Central Election Committee 2012). These examples all indicate that gender equity education has improved the status of women in Taiwan.

Issues Related to Equity of Educational Opportunity

After World War II, scholars such as Boudon (1974) indicated that quality in an education system was not the only factor that could influence a society to be more equitable. This is because the demand for a higher level of education in a society ultimately favors the most competent ones and usually those from a higher social background. Blau and Duncan (1967) also indicated that there is a positive correlation between family backgrounds and educational opportunity. In terms of income distribution, Taiwan used to be considered a relatively equitable society and has been seen as fair with regard to educational opportunity. Nevertheless, in comparison to Western developed societies, Taiwan shows similar trends in terms of a close tie between family background and academic achievement.

The Taiwanese high school and college entrance examination system played a role between the 1950s and 2000 as one of the major educational filters for tracking students into different type of schools. For cultural reasons as well as those of tradition, Taiwanese parents are most willing to invest in their children's education by sending them to cram schools or private talent classes. Ling (2001) pointed out that the major threshold for student tracking took place on the entrance exam of senior high schools, which classified students into different types of schools according to their test results, and which in turn led to different career opportunities.

In Taiwan, as in any other Asian society, the higher the socioeconomic status of the family, the higher the educational expectations. Unlike in Western societies, where cultural capital counts, in the Taiwanese context, it is family educational resources and extra tutoring lessons such as attendance at a cram school that make the difference in the schooling process (Zhang and Huang, 1997). According to Stevenson and Baker (1992), Japanese students receive better chances in universities if there are more educational opportunities outside the school, such as a cram school or private tutoring. In Taiwan, the case is hardly different. Family background continues to be a major factor in determining children's educational opportunity.

Another area of concern related to equity concerns educational opportunities for indigenous people. Of those students whose education opportunities have fallen behind those of the majority, about 2 percent are aboriginal people. There is little similarity between the number of students attending higher-education institutions (HEIs) and indigenous people who have the opportunity to attend those institutions. According to recent statistics, about 11.03 percent of indigenous students have the opportunity to access higher education, and of that number, 25.70 percent of them participate. This means that about 3 percent of indigenous people are enrolled in the higher-education system (Council of Indigenous People 2010).

It is the case that since marketing and deregulation were introduced into Taiwanese education reform schemes beginning in the 1990s, this trend has been reinforced. As more and more reform programs come into play, such as different versions of textbooks and multiple channels of entrance exams for high school and university, the grading competition among schools and families accelerates. According to *Business Week in Taiwan*, Taiwan's former profile as one of the most equitable societies in Asia has moved into a different phase in the last ten years.

In consonance with the 2001 National Annual Statistics, there has been a growing trend related to income distribution in Taiwanese society, to the extent that there is a significant difference between the have's and the have-not's, with the top-ranked families earning an income of about 161 times more than their counterparts at the bottom of the rankings. The previous year, in 2000, the correlation difference was only about forty times, and about twenty years further back, in 1991, the difference between the top and the bottom rankings was less than twenty times.

In 2003, when the average of the top 20 percent and the bottom 20 percent are compared, the annual income difference was about six times. It is noted that in the last few years, lower income families have earned less, as seen in the fact that ten years ago, the annual income difference did not even reach five times, when the same top and bottom percentages were compared. The twice-elected President Chen (2000 and 2004) came from a poor family at the bottom of the income ranks, and Taiwan took great pride in this. However, the dream of reaching a high-level position in society if one comes up from the bottom has come to seem less and less plausible.

Problems related to the educational budget and the authority for oversight are expected to appear in 2012, with responsibility for 180 national general and vocational senior high schools formerly under the authority of the Central Region Office being shifted to local governments, especially after the reorganization of new five Special Municipalities (Government Information Office 2010).

References

Ball, Stephen J. 1998. "Big Policies/Small World: An Introduction to International Perspectives in Education Policy" *Comparative Education* 34 (2): 119–130.
Boudon, Raymond. 1963. "Quelques Fonctions de la Formalisation en Sociologie." *European Journal of Sociology* 4: 191–218.

Central Election Committee (CEC). 2012. *CEC Website*. Taipei: CEC. Available online at: http://www.cec.gov.tw.
Chen, Joseph C. 2001a. "Being a Mentor—The Self-Identity of Primary School Teachers." *Primary Education Journal of NTNU* 52 (3): 25–28.
———. 2001b. "The Moral Education under the Trend of Biotech Development." In *International Conference of the Citizen Quality and Teachers Training*. Taipei, National Taiwan Normal University
Cohen, Marc J. 1988. *Taiwan at the Crossroads: Human Rights, Political Development and Social Change on the Beautiful Island*. Washington, DC: Asia Resource Centre.
Coleman, James Samuel. 1990. *Equality and Achievement in Education, Social Inequality Series*. Boulder, CO: Westview.
Council of Indigenous Peoples. *Introduction* 2010. Taipei: Council of Indigenous Peoples. Available online at: http://www.apc.gov.tw.
Cummings, William K. 2003. *The Institutions of Education*. Oxford: Symposium Books.
Dai, Xi Xi, Ka Ho Mok, and Ang-Rong Xie. 2002. *The Marketization and Higher Education: A Comparative Study of Taiwan, Hong Kong and China*. Taipei: Higher Education Publishing.
Dale, Roger 2001. "Constructing a Long Spoon for Comparative Education: Charting the Career of the 'New Zealand Model.'" *Comparative Education* 37 (4): 493–500.
Einhorn, Bruce. 2005. "Why Taiwan Matters?" *Business Week*, May 16.
Elwyn, Thomas. 2000. "Researching Values in Cross-Culture Contexts." In *Education for Value*: Morals, Ethics and Citizenship in Contemporary Teaching edited by Roy Gardner, Jo Cairns, and Denis Lawton, 257–265. London: Kogan.
Gender Equity Education, MOE. 2012. *Origin and History*. Taipei: Gender Equity Education, MOE. Available online at: https://www.gender.edu.tw.
Giddens, Anthony. 1994. *Beyond Left and Right—The Future of Radical Politics*. Cambridge: Polity Press.
Giroux, Henry A. 1985. *Theory and Resistance in Education*. New York: Bergin & Garvey.
Government Information Office. 2010. *The Republic of China at a Glance*. Taipei: Government Information Office. Available online at: http://www.gio.gov.tw.
Levin, Benjamin. 2001. *Education Reform from Origins to Outcomes*. London: FalmerRoutledge.
Lew, William F. 1981. "The Educational Ladder." In *The Taiwan Experience, 1950–1980* edited by J. C. Hsiung. New York: Praeger, 82–85.
Ling, Da-Sen (2001). "The Effect of Family Educational Resources on Tracking and Educational Status Attainment." *The National Cheng-Chi University Journal of Sociology* 31: 45–75.
Mazurek, Kas, Margret A. Winzer, and Czeslaw Majorek. 1999. *Education in a Global Society: A Comparative Perspective*. New York: Pearson Education.
Ministry of Education (MOE). 2010. *Educational Statistical Indicators* 2010. Taipei: MOE. Available online at: http://english.moe.gov.tw.

Murray, Thomas, ed. 1992. *Education's Role in National Development Plans: Ten Country Cases.* New York: Greenwood.

Shor, Ira. 1992. *Empowering Education: Critical Teaching for Social Change.* Chicago: University of Chicago Press.

Stevenson, David L., and David P. Baker. 1992. "Shadow Education and Allocation in Formal Schooling: Transition to University in Japan." *American Journal of Sociology* 97 (6): 1639–1657.

Thomas, Jim. 1993. *Doing Critical Ethnography (Qualitative Research Methods).* Beverly Hills, CA: Sage.

Tsai, Shu-Ling, and Yossi Shavit. 2002. "Higher Education in Taiwan: Expansion and Inequality of Educational Opportunity." Paper presented at the *XV World Congress of the International Sociological Association*, Brisbane, Australia: ISA-RC28, July 7–13, 2002.

Tu, Wei-Ming. 1995. "The Mirror of Modernity and Spiritual Resources for the Global Community." *Sophia* 34 (1): 79–91.

Xie, Wen-Quan. 2007. *Chinese Encyclopedia.* Taipei: Chinese Culture University.

Yang, Shen-Keng. 2001. "Dilemmas of Education Reform in Taiwan: Internationalization or Localization?" Paper presented at the Annual Meeting of the Comparative and International Education Society, Washington, DC, March 14–17, 2001.

Yao, Xin-Zhong. 2000. *An Introduction to Confucianism.* Cambridge: Cambridge Press.

Zhang, Shan-Nan, and Yi-Zhi Huang. 1997. "The Causal Relationship of Ethnicity and Academic Achievement," Paper prepared for presentation at the International Conference for Educational Research on Education of Minority Groups, Han, and Aboriginal People, National Taitung University of Education, Taitung, Taiwan.

Zhou, Yu-Wen. 2000. "Confucianism and Competition of Education." In *International Conference for a Study on the Competition of Education in Confucian Asia for Center for Educational Research*, edited by S. W. Yang, 204–210. Taipei: National Taiwan University.

Chapter 5

The Taiwan Education System

The education system in Taiwan, similar to other education systems in East Asia, has undergone an enormous transformation over the last two decades. Education has become interconnected with the trends of globalization and internationalization, the development of information communications technology, and a set of political, sociological, economic, and management changes. For example, internationalization is taught through foreign language and history classes, and technology has made its way into Taiwanese classrooms in the form of the Internet, electronic blackboards, computers, and televisions, while classroom management policies have also undergone enormous changes such as the ban on physical punishment in classrooms. These shifts together have had a multifaceted impact on education in Taiwan. In particular, the ideology of globalization and localization acts as one of the driving policy agendas in Taiwan.

In Taiwan, the Educational Executive Organization is divided into the Central Authority and the Local Authority. The Ministry of Education (MOE), one of the eight main ministries under the Executive Yuan, works as the executive branch of the central government and directs the entire body of national education institutions, including social educational institutions, private universities, and private senior high schools. On the other hand, the Bureau of Education, the subordinate unit of the municipality and the county, is in charge of municipal/county schools at all levels, social educational institutions, private primary and secondary schools, and non-national social educational institutions.

The Central Region Office is also part of the MOE, and is in charge of the curriculum and the placement of interns, according to the needs of supply and demand. This office is concerned as well with the registration and examination of teachers in schools below the secondary level. Additionally, the Central Region Office manages the release of certifications and oversees state schools, special education, and education in senior high schools and technological and vocational high schools.

As for national social educational institutions, they can be classified into eleven different categories according to the affairs that they manage, including libraries, museums, art museums, music halls, theaters, memorial halls, sports venues, zoos, youth activity centers, and other related social education centers (Government Information Office 2010a).

Central Authority: Ministry of Education

The role of the MOE, in accordance with Article 162 of the national constitution, is to supervise schools at all levels, national or private, and cultural institutions as dictated by law. The MOE only possesses the rights of "legal supervisor" rather than "profession supervisor." Therefore, the MOE adopted the *Department of Education Organization Act*, revised almost 40 years ago, on July 25, 1973, to manage all the national education institutions. According to Article 1 of the act, the MOE is in charge of the national education system, culture, and businesses related to educational administration. Article 2 states that the MOE has the responsibility to select and supervise the local chief executive in order to implement management by the MOE, while Article 3 mentions that if the MOE's chief executive signs an order or a sanction, this is regarded as illegal, as it is believed to be an abuse of authority (MOE 2011a).

The MOE can appeal an issue or policy to the Executive Yuan's interministerial coordination meeting, which has the final say or approval on national educational policy making. The MOE has been, however, the leading authority over the seventeen Bureaus of Education in the education system since December 25, 2010. These bureaus are, in practice, one of the subordinate units under each municipality and the county. This arrangement sometimes causes conflicts between local and central governments. For example, a serious confrontation and debate between the Taipei Educational Bureau and the MOE regarding the publication of single or multiple versions of middle-school textbooks occurred in 2007 (Zhang 2007).

The MOE is the national education authority and responsible for managing the ministry's affairs, organizations, and staff. The staff is less than seven hundred individuals, including personnel in the Central Region Office. The MOE has the responsibility for dealing with all teachers and students throughout the country, which accounts for about one-fourth of the national population, not to mention the students' parents (Chou 2008).

The ministry has numerous responsibilities, in addition to the requirement that it must maintain active communications and negotiations with other governmental units. According to the Organizational Act for the Ministry of Education, all proposed twenty-nine units and commissions mentioned above deal with school matters directly (Ministry of Education 2011a).

In a report from the MOE titled "Mission and Policy of Educational Administration: The Prospective 10 Golden Years," issued at the 8th National Education Conference in 2010, the driving idea was to lead the development of national education in the best direction for the next decade, since many education reform policies have been issued and implemented since the mid- 1990s (MOE 2011b). Much more is expected from the education general authority (i.e., the MOE). The same problems exist, in addition to new problems identified during the reform era of the 1990s. The number of college graduates is large, yet the country continues to struggle with how to compete with the rest of the world in terms of economic and social development. Questions about whether Taiwan's next generation is equipped with enough educational preparation for the world of the future are still prevalent. Since 2003, the issue has been debated of whether the mixed education reform outcomes in Taiwan are attributed to the frequent changes of the education ministers (over eleven ministers in the last twenty-five years), or whether it is a result of a lack of strategic planning and follow-up evaluation of the policies that have already been implemented. Or is it the result of a lack of two-way communication between teachers and parents? Or is it because the Chinese credential and examination-based culture continues to prevail? These questions are too complicated to have a single clear answer. If one examines the profiles of the education ministers over the last quarter century in Taiwan, it is apparent that very few of them share a consensus or consistent policies in the field of education. The following observations can be made about these various ministers who have overseen education in Taiwan since the late 1980s:

1. Gender: They are invariably male, including their personnel, staff, assistants, and the directors of all units.
2. Preparation: The majority received graduate education overseas, mainly in the United States. More than half have a PhD, and worked in academia or a technology field before taking their post. In some cases, they were a minister in another government department or were a university president, a national adviser, or a researcher in a university or the Academia Sinica.
3. Relationship with political party: Most of them maintained contact and had friendly relations with the Kuomintang (KMT) as one of

the ruling parties. As for those involved in social movements, one former university professor participated in both the March Student Movement in 1990 and the 401 Education Reform Movement in 1994.
4. Office tenure: They held office for an average of 2.4 years or less after the lifting of martial law. It is easy to see that education reforms can be taken in diverging directions or might not be consistently followed, as ministers often change. The frequent change of ministers has historically been a key factor in the unsatisfactory results that education reform has achieved so far (MOE 2011c).

There are some points that are worth mentioning in order to better understand what the cost of these trends has been (Chou 2008):

1. The ministers' shorter tenure in office has had a critical impact on policies. For instance, the plan entitled "Expanding Senior High Schools and Universities," issued while Minister Chin Wu was in office, less than two years, was somewhat different from what was pursued by the *410 Education Movement*, which promoted the expansion of public high school and university and other reform initiatives. According to Wu's *Three Directions to Building the National Super Manpower Highway*, improving the quality of general education, upgrading technological and vocational education, and promoting long-term, lifelong, and vocational training were considered the three top priorities. As a result, many vocational high schools and colleges were permitted to upgrade, a short period of time, the level of higher education they provided at the expense of the quality of the education (Chou 2008). Also, Minister Kirby Yang's *921 Earthquake Project on the Reconstruction of Primary and Secondary Schools* and *Education Basic Law*, and Minister Ovid Tzeng's *Children's Reading Movement* are policies that were forged out of great intentions and had a lasting impact on Taiwan's education system. Nevertheless, it cannot be expected that the best results will be achieved due to the ministers' lack of tenure, because more time is needed in order to consistently implement policies.
2. The ministers are assigned as political appointees, and they possess more rights than responsibilities after they step down. Unlike other tenured civil servants in the education sector, ministers of education are political appointees, who generally have held this position for a short time period. Ministers come and go very rapidly, as is also the case with department directors in the ministry, especially those senior assistants of the minister, who have a more important role, since they are responsible for the policies and practices that are instituted and

move along steadily. Therefore, managing, delegating tasks, and assigning personnel to their positions are a big challenge for the minister. The minister can also attempt to review ongoing policies and departments. However, owing to the complexity of personnel management and finance budgeting, most ministers lacked the tenure and expertise to fully implement their new ideas and innovations.
3. It is hard for a minister to remain neutral due to the influence of political power. It is clearly stated in the *Education Basic Law* (Article 6) that education should be nonpolitical and neutral, and that no school should help to promote any specific political idea or group. Although rumors always surround the mention of important education policies where there is pressure from elected representatives to follow the main policies, in the end, the minister's behavior is evaluated by the public, and therefore it is imperative for him to remain professional and neutral, and to possess moral values as well as integrity.

Local Authorities: Municipal and County Education Bureaus

Divisions in the education bureaus in municipalities and counties are related to the implementation of national policies in the local context. All education bureaus are responsible for early childhood, primary, and secondary education In other words, below the junior high school level, all these bureaus are guided by local educational authorities who oversee all educational affairs related to both public and private schools, including facilities, curricula, teaching materials, teaching equipment /instruments, enrollment, military training, scouting education, cooperative education, the establishment and reorganization of schools, preschool education, special education, education related to international and cultural exchange, the assessment and examination of teachers' qualifications, teacher registration, teachers' additional study and professional training, and so on.

Other Related Educational Institutions

Academia Sinica

Founded in 1928, the Academia Sinica is the highest academic institution in Taiwan. Directly supervised by the office of the president, it takes responsibility for supporting research in the humanities and the sciences, nurturing talented personnel, and providing guidance and rewards for scholars (Academia Sinica 2007). In other words, their responsibility is to raise and maintain the nation's level of scholarly research in both the humanities and scientific fields as well as to remain in the loop for relevant and competitive alternate research in terms of productiveness and overall knowledge.

Chou (2010) observed that most of the academicians who are responsible for the nation's research policies have a background in the field of science and technology. Also, very few of these researchers are female or of different ethnicities. The majority of scholars know little about domestic education issues, because most of them hold permanent professional jobs overseas. The question is, are these respected scholars actually able to handle such an important role in providing constructive and timely policy advice and strategy? The government grants academics great authority in key positions for creating national policy on science, the economy, and so forth. The great master plan of education reform since 1994 was also initiated and implemented by a former director of Academia Sinica. Universities' evaluation indicators and appraisal also originated from the recommendations of their scholars. For instance, through the recommendation of two prominent economists in Academia Sinica, the Science Citation Index (SCI) and the Social Science Citation Index (SSCI) have become the two most crucial databases for academic evaluation indicators in Taiwan, which has resulted in tremendously mixed feelings and social debate over the lack of attention given to the humanities and social sciences.

In the last few years, with the cooperation of the national universities, which have shared professional personnel, collaborated on academic research, trained graduate students, and together implemented courses for overseas students, the education system has experienced all these aforementioned changes and much more. Yet, there is also a certain degree of competition among them for research subsidies offered by the government, such as from the National Science Council (NSC) and the MOE. However, the Academia Sinica takes the lead in this competition due to its capacity to support full-time research, which is more extensive than that of the other national universities. Apart from that, its funding overall is superior to that of the other universities because it is under the president's office instead of MOE,

National Science Council (NSC)

The National Science Council was established in 1959, and it is the sole organization in charge of promoting the development of scientific technology for the government. The main responsibility of NSC is to promote the national development of science and technology, support academic research, and develop science parks.

In order to enhance the level of national competitiveness in higher education, the NSC adopted the SSCI, SCI, and the Engineering Index (EI), as the gold standard for evaluating the level of academic research of Taiwan's universities and faculty members. The primary evaluation process involved a counting of the actual number of faculty publications in these three citation index databases as to determine institutional ranking and public budget allocation. The government further promoted the SSCI and so forth as the standard for "gate-keeping knowledge" that determines what constitutes valid forms of academic knowledge. The overt emphasis on the imported, US-based, English-oriented "official knowledge," has significantly degraded the culture-based research production, which has traditionally been at the heart of humanities and social science research. Materials published in non-English languages, "non-scientific" research, and even research on Taiwan-related issues is generally given less recognition and prestige. Such issues have altogether resulted in making the individual publication process a controversial issue in Taiwan. In addition, in order for scholars to obtain research funding, university faculty members and researchers must first apply for NSC project approval. Applicants who have written books or done innovative work related to arts and the humanities are often disadvantaged if their scholarship falls beyond the academically approved publication indexes. Consequently, the need to employ other means of assessment and evaluation remains a key issue in Taiwan higher education realms, and there is an increasing demand to find multiple and alternative ways to improve the evaluation of scholarship.

Taiwan Education System

As the second country in Asia to extend compulsory education to nine years (the first being Japan), Taiwan's present educational structure supports approximately twenty-two years of formal study. As previously noted, the current six-three-three-four education model has remained intact since it was first introduced in 1922 in China and then later reinstituted in Taiwan after World War II. Citizens of Taiwan enjoy the highest rate of access to education at all levels, and the illiteracy rate among people aged fifteen and over has declined to nearly 2 percent, the lowest in Chinese history.

On average, the entire education process consists of two years of preschool, six years of primary school, three years of junior high school, three years of senior secondary school, four to seven years of college or university, one to four years of a master's degree program, and two to seven years of a doctoral degree program (see Figure 5.1). At age six, children attend primary school, and continue for nine years of compulsory education. After age fifteen, most young people take the high school entrance exam

SCHOOL AGE	NORMAL AGE										
25	30	HIGHER EDUCATION	DOCTORAL PROGRAM								
24	29										
23	28										
22	27										
21	26										
20	25										
19	24										
18	23		MASTER'S PROGRAM								
17	22										
16	21		UNIVERSITY & COLLEGE	COLLEGE OF TECHNOLOGY (4 YRS.)	COLLEGE OF TECHNOLOGY (2 YRS.)	TECH. & JR. COLLEGE EDUCATION					
15	20										
14	19				JUNIOR COLLEGE (2 YRS.)						
13	18										
12	17	SR.SEC. EDUCATION	COMPREHENSIVE HIGH SCHOOL	SENIOR HIGH SCHOOL	SENIOR VOCATIONAL SCHOOL		JR. COLLEGE (5 YRS.)		SUPPLEMENTARY AND CONTINUING EDUCATION		
11	16										
10	15										
9	14	NINE-YEAR COMPULSORY EDUCATION		JUNIOR HIGH SCHOOL				NINE-YEAR COMPULSORY EDUCATION		SPECIAL EDUCATION	
8	13										
7	12										
6	11										
5	10		PRIMARY SCHOOL								
4	9										
3	8										
2	7										
1	6										
	5	PRE-SCHOOL EDUCATION	KINDERGARTEN					PRE-SCHOOL EDUCATION			
	4										

Figure 5.1 The Current School System in Taiwan.
Source: Ministry of Education (2010).

and are divided into three tracks: an academic route for higher education, vocational school for practical training, and job-related training.

Education is not compulsory for children aged between two and six years old, but parents of children in this age group usually send them to kindergarten. Apart from the nine-year compulsory education system, the Taiwanese MOE also implemented a trial ten-year compulsory education program in the 1990s, so that junior high school students who are interested in beginning a program in vocational training can do so, beginning in the last year of junior high school and continuing for another year (Ministry of Education 2010).

Since 2001, students who wish to be admitted to senior high schools, vocational high schools, and postsecondary schools are required to pass the Basic Competence Test (BCT) for Junior High School Students, which includes written tests of Mandarin, English, math, social studies, science, and essay writing (BCTEST 2011). Some people criticize the Basic Competence Test for placing unnecessary pressure on junior high school students who are already under a lot of academic stress (Hu and Lin 2010).

In order to enter university, high school students in the past were required to take the Joint College Entrance Examination, but in 2002, the MOE launched the Department Required Test and General Scholastic Ability Test to replace the Joint College Entrance Examination. Once students are enrolled, university undergraduate programs require four years of study; however, students who are unable to fulfill their requirements within the designated time may be granted extensions of up to two years. Specialized undergraduate programs such as dentistry or medicine require six to seven years, including an internship period of one year. Students who enter graduate school as part of their on-the-job training may also be granted an extension.

Lifelong learning opportunities are available to people of all ages, especially senior citizens. The MOE and local education bureaus, coupled with many nongovernmental organizations (NGOs) have established education programs for people from all walks of life, especially for those aged sixty and above, with a minimal tuition fee or free of charge in some cases. Programs include a variety of tailored short courses at universities and community colleges.

An Overview of Schools at All Levels

Preschool to Junior High School

As mentioned above, most Asian parents tend to place a high priority on their children's education. Taiwan is no exception in this respect, and parents start their children's education beginning in early childhood in order to prepare them to succeed in Taiwan's highly competitive education system. Nevertheless, the majority of kindergartens and nurseries are privately owned, and they have relatively high tuition fees; therefore, these costs place a heavy burden on families with an average income. Elementary schools were originally encouraged to set up public preschools in order to accommodate children of middle-class families. In school year 2009–2010, more than 181,628 children aged 3–5 years old attended 3,154 (MOE 2010) registered preschools, with the attendance rate at 29 percent (the total school-age population of children between 3–5 years old reached 621,318).

In addition, the net enrollment rate of primary students was 99.4 percent, of secondary school students 97.3 percent, and of high school students 47.1 percent (MOE 2010). As the birthrate rate has declined, the class size in each primary school class in elementary schools has been twenty-six; in middle school classes, thirty-three; and in high school classes, forty. Compared to schools in the mid-1990s, most schools are currently experiencing a reduction in enrollment overall and also in class size.

Senior High School

Up to the high school level, two tracks of education coexisted for the last few decades. Regular high schools comprised 60 percent of the student population, admitting students with a scholastic aptitude whose education goal is to be admitted to the university. Senior vocational schools and institutes of technology accept students with an aptitude for practical learning and the job market.

The three-year senior high school program prepares 15- to 18-year-old students for admission to higher education. Most senior high school graduates nowadays are entitled to select between two paths, whether that is attending a regular university/college or studying at an institute of technology for a four-year period. In the second year of high school, students are streamed into different tracks of classes based on their interests and aptitude. These categories include science and technology, the social sciences and liberal arts, medical science, and agriculture.

Senior Vocational School

While high schools prepare students to move further on the academic track, senior vocational schools aim to equip students with practical skills suitable for the job market or particular professions. Schools generally specialize in a given field, such as business, agriculture, nursing, or technology. Many senior vocational school graduates will seek employment or set up their own small businesses with the specialization certificates that they obtain from their educational programs, while others will continue with further education at institutes of technology, junior colleges, regular colleges, and universities.

A total of 362,514 students were enrolled in senior vocational schools in academic year 2009–2010 (MOE 2011d). In order to broaden students' and teachers' horizons, the MOE has begun to subsidize international exchange programs for vocational schools and encourage them to organize international symposia.

Comprehensive High Schools

To increase the number of years that students study and allow them to have more opportunities for self-exploration between academic and vocational training, several experimental high schools have combined their vocational and academic programs since 1996. In these cases, students are encouraged to select from a wide range of coursework before deciding whether to continue on an academic or a vocational track. In addition to general high school subjects, such as Mandarin, English, physics, chemistry, mathematics and social studies, various technological courses are also available for students who seek more practical preparation for more productive workforce outcomes.

Higher Education

As in many Asian countries, higher education in Taiwan represents a diverse outlook based on different educational purposes. Taiwan's HEIs are comprised of four-year colleges, universities, institutes of technology, and two- to five-year junior colleges.

Junior Colleges and Institutes of Technology

Taiwan has been renowned for its junior colleges, which are vocation oriented and focused on practical business, technological training, and the applied sciences. However, many colleges have been upgraded to institutes and universities of technology as higher education has expanded over the last fifteen years, although a very few, especially nursing schools, still offer junior college programs.

Among these vocational training institutes, a traditional five-year junior college (including the former teacher's college) admits junior high school graduates for specialized or semiprofessional training. Another two-year junior college accepts graduates of senior high schools and senior vocational schools to major in programs such as foreign languages, hotel management, tourism, business administration, computer science, nursing, agriculture, forestry, fishery, home economics, architecture, civil engineering, and so on. In addition, students are encouraged to have relevant work experience in order to link their study to the practical job market.

Universities, Colleges, and Graduate Schools

There were a total of 149 universities and colleges in Taiwan as of 2010. The majority of programs at these institutions last four years, although those for training teachers, architects, and lawyers require five years, while medical programs take up to seven years. On the other hand, some universities also offer two-year institutions of technology, which generally admit junior college graduates, while four-year institutions of technology admit senior vocational school graduates.

Special Education

In addition to mainstream education, education for special-needs students is also in great demand. Special education in Taiwan includes programs for individuals with special needs due to mental and physical handicaps, learning disabilities, or gifted and talented abilities. In recent years, in contrast to the way in which such students were segregated in the past, students with special talents or challenges have been mainstreamed into schools from elementary through senior high school that have special facilities to meet their needs. This is an effort to comply with the worldwide trend in other developed nations, that is, to provide inclusive education for special-needs children. The majority of impaired as well as gifted students attend regular classes with other students prior to joining the more resource-rich classrooms with visual and audio aids for specialized follow-up counseling and training. More advanced students are, in most cases, generally registered for special classes in which they receive focused instruction to enhance their talents and abilities.

In the case of schools for the visually and auditorily impaired, as well as for the most physically or mentally challenged students, the programs are run in the same way as the current mainstream general-education system. Almost entirely supported by the government, these schools for students with special needs offer classes from preschool through senior vocational school levels. In terms of gifted students, during the 2008–2009 school year, more than six thousand students with special talents were identified as having acute abilities in math and science subjects as well as in fine arts, the performing arts, or sports overall.

Alternative Education

The need for alternative education has drawn people's attention during the last decade, as more and more children with special needs have not fit in at regular schools. These alternative education models were established to provide native students with a different, less stressful learning experience. For example, Taipei County's Seedling Elementary School, established in 1994, places its focus not only on traditional school courses, but also concentrates on children's bond with nature and aboriginal culture. The school is set in the middle of a green, natural environment, featuring tree houses, forest trails, streams, and an ecological pond for students to observe. Seedling Elementary School stresses a good teacher-student relationship, and since it is set in an aboriginal area, students get to learn about aboriginal culture firsthand and explore the natural landscape that surrounds the school (Seedling Elementary School 2010). Nantou County's Forest Elementary School, established in 1990, also emphasizes nature and hands-on learning. Forest Elementary School has a different grading system as well; rather than giving single numbers or letters as grades, the teachers write a report on each student's personal development and evaluate the students by their daily performance and attitude rather than examination grades (Forest Elementary School 2010).

These special schools stress a tension-free, humanistic education, and provide an alternative education pathway for Taiwanese students, who are usually heavily bound by examinations, cram schools, and parents' high academic expectations. Though some critics have concerns over whether students graduating from these types of alternative schools will be able to adjust to the normal Taiwanese education institutions, there have not been any significant reports of student maladjustment. The founding of alternative schools represents the government's intention to develop a system of education that produces students who are not only knowledgeable but also well-rounded, open, close to nature, and happy. In Taiwan's current academic-driven education system, it would be hard for an ordinary school to provide what alternative schools can give to students, that is, an open, stress-free, and natural learning environment.

In addition, schools based on the Waldorf method also deserve some attention. Adopting its philosophy from the Austrian Rudolf Steiner's work, Waldorf schools advocate a holistic approach towards children's learning. For instance, the CIF-Xing Waldorf School in Yilan County, in the northeast region, has been well received by parents who are enthusiastic for a philosophy of self-learning and independent study, such as a strong emphasis on creativity and individual talents. Unlike in the public school system, students enrolled in this type of school can have more practical learning opportunities for skill development in a broader range of craft fields, woodworking, and organic gardening. The Taiwanese Waldorf system has received positive reports, including favorable feedback related to students' mental and intellectual maturity and their higher motivation for self-learning, as well as their physical and psychological well-being (Government Information Office 2010a).

Education for Ethnic Minorities

Taiwan's ethnic minorities account for 3 percent of the population. The Aboriginal Student Education Law, launched in 1998 and revised in 2004, reconfirmed the practice of affirmative action in the mainstream education system and financially supported aboriginal students from the lower levels up to higher education. In addition, universities are encouraged to set up colleges and departments for aboriginal studies and give preference to aboriginal students.

Adult and Social Education

With the emergence of an aging society, the government is sponsoring a number of supplementary and continuing education programs for adults through public funding. A wide range of institutions and education-relevant events, such as art exhibitions, cultural centers, libraries, zoos, museums, parks, orchestras, and observatories are encouraged to embrace adult students at all levels.

Public supplementary schools are affiliated with regular primary and secondary schools and operate in the form of distance learning, night schools, and weekend classes. Supplementary adult education, in the meantime, offers courses for the general public from the elementary level all the way throughout senior high school, senior vocational school, junior college, and college. Upon completion of their respective courses, followed by their passing examinations in each subject, such adult graduates can be granted mainstream-equivalent diplomas.

Among the social education institutions discussed earlier, the National Association for the Promotion of Community Universities (NAPCU), founded in 1999, is one of the first private-sector organizations in Taiwan to promote the establishment of community colleges by offering a variety of practical, remedial, and enriched programs suitable for adults. To date, nearly ninety community colleges and tribal community colleges for indigenous peoples have been established nationwide since 1998, and they enroll more than 200,000 adult students each year. In so doing, these community colleges in Taiwan have played a key role in education reform and social movements, paving the way for Taiwan to become a civil as well as a lifelong learning society (MOE 2006).

The MOE also provided funding up to US$30 million in subsidies during the last decade for this type of education, which, though privately operated, is expected to offer more courses suitable for the general public and senior citizens. Some of its graduates demanded an alternative diploma/certificate from the MOE, but the government did not approve the appeal for fear of pressure from regular HEIs.

In order to enhance the open-door policy of university education, the MOE launched a program in 2008 that provided senior citizens with "mini-courses" on college and university campuses. Inspired by American adult-education programs, the Taiwan programs and courses were designed to meet the physical, mental, and spiritual needs of the elderly, and included such topics as aging, geriatric psychology, art appreciation, and marine studies. Though these programs last only for a week or so, they represent a milestone for Taiwan, as senior students live on campus and interact with younger generations through their rich life experience. Consequently, another 368 centers, sponsored by the MOE and local county governments, were set up throughout the island, which provided more learning resources to senior citizens by 2010 (Government Information Office 2010b).

Apart from the education pathways discussed above, social education is available to all citizens of Taiwan, including "supplementary and continuing education, on-air education, adult and lifelong learning, national language education, citizen's education, art education, library education, museum education, audio-visual education, family education, and guidance in spiritual renewal" (MOE 2009). Among these social-education programs, supplementary and continuing education programs are more formal than the others, and are designed to supplement regular education, raise education attainment, teach practical skills, and upgrade productivity (MOE 2009). Social education provides citizens not enrolled in school as well as working youths in Taiwan with an alternative way to acquire basic education, advanced studies, and/or short-term supplementary education, and thus to achieve their educational goals. The curriculum is classified into three main categories: basic education, advanced education, and short-term supplementary education. The study periods vary according to their curriculum design. The efforts described above also show Taiwan's devotion to enhancing civilian competitiveness and competence in the global world.

Extension Education

The number of higher-education institutions in Taiwan has increased, from 7 in 1950 to 164 in 2008, among which are now 100 universities, 49 colleges, and 15 junior colleges (MOE 2010). In effect, vocational junior colleges offering two-year degrees are being phased out and upgraded to universities/institutes of technology that offer four-year degree programs. With the maturation of the knowledge economy, a major challenge for higher education in Taiwan (and elsewhere) is actually to provide broad access while sustaining or improving the quality of education. However, such a drive towards opening up higher education to the masses has led to the decline in the average qualifications for academics in many countries (Altbach, Reisberg, and Rumbley 2009). In essence, education has gone from being the province of elites to a commodity accessible to anyone.

As the number of HEIs increases, colleges and universities have found themselves facing stiff competition in the recruitment of faculty. As a result, many HEIs have begun to establish so-called continuing/extension education centers, which provide accredited and nonaccredited courses as well as short- and medium-term vocational training for adults from various walks of life who live off campus to continue learning and obtain further knowledge and skills. The goal of such centers is actually focused on satisfying the needs of the community, local industry, and local professional development. Furthermore, the formation of such centers is in compliance with the lifelong learning policy of the MOE, whose mission is to provide credit and noncredit programs.

Extension education centers actually provide various courses or programs for industry professionals and general adults so as to promote lifelong learning and serve the public at large. The courses offered by such centers are not part of a degree program, and therefore cannot lead to a bachelor's or master's degree, while those offered through continuing education centers are part of a degree program and thus can lead to a degree. In essence, courses are designed based on consideration of the social needs and the academic specialties of the higher-education institutions' faculty members or at the request of the government or businesses.

Basically, two different types of courses are offered: credit courses and noncredit courses. Credit courses are available in different fields at the graduate or undergraduate level. Students are selected according to a specific guideline issued by the MOE. Students of credit courses (programs) are eligible to apply for credit certificates if they pass the courses they take. With the certificates, they can have those credits waived when they enter the regular programs at an institution. Noncredit courses are designed to be as practical as possible so that students may acquire/improve their job skills or satisfy their particular needs based on what they learn in class.

In addition, in order to further reach out to the Taiwanese community beyond Taiwan, in May 2002, the Measures for the Implementation of University Extension Education were revised to allow universities in Taiwan to open extension programs abroad. This change in policy was made in light of local universities' desire to offer extension programs to citizens of Taiwan in Southeast Asia and mainland China, as these two areas have the highest concentration of Taiwanese expatriates.

On the other hand, the cross-strait relations between Taiwan and mainland China have relaxed. On November 3, 2008, the Taiwanese government began allowing people from mainland China to attend extension education programs organized by Taiwan's universities in Kinmen, Matsu, and Penghu (the outlying islands of Taiwan). The government also eased restrictions on student qualifications and teaching credentials for domestic universities offering extension education on the mainland to facilitate the globalization of enterprise operations and the internationalization of higher education (MAC 2008).

International Education

As Taiwan interacts more and more with the global community, an increasing number of international schools are being set up in Taiwan. The majority of these seventeen schools, which admit students of foreign origin, including American, European, Japanese, and Korean students, among others, offer international coursework covering primary and secondary education. Instruction is conveyed in English or other foreign languages based on the curricula. These international schools provide comprehensive education to the children of foreign nationals living in Taiwan.

Another type of bilingual schools for local students has recently been established across the country, and these schools often integrate Chinese and English into the curricula and coursework. These schools tend to employ faculty and staff of international backgrounds. Most them emphasize a multicultural campus life that adopts the Taiwan national curriculum as well as bilingual programs. The latter serves students in the English-speaking community who either seek a college preparatory education relevant to an English-speaking country or plan to transfer to the local school system. The curriculum consists of bilingual (English and Mandarin) content on a semester system with a two-hundred-day school year. Subjects that are offered include English, Chinese, mathematics, science, and social studies, and many electives, such as drama, painting, choir, French, Japanese, creative writing, earth science, and AP statistics (International School Friends 2008).

Regarding students from overseas, there are approximately twenty-seven Chinese language centers that are affiliated with universities and staffed by instructors who specialize in Teaching Chinese as Second/Foreign Language (TCSL). Taiwan currently hosts more than ten thousand students who are learning Mandarin Chinese. About 58 percent hail from Asian countries, and 24 percent come from the United States. The largest language center in Taiwan is the National Taiwan Normal University (NTNU), which hosts about sixteen hundred students from, in descending order of number of students, Japan, South Korea, the United States, Southeast Asia, Europe, and Central and South America. The students may take basic language and culture courses, including calligraphy, seal carving, tai-chi, and traditional arts and music. Students who pass the Test of Proficiency—Huayu (Mandarin Chinese) may pursue further studies in most disciplines.

Not only is there an influx of international students to Taiwan, but Taiwanese students now enjoy more opportunities to study abroad. Statistics show that Taiwanese students applied for more than 32,162 student visas in 2001, and 3,7800 in 2008 (MOE 2011e). The majority of students attended U.S. universities, accounting for 26,685 students in 2010 (Institute of International Education 2011). The top five destinations of Taiwanese studying abroad for the years 1996–2007, as determined by the number of student visas granted, were the United States, the United Kingdom, Australia, Canada, and Japan. Since 2004, the Taiwan government has increased the number of scholarships and student loans to local university graduates for advanced studies or to conduct research abroad (National Chengchi University 2011). In addition, a series of scholarships subsidizing students who study abroad or attend exchanges or joint degree programs were set up in 2006 in the hope of encouraging more Taiwanese to reach out the world for advanced education (Cheng 2007). In conclusion, all of these new trends in education represent Taiwan's dedication to meeting the new challenges of globalization while coping with its rising awareness of local demand.

Educational Statistics

The following section will outline some of the key educational statistics to highlight the transitional profile of Taiwan's education system as it progresses toward becoming a member of the global village. Educational development in Taiwan over the past five decades is briefly represented in the following statistics.

The Number of Graduates Admitted to the Next Level

The acceptance rate for students has increased steadily since 1968. According to a 2004 report on education in Taiwan, the percentage of graduates admitted to the next level of education during school year 1965–1966 was 58.2 percent at the primary school level, 78.5 percent at the junior high school level, and 38.3 percent at the senior high school level. The percentage of primary graduates admitted to junior high schools entered a period of phenomenal growth in the beginning of the 1970s. The growth then became steady in the years that followed. By 2010, the average percentage of graduates admitted to the next level of education had reached 99.73 percent at the primary school level, 97.63 percent at the junior high school level, 95.56 percent at the senior high school level, and 76.91 percent at the senior vocational school level (MOE 2010).

The increase in Taiwanese citizens' level of education over the past few decades is certainly notable, and the Taiwanese government is now pushing for improvements in the education system itself. Female graduates' enrollment rate has risen since the implementation of nine-year compulsory education, begun in 1968. According to the statistics, in 1966, 69.38 percent of male primary school graduates attended junior high schools, whereas only 47.42 percent of female students did so. The percentage of primary graduates admitted to junior high school soon rose to 88.70 percent of male students and 72.28 percent of female students in 1971, and to 99.77 percent of male students and 99.70 percent of female students in 2010 (MOE 2011f).

During school year 2008–2009, more than one out of five persons in Taiwan was a student, and among these individuals, students in primary education and higher education accounted for the majority per one thousand residents.

The Teacher-Student Ratio

The number of students per teacher in a classroom has been decreasing over the years, and this was especially the case when the birth rate started to decline in the late 1990s. According to official statistics from the Ministry of Education (MOE 2010), the average teacher-student ratio is 1:18 across all school levels (1:16.5 for public schools, and 1:25 for private, respectively), but private institutions tend to have a much higher teacher-student ratio than their public counterparts, except for private colleges, which suffer from severe shortages of students, due to Taiwan's declining birth rate and these institutions' remote locations. Another study comparing teacher-student ratios for the last decade indicated that the number decreased from 23.8 in 1992 to 19.7 in 2002 (Directorate General of Budget 2010), but the average budget spent on students doubled in those periods, except at the university level, where the budget declined by one-sixth over the last decade as a result of the expansion of higher education.

Regional Discrepancy

The average national statistics cannot overrule the fact that there is an increasing regional gap between rural and urban schools. Some suburban schools are packed with a few thousand students, while the rural schools are suffering losses in their student populations. As the birth rate declined drastically over the past ten years (to 1.1 babies per couple in 2009), many remote primary and secondary schools were faced with the choice of closing down or merging with other schools. The trend of closing schools has gradually made its way up to higher education, especially in those private institutions located in less accessible areas.

REFERENCES

Academia Sinica. 2007. *History and Mission*. Taipei: Academia Sinica. Available online at: http://www.sinica.edu.tw.

Altbach, Philip G., Liz Reisberg, and Laura E. Rumbley. 2009. *Trends in Global Higher Education: Tracking an Academic Revolution*. Paris: UNESCO.

Basic Competence Test (BCTEST). 2011. *Introduction 2011*. Taipei: BCTEST. Available online at: http://www.bctest.ntnu.edu.tw.

Cheng, Ru-Yun. 2007. A Study on Overseas Education Policies of Asia-Pacific Countries. National Taiwan University of Technology, Taipei: Unpublished master's thesis.

Chou, Chuing Prudence. 2008. *Mr. President: How are You Going to Deal with Education in Taiwan?* Taipei: Psychology.

———. 2010. "Expectation of Academicians and Academic Sinica 2010." Taipei: Chine Review News. Available online at: http://www.chinareview news.com.

Directorate General of Budget. 2010. *Summary of Country Profile.* Taipei: Directorate General of Budget. Available online at: http://ebas1.ebas.gov.tw.

Forest Elementary School. 2010. *Forest Elementary School Is Accepting Entrance Applications 2010.* Taipei: Humanistic Education Foundation. Available online at: http://hef.yam.org.tw.

Government Information Office. 2010a. *The Republic of China at a Glance, 2010.* Taipei: Government Information Office. Available online at: http://www .gio.gov.

———. 2010b. *Alternative Education.* Taipei: Government Information Office.

Hu, Qing-Hui, and Xiao-Yun Lin. 2010. *Basic Competence Test Skills.* Taipei: Liberty Times. Available online at: http://www.libertytimes.com.tw.

Institute of International Education (IIE). 2011. *Open Doors 2011: International Student Enrollment Increased by 5 Percent in 2010/11.* New York: IIE. Available online at: http://www.iie.org.

International School Friends. 2008. *International School 2008.* World Community of Students of International Schools. Available online at: http://www.inter national-schoolfriends.com.

Mainland Affairs Council (MAC). 2008. *Major Measures of the Government's Mainland Policy.* Taipei: MAC. Available online at: http://www.mac .gov.tw.

Ministry of Education (MOE). 2006. *Community Colleges Raise Awareness of the Importance of Lifelong Learning.* Taipei: MOE. Available online at: http://eng .tmue.edu.tw.

———. 2009. *Special Education.* Taipei: MOE.

———. 2010. *2010 Education Statistics Indicators.* Taipei: MOE.

———. 2011a. *Educational Laws.* Taipei: MOE. Available online at: http://edu .law.moe.gov.tw.

———. 2011b. *Educational Laws.* Taipei: MOE. Available online at: http://140.111.34.34.

———. 2011c. *Employee Listing.* Taipei: MOE. Available online at: http://history. moe.gov.tw.

———. 2011d. *Education Statistics.* Taipei: MOE.

———. 2011e. *Education Statistics.* Taipei: MOE. Available online at: http:// www.edu.tw.

———. 2011f. *Education Statistics.* Taipei: MOE.

National Chengchi University (NCCU) 2011. Scholarships. Taipei: NCCU. Available online at: http://oic.nccu.edu.tw/chinese/scholarship.php.

National Commission on Excellence in Education. 1983. *A Nation at Risk: The Imperative for Educational Reform*. Washington, DC: U.S. Department of Education. Available online at: http://www2.ed.gov.

Seedling Experimental School. 2010. *Introduction*. Wulai Township, Taiwan: Seedling Experimental School. Available online at: http://www.seedling.tw.

Zhang, Fang-Quan. 2007. *Problems and Srategies Regarding Textbook Debate*. Taipei: Chian Cheng Middle School. Available online at: http://ppk.tp.edu.tw.

Chapter 6

Course, Curriculum, and Textbooks

At the primary level, school subjects include the national language (Mandarin), mathematics, English, indigenous languages, civics, physical education, social studies, science, and fine arts such as music and drawing. In junior high school, geography is included, and social studies may be split into history and geography classes. Other subjects, such as home economics, biology, and computer science are also taught, while English courses, which students take beginning in primary school, may be divided into listening, reading, and composition classes. In 2001, the government promulgated a set of guidelines—the Nine-Year Spiral Curriculum—for Grades 1 through 9 to integrate elementary and junior high school curricula. The guidelines aim to help students develop self-understanding, respect for others, self-expression, a capacity for lifelong learning, and respect for the law and global perspectives. The integrated curricula also designate seven major areas of learning: languages, health and physical education, social studies, arts and humanities, mathematics, and natural and life sciences, as well as interdisciplinary activities.

Among these new learning domains, languages constitute 20 percent to 30 percent of the overall curricula, with the other six areas accounting for equal shares of the remainder. To help prepare students for life in an increasingly interconnected world, English is a compulsory subject from Grade 3 on, and numerous elementary and junior high schools around Taiwan employ native English-speaking teachers. Besides English and the official lingua franca, Mandarin Chinese, students in Grades 1-6 are required to study one additional local dialect of Taiwan, which then becomes optional in junior high school.

The Ministry of Education (MOE) has also highlighted the importance of learning and reading English. Based on the general guidelines of the elementary curricula for Grades 1 through 9 (MOE 1997), English language-learning programs for Grades 5 and 6 were implemented in school year 2001. Four years later, in school year 2005, an English language program was implemented for Grade 3 in the hope of improving Taiwanese English proficiency.

Influenced by the worldwide trend of educational restructuring and reform that has taken place since the 1980s, Taiwan started to implement its goals in the *Action Plan for Educational Reform* in 1996, which aimed to accommodate the needs of each student and help him or her to fulfill his or her educational goals (Fan 2006). Recently, much effort has been directed toward low achievers or underachievers, thanks to the belief that early intervention and remedial instruction will facilitate those children at risk to have a head start in learning (Pikulski 1994; Shanahan and Barr 1995; Berk 1996).

Evolution of the English Curriculum

The English curriculum in Taiwan underwent some major revisions both before and after the implementation of the nine-year compulsory education system in 1968 (Chern 2002). According to Shih (2000), the curriculum standards mandated prior to 1968 followed the grammar translation theory; the standards mandated in 1971 focused on reading and writing, with a slightly greater emphasis on listening and speaking than in the past. The aim of English instruction was to help students pass the entrance examinations to be admitted to senior high schools and universities, the so-called "teach-to-the-test" practice (Su 2000). At the university level, although there is no pressure from other entrance examinations, the focus of the English curriculum is still on reading and grammar translation. Since 2002, the trend of students taking the General English Proficiency Test (GEPT) has led the focus of teaching and learning to be on four skills: listening, speaking, reading, and writing. Presently, from the perspective of paradigm shifts, English instruction tends to be communicative language teaching, which appears to be a recent development.

Importance of English for Specific Purposes (ESP) in Taiwan

ESP has been around since the early 1960s (Strevens 1977). It actually originated from the massive expansion of scientific, technical, and economic activities on a global scale, which resulted in the increased demand for communication through English (Dudley-Evans and St. John 1998). In addition, with the usage of English varying from context to context, English language practitioners thus felt the pressure to adapt to the needs of the learners within their specific environment. It is noted that advocates of ESP practice an approach to language teaching in which all decisions as to content and method are based on the learner's reasons for learning (Law 1996).

In Taiwan, English was once a required course for college students that emphasized the reading of literature (Chia et al. 1998). However, in 1993 the MOE abolished the mandatory English reading requirements in higher-education institutions (HEIs) due to growing concerns that both English language teaching and the curricula had been ignoring students' needs (Law 1996; Chia et al. 1998; Liaw 2009). This phenomenon opened up opportunities for Taiwanese HEIs to freely design their own English language courses based on a content focus or a designated-skill focus. In spite of this, such courses were still not developed on the basis of an analysis of the English language needs of college students (Chia et al. 1998). Therefore, there is a serious need to develop an ESP course that covers the two absolute components that Strevens (1988) mentioned: needs assessment and discourse analysis.

For the past decade, HEIs in Taiwan have been encouraging course programs to be taught in English, offering more ESP courses, and requiring students to pass the Test of English for International Communication (TOEIC) prior to graduation (Chien et al. 2008). These measures were actually brought to the fore by the need for HEIs to become internationally competitive in an age of globalization and internationalization (Butler 2005; Chang 2005), which has led to changes in the goals of teaching English (Borsheim, Merritt, and Reed 2008).

English has been highly regarded as the de facto language in the fields of banking, commerce, trade, research, technology, and tourism (Tsai 1998). Furthermore, as Taiwan engages more centrally as a player on the global economic stage (Mok 2005; Zaharia and Gilbert 2005), the trend of studying English as a medium of communication in the business arena has become an increasingly important element in the education of Taiwanese students. What is more, Taiwan's language and linguistic academic domain has recently placed great significance on ESP, as indicated by the establishment of the Taiwan ESP Association in 2008 (Taiwan ESP Association 2010). Clearly, ESP in Taiwan, more specifically learning Business English, has become a strong necessity for future graduates' careers.

Changes in the Curriculum

In addition to the 2001 guidelines, new teaching methods and a wide selection of textbooks have been introduced. Today, each school has its own curriculum development committee, which reviews teaching materials in light of the school's individual approaches and the needs of students. To move on to senior high school, junior high school graduates are required to take the Basic Competence Test, which covers five subjects: Chinese, English, mathematics, natural science, and social science. The Practical Vocational Program is an alternative for those students who are interested in hands-on experience. These courses are offered at the beginning of the third year of junior high school. Students may enroll in vocational schools after graduation.

As mentioned earlier, there are two types of institutions beyond junior high school: senior high school for the academic track, and senior vocational school for the nonacademic track, which places more emphasis on vocational training and career planning, both of which require three years to complete. In terms of subject matter, a total of twenty-two subjects cover three years of high school instruction. According to the new curriculum guidelines released in 2010, most senior high school courses include the national language (Mandarin) and literature, English, mathematics, history, geography, civics and society, physics, chemistry, biology, earth science, music, art, arts and life, integrative activities, life technology, home economics, physical education, health and nursing education, information technology, career planning, national defense education, life education, and a second foreign language.

The courses taught each semester range from fifteen to sixteen subjects, on average, which is a relatively high number compared to some Western countries. On the other hand, vocational high schools have a much more complex system, with subject matter and programs geared toward vocational training and practical skills. In spite of this, more than 90 percent of vocational students also choose to attend college and a university of technology instead of seeking jobs, due to the recent expansion of vocational higher education, lower salaries, and parental expectations.

As Taiwanese society has become more open and diverse, other dialects such as Taiwanese, Hakka, and indigenous languages are finding their way into the educational system, even though Mandarin Chinese is still the only official language taught in schools. The mixture of foreign languages and indigenous languages can be said to represent Taiwan's ambition in terms of the movements of globalization and localization that are taking place.

At the level of higher education in Taiwan, the broad divisions are usually categorized into streams, such as the College of Humanities and Sciences, the College of Social Sciences, the College of Medical Sciences, the College of Engineering, the College of Professional Schools, and so forth. Most of the universities and colleges are supervised by the MOE, except for the Military Academy and the Police Academy.

To better understand what comprises university core teaching in Taiwan, it is worthwhile to introduce some coursework examples as follows. First, there is general and liberal arts education, of which the former covers a wide range of required courses such as Chinese literature, foreign languages, physical education, and community service; the latter covers eight areas: literature and arts, historical thinking, world civilization, philosophy and moral reasoning, civic awareness and social analysis, quantitative analysis and mathematics material science, and life science. These courses are designed to enhance a diverse dialogue and integration among different academic fields, to stimulate old and new ways of thinking, and especially to cultivate students' cultural literacy as they embrace globalization and localization in a lifelong learning society.

Second, courses required by department/graduate institutions consist of half of the graduation credits, which normally range from 128 to 148 credits (one credit equals one hour of class per week, with eighteen weeks per semester). Third, students are at liberty to choose elective courses and credits campus-wide or through the intercampus system. One exception is that students who have passed the prerequisite test that is part of teacher education programs are qualified to take courses in the preservice teacher training program, which will grant teacher candidacy after a postgraduate six-month internship.

The Philosophy Underlying Curriculum Reform

Since the 1980s, along with following international movements towards restructuring, curriculum reform has been prioritized not only in terms of the courses taught in schools but also as an arena for the representation of the values and interests among different social groups. The curriculum, as a medium for the construction of social and cultural identity, represents a place where power struggles and conflicts of interest may arise. Curriculum debates worldwide have gone beyond subject matter and "what is taught" to issues of national identity, such as "who we are" (Mao 2008). The current Taiwan curriculum reflects not only what Taiwan really is in terms of education, but also what it will be in the future under the overwhelming impact of internationalization. It is believed that the upcoming curriculum reform, which extend mandatory education from nine years to twelve, especially in the subjects of Chinese literature and history, characterizes the ambivalence in the "Taiwanese identity," which is interwoven with issues of localization and globalization.

Along with Taiwanese social movement of the 1980s, the curriculum has been undergoing reforms that attempt to promote the "Taiwanese identity" by reshaping the country's own sociopolitical and cultural boundaries, and thus separating her from her former pro-Chinese identity. The most significant change is the emergence of indigenous languages and local dialects (i.e., the mother tongue) in primary schools, which in the past were banned completely and now, thanks to social solidarity, have been returned schools. Specifically, Chinese content in social studies textbooks was reduced to a great extent and replaced by local Taiwanese history and geography. The profound promotion of a national spirit and the Chinese identity, along with the inclusion of more modern topics such as gender issues, multiculturalism, and so on began to transform Taiwan into a country with a more open-minded, contemporary, and updated worldview (Su 2007). Despite the large number of courses in Taiwanese schools, such changes can be clearly observed in textbooks and education policies.

The Reform of Textbooks

The privatization of textbooks is also a hot issue in recent education reform. Textbooks have traditionally been monitored and published by the central government and served as a social medium for the construction of political ideologies and social cohesion. The trends toward "Chinization" and patriotism after Taiwan was restored to China following the Second World War led to uniform official school textbooks, the prohibition of Taiwanese dialects in schools, and restrictions on the performance of indigenous arts, all methods that the government used in order to promote a strong Chinese national identity (Yang 2001). Later, along with the political reform and social protest movements in the 1970s and 1980s, the issue of textbooks became a burgeoning topic of debate. Traditional textbooks have been criticized for reinforcing the dominant cultures of the governing party without considering the specific perspectives and voices of gender and different cultural and ethnic groups. Parallel with the trend toward diversification and liberalization in Taiwanese society and education, a new textbook publication system was introduced in 1996 to decentralize the textbook market. The updated system entitles private companies to publish textbooks and teaching materials after they are reviewed, screened, and approved by the National Institute for Compilation and Translation (NICT) under the authority of the MOE (Pan and Yu 1999). This approach implies that the

MOE is still responsible for setting the standards for the curriculum and overseeing educational quality control (Chou and Ho 2007).

Many centralized governments transmit their ideology to the younger generation by publishing nationally standardized textbooks (Altbach and Kelly 1986). Such texts were published and used before 1995 as a way of reinforcing a centralized political and ideological uniformity in education. According to Hwang (1999), though the relaxation of the textbook market in Taiwan has literally created more options for schools and teachers to choose from, "the introduction of market forces in the textbook market does not necessarily reduce the monopoly of government's role in textbook publication" (87). While giving schools and publishers more autonomy to design their own "school-based curriculum," the MOE still regulates the curriculum guidelines and criteria for textbook content. In most circumstances, textbooks still play the role of articulating values and transmitting the official ideology preferred by specific political groups. Does the question of whether or not Taiwan's textbooks, which are published by the private sector, can remain neutral in conveying subjective knowledge and values deserve more attention? Does the government constrain its agenda and values so that education, in terms of textbook content, can be immune to political upheaval and changes in government administrations? These questions remain unanswered as Taiwan undergoes a globalization process.

The conflict related to Taiwan's pursuit of independence versus its political unification, ongoing since the late 1980s, has also been part of the process of localization. In practice, the number of school textbooks containing Chinese content were reduced to great extent starting in 1988, when President Lee, the first local leader in Taiwanese history who was brought up during the period of Japanese colonization, assumed the presidency. At this time, local dialects and indigenous languages were introduced into the primary schools and became required courses along with Chinese and English. History and Chinese courses were tailored more to Taiwanese instead of Chinese issues. Instruction now focused extensively on local issues and the Taiwanese identity, such as the calls for the country to be known as Taiwan rather than the Republic of China, the shift of textbook content in elementary and secondary schools from Chinese to Taiwanese subject matter, and the increased Taiwanization/indigenization of the national civil service examination by the Examination Yuan.

On the other hand, one can always ask whether or not textbooks at different stages reinforce the dominance of the traditional Chinese cultural identity. How are issues related to gender and various cultural and ethnic groups represented in the content? Furthermore, how were issues of political ideology, along with Taiwan's political and socioeconomic deregulation, presented in textbooks after the democratization process in the late 1980s? Su (2007) attempted to answer these questions by conducting a content analysis of two sets of social studies textbooks for Grade 4 from 1978 to 1995 (the first set was published between 1978 and 1989, the second between 1989 and 1995). The research findings indicated that not only the historical interpretation but also the ideology of a unified Chinese national identity was emphasized in both series of social studies textbooks before 1995 (Su 2007). The two series often legitimated the notion that Taiwanese ancestors migrated from mainland China, and the Kuomintang (KMT) ruling party used these texts as a way to assert political legitimacy by conveying special values, assumptions, and principles that reflected the interests of the political authorities (Williams and Dyke 2004). As a result, many sensitive and controversial political and cultural issues were removed from the textbooks (Anyon 1979). For example, both sets of textbooks contrasted the differences in life between the period of Dutch/Japanese political and economic oppression and the period of prosperity under the Chinese without portraying in detail the integration and prosperity of Taiwan as a Japanese colony between 1895 and 1945 (Su 2007).

Localization in Taiwan is a phenomenon with roots that reach back to the Japanese occupation. In order to form her own national and cultural identity, Taiwan tried in every possible way to dismantle and eradicate the Japanese colonial influence and also to escape from China-oriented nationalism. These notions have led to an influx of teaching materials that are focused on local history and geography as well as the local arts in the curriculum reform at every level of the education system. Hence, the localization of Taiwanese education is taking shape.

References

Altbach, Philip G., and Gail P. Kelly. 1986. *New Approaches to Comparative Education*. Chicago: University of Chicago Press.
Anyon, Jean. 1979. "Ideology and United States History Textbooks." *Harvard Educational Review* 49 (3): 361–386.
Berk, Laura. E. 1996. *Infants, Children, and Adolescents*. Needham Heights, MA: Allyn & Bacon.
Borsheim, Carlin, Kelly Merritt, and Dawn Reed. 2008. "Beyond Technology for Technology's Sake: Advancing Multiliteracies in the Twenty-First Century." *Clearing House: A Journal of Educational Strategies, Issues and Ideas* 82 (2): 87–90.
Butler, Yuko Goto. 2005. "Comparative Perspectives Towards Communicative Activities among Elementary School Teachers in South Korea, Japan, and Taiwan." *Language Teaching Research* 9 (4): 423–446.

Chang, Qin Sheng. 2005. *Internationalization of Higher Education from the Perspective of Globalization 2005*. Taipei: MOE. Available online at: http://english.education.edu.tw.

Chern, Chiou-Lan. 2002. "English Language Teaching in Taiwan Today." *Asia-Pacific Journal of Education* 22 (2): 97–105.

Chia, Hiu-Uen, Ruth Johnson, Hui-Lung Chia, and Floyd Olive. 1998. "English for College Students in Taiwan: A Study of Perceptions of English Needs in a Medical Context." *English for Specific Purposes* 18 (2): 107–119.

Chien, Ching Ning, Wei Lee, and Li Hua Kao. 2008. "Collaborative Teaching in an ESP Program." *Asian EFL Journal* 10 (4): 114–133.

Chou, Chuing Prudence, and Ai-Hsin Ho. 2007. "Schooling in Taiwan." In *Going to School in East Asia*, edited by G. Postiglione and J. Tan. New York: Greenwood. 344–377

Dudley-Evans, T., and M. St. John. 1998. *Developments in ESP: A Multi-Disciplinary Approach*. UK: Cambridge University Press.

Fan, Sun-Lu. 2006. *Speech by Vice Minister of Education Fan Sun-Lu 2006*. Taipei: MOE. http://english.moe.gov.tw.

Hwang, Jenq-Jye, 1999. *Curriculum Reform in Taiwan*. Taipei: HanWen

Law, Wing Wah. 1996. "The Taiwanisation, Democratisation and Internationalisation of Higher Education in Taiwan." *Asia Pacific Journal of Education* 16 (1): 56–73.

Liaw, Meei Ling. 2009. "Panel Discussion: Contexts in ESP." Paper presented at the 2009 International Symposium on ESP & Its Application in Nursing & Medical English Education, Kaohsiung, Taiwan, November 7–8, 2008.

Mao, Chin-Ju (1997). "Constructing a New Social Identity: Taiwan's Curricular Reforms of the Nineties," *International Journal of Educational Reform* 6 (4): 400–406.

———. 2008. "Fashioning Curriculum Reform as Identity Politics—Taiwan's Dilemma of Curriculum Reform in the New Millennium." *International Journal of Educational Development* 28 (5): 585–595.

Ministry of Education (MOE). 1997. *General Guidelines of Grade 1–9 Curriculum of Elementary and Junior High School Education*. Taipei: MOE. Available online at: www.apecneted.org.

Mok, Ka Ho. 2005. "Fostering Entrepreneurship: Changing Role of Government and Higher Education Governance in Hong Kong." *Research Policy* 34: 537–554.

Pan, Hui-Ling, and Chien Yu. 1999. Educational Reforms with Their Impacts on School Effectiveness and School Improvement in Taiwan, R.O.C." *School Effectiveness and School Improvement* 10 (1): 72–85.

Pikulski, John J. 1994. "Preventing Reading Failure: A Review of Five Effective Programs." *Reading Teacher* 48 (1): 30–39.

Shanahan, T., and R. Barr. 1995. "Reading Recovery: An Independent Evaluation of the Effects of an Early Instructional Intervention for At-Risk Learners." *Reading Research Quarterly* 30: 958–996.

Shih, Yu-hui. 2000. "General English Education at the University Level in Taiwan." Paper presented at the JACET 39th Annual Convention: English

Education in the East Asia for the 21st Century, Okinawa, Japan, September 14–16, 2000.

Strevens, Peter. 1977. "Special Purpose Language Learning: A Perspective." *Language Teaching and Linguistics Abstracts* 10: 145–163.

———. 1988. "ESP After Twenty Years: A Re-Appraisal." In *ESP: State of the Art*, ed. M. Tickoo. 1-Singapore: SEAMEO Regional Centre. 1–13.

Su, Fu-Hsing. 2000. "New Goal Orientation of English Education for Young EFL Learners." In *Conference of ELT Curriculum for Young Learners in East Asia*, 107–120. Taipei: National Taiwan Normal University and British Council.

Su, Ya-Chen. 2007. "Ideological Representations of Taiwan's History: An Analysis of Elementary Social Studies Textbooks, 1978–1995." *Curriculum Inquiry* 37 (3): 205–237.

Taiwan ESP Association. 2010. *Taiwan ESP Association Introduction 2010*. Taipei: Taiwan ESP Association. Available online at: http://www.tespa.org.tw.

Tsai, Chuan-tzu. 1998. "The Effects of Cooperative Learning on Teaching English as a Foreign Language to Senior High School Students." MA thesis, National Kaohsiung Normal University, Kaohsiung, Taiwan.

Williams, R., and N. V. Dyke. 2004. *The International Standing of Australian Universities, 2004*. Melbourne: Melbourne Institute, Faculty of Business and Economics, University of Melbourne. Available online at: http://www.melbourneinstitute.com

Yang, Shen-Keng. 2001. "Dilemmas of Education Reform in Taiwan: Internationalization or Localization?" Paper presented at the Annual Meeting of the Comparative and International Education Society, Washington, DC, March 14–17, 2001.

Zaharia, Sorin E., and Ernest Gilbert. 2005. "The Entrepreneurial University in the Knowledge Society." *Higher Education in Europe* 31 (1): 31–40.

Chapter 7

Budget Allocation Features

Regulations of the Constitution, Laws, and Acts

The constitution (Article 164) stipulates that the government's educational expenditures at all levels account for at least 15 percent of the general government net revenues (including science and culture), while expenditures are 25 percent in the provinces and 35 percent under the local governments (including municipalities and counties) (Office of the President 2011). However, after the abolishment of the lower budget limitation during the fourth revision of Article 10 in 1997, the stature of Taiwan province was suspended (Taiwan decided to become independent and not a part of mainland China) together with the further budget allocation features.

Since then, only the central and the local governments (including municipalities and counties) have taken responsibility for educational budget allocations. To save education funding from being neglected, the *Education Basic Law* (Article 5), launched in 1999, specified that all local governments should draw up an ample budget for education and coordinate resources appropriately, particularly to safeguard grants for remote and special education (MOE 2006).

In 2005, the law was amended to ensure that educational funding would be used on educational affairs only, as a way of avoiding any abuse of local public funds, which political elections and votes can strongly influence. Prior to that, the *Education Basic Law* and the *Educational Budget and Management Act* were put into effect in 2000, and these measures required, in Article 3, that the educational budget must not be less than 21.5 percent of the previous three-year average of the government's net revenue (MOE 2000). Regarding governance and the funding agency, higher education in Taiwan has been governed by the Ministry of Education (MOE), with most of the senior high schools in the hands of the Central Office under the MOE (formerly the Provincial Department of Education before 1997), and primary and junior middle schools (years one to nine) under the control of local governments.

Expenditure from Public and Private Sources

When Taiwan's central government withdrew from mainland China in 1949, the gross domestic product (GDP) of Taiwan was NT$927.04 million, around US$185.408 million (NT$ to US$=5:1), and her per capital income was around US$100 annually in the 1950s (Copper 1988). Taiwan was one of the poorest countries in Asia; however, the literacy rate was around 60 percent (Wu 1991), one of the highest in the region (Huang 2006). In fiscal year (FY) 1951, the government's education expenditure at all levels accounted for US$5.325 million (which accounted for 9.93 percent of the total government expenditure), but it increased to around US$24.621 billion, 25.1 percent of the government's annual expense, in 2009, according to national statistics compiled by the MOE. In FY 1951, expenditure on public and private education at all levels totaled US$5.325 million, occupying 1.69 percent of Taiwan's gross national product (GNP), and in FY 2009 it reached US$24.621 billion, 6.17 percent of the GNP, which has increased 4.48 percent during the past half century (MOE 2010a).

In observing the state of public and private educational investment, it is possible to see that public expenditure began going down after reaching its peak in 1993, while private expenditure, in contrast, kept growing, rising twice at impressive rates in 1982 and 1997, and sharing over a quarter of the proportion after 2005 (MOE 2010a).

Since the late 1980s, governments in Taiwan have responded to the worldwide trend of neoliberalism and globalization alongside political democratization and a process of economic transformation. Many countries are reorganizing their education systems, seeking to increase the relative autonomy and responsibility of individual institutions. Through deregulation and liberalization, each institution is expected to become more competitive and accountable, with the result that an overall market mechanism within the education system will be created (Giroux 2002).

Accordingly, Taiwan has adopted reforms to improve education quality by decentralizing governance and finance, and increasing school personnel's outcome-based accountability.

Under such an economic ideology, it is believed that in order to share the governmental burden and enhance accountability, the private sector should be encouraged to invest in education so that privately-owned education institutions can be as competitive as their public counterparts. In so doing, people will have more opportunities to receive a quality education based on market competition. In amendments to the *Education Basic Law* (Article 7) and the *National Education Act* (Article 4), we can also see the government's attitude of encouraging the private sector to exert control in schools. Both Taipei city and Taipei county set up their own private management of public school regulation in 2000 and put it into action immediately, with the rest of the country soon following. Since then, an increase in private investment has taken place in all aspects of education, while public funding has begun to be withdrawn.

As for the development of private schools in Taiwan, this can be traced back to the late 1960s and early 1970s (National Policy Foundation 2007). At that time, Taiwan was focused on implementing nine-year compulsory education, and it invested most of its educational funding in establishing junior high schools and meeting requirements for primary and secondary education. Therefore, the government encouraged the private sector to run senior high schools, junior colleges, and universities, which resulted in a field share of 8:2 (private: public) for many years. Yet, for the sake of expediency, when poor teaching quality and a poor educational environment in some private vocational schools aroused severe criticism from the public, the establishment of private schools was stopped completely from 1974–1986. Moreover, the *National Education Act*, passed in 1979 and amended in 1999, specified that the government should manage compulsory education. In 1985, however, the MOE announced a *Guideline for Establishing New Private Schools*, which enabled private schools to nurture professional personnel in the fields of business, engineering, and medicine. Not until 1999 did the government revise the preceding regulation and permit the new establishment of private schools at all levels.

As we all know, investment plays a crucial role in guaranteeing the quality and development of education. Over the past decade, the overall funding for education in Taiwan has increased, but government investment is declining, threatening the quality of schools and their operation. For example, in FY 1995, the total fund for education was US$16.976 billion (the exchange rate 26.49 in 1995, and 32.18 in 2005), which accounts for 6.37 percent of the national GNP, of which 5.20 percent was from the public sector and 1.17 percent from the private sector. In FY 2005, the total fund reached US$21.302 billion, which accounted for 5.74 percent of the national GNP, of which 4.24 percent was from the public sector and 1.5 percent from private sources. The decrease in public expenditure has led to the rise of private investment on a yearly basis, which has also resulted in a new form of educational class. That is to say, those who can afford the extra costs can obtain more educational resources. In this case, there may not be as much social class mobility as in the past.

Unit Cost Per Student

When the educational expenditure per student at all levels (see Table 7.1) was considered, it was found that the overall budget appeared to be growing. Upon comparison there is a clearly tendency of each education stage with that of grand total in subfigures, there among, the unit cost of education in universities and colleges and compulsory schools is growing greatly, which appears to be the highest educational expenditure that has been invested in these sectors for the past few years.

Preschool Education

According to the MOE's statistics, the enrollment rate at the preschool level is low. Based on the educational expenditure per student (see Table 7.1), the

Table 7.1 Educational Expenditure per Student in Taiwan

								Unit: US$
Year	Grand	Preschool	Primary	Junior	Senior	Senior	Junior	Universities
	Total		Schools	High	High	Vocational	Colleges	&
				Schools	Schools	Schools		Colleges
1980	448	189	236	357	561	674	935	1,695
1985	700	474	335	533	749	862	1,427	2,450
1990	2,120	1,294	1,115	1,571	2,144	2,467	2,456	7,009
1995	3,248	1,797	2,367	2,882	3,183	3,619	3,314	7,498
2000	3,407	1,985	2,426	3,750	2,946	3,518	2,930	5,440
2005	4,081	2,341	2,726	3,915	2,874	3,283	3,785	5,344
2008	4,726	3,210	3,122	4,117	3,213	3,482	3,701	5,832

Source: MOE (2010a) Educational Statistical Indicators (www.moe.gov.tw).

investment in preschool is the lowest portion among all levels, except that it does not belong to compulsory education, and it also entails expensive costs charged by private kindergartens. If we take the expenditure per student in 2009, for example, the preschool investment is not only far below the average of all levels but also below half of higher education's average investment. Moreover, while the university's enrollment rate rises to 64.98, that of preschools is only 28.71, a little more than one-fourth of its school-age population. What is more, there are too few public kindergartens to enroll all of the eligible children; therefore, about 60 percent of children are forced to attend private kindergartens.

Preschool education consists of not merely teaching children to recognize numbers and the letters of the alphabet, or to memorize poems and sayings, but also to develop their personality, to help them grow. Preschool education focuses mainly on, but is not limited to, instilling the correct values in children, nurturing behaviors necessary for everyday life, and inculcating in them a positive attitude, such as a sense of responsibility, the ability to distinguish clearly between right and wrong, and an understanding of morality. Professional teachers become the key factor that determines the quality of a kindergarten. Although the teacher-student ratio of private kindergartens is just 9.95, which is far below any of the school levels, private kindergartens are still more competitive.

It is claimed that public kindergartens meet a higher standard than the private ones. In addition to having an enhanced learning environment and professional teachers, kindergartens accept only those children who are between four and six years old. In contrast, private kindergartens are easily established and are able to accept children from infancy to six years old. Generally speaking, parents tend to send their three-year-old children to private kindergartens that are located near their homes or are on the way to their office so that the children can learn basic knowledge and how to get along with their peers. Due to limits on enrollment, those children who are able to attend public kindergartens have to be carefully selected, and the remaining children—the majority—have no choice but to enroll in private kindergartens.

When tuition and monthly fees are considered, according to the data of the MOE, the unit educational expenditure of private kindergartens is four times that of public kindergartens, not to mention that some of the private ones flaunt themselves as an all-English learning environment and charge as much as ten times more than public ones. Since there is not yet a supervising institution to oversee the quality of private kindergartens, parents with a higher income usually choose to invest more for an educational setting that offers better care and better nurturing (Academia Sinica n.d.). In order to integrate kindergartens and nursery centers into the extension of compulsory education to twelve years, the government has issued various acts meant to grant subsidies to and alleviate the educational burden of vulnerable and aboriginal groups, and these laws and regulations have contributed to raising the enrollment rate in preschools (Education Yearbook 2008). Yet the status of other minority groups (vulnerable and aboriginal groups) remains unimproved.

Compulsory Education

Enrollment statistics during 1991–1998 provide evidence that the number of students was in gradual decline during this period, and this to due to the low birthrate. The unit cost per student, however, increased yearly during this same time. One exception is the proportion of the government's expenditure on education, which experienced an increase from 16.57 percent to 25.10 percent, something that is also due to the implementation of a policy of reducing class size. According to the Education Reform Report (Academia Sinica n.d.), this reform addressed the goal of downsizing in classes and schools for the first time, but also promised to cover all extra expenditures, such as teachers, school infrastructure, and so on. That is to say, although more funds were invested, the result was that the unit cost grew. This is a long-term project; therefore, this trend is expected to keep rising in the decades to come.

Local community governments allocate funding for compulsory education, yet the student cost unit of junior high schools is always higher than that of primary schools. For example, in 2009 the difference in expenditure per student rose to US$1149, as seen in Table 7.1. That is to say, when the number of students becomes the only factor in the calculation of unit cost, the smaller dividend (number of students) can obtain a higher quotient (unit expenditure per student).

Upper-Secondary Education

If the enrollment statistics for senior high schools and senior vocational schools are considered, as also seen in the MOE 2010 Educational Statistical Indicators, it is clear that the overall status of upper-secondary education has changed greatly since the 1990s. The total enrollment of upper-secondary education has increased, although there was a reduction every year in compulsory education in previous periods. As preparation for the twelve-year compulsory education that was to be instituted, the government tried to balance the difference between senior high and senior vocational schools by controlling the number of schools, which had an impact on the expenditure allocation, the number of teachers, and also the higher enrollment rate at upper-secondary institutions.

In 1995, the number of senior high schools for the first time surpassed that of senior vocational schools. At almost the same time, the number of students in senior vocational schools decreased greatly and slowed down after year 2002. Part of the attraction of senior high schools comes from the influence of Confucianism on the curriculum and the related idea that "All things are beneath study," which is why junior high graduates always set as their main goal the passing of the senior high school exam. Regarding the number of teachers, this change also coincides with the tendency for the number of schools to increase or decrease. The expansion of the number of senior high schools forced a reallocation of educational expenditure, which led to the decrease of unit cost per student and passed the extra burden on to students and their families as a result.

Higher Education

According to Table 7.1, Taiwan's government has established higher education as its highest priority when allocating educational expenditure, and thus, a comparatively small number of students possess the biggest share of resources. This disparity in resources can also be traced to the extensive movement to restructure schools that took place later. Obviously, the expanded number of schools brings in more students. For example, there were 183,000 more students from 1991 to 1998, which slowed the pace of the growing unit cost. The increased number of universities in the last decade has continued, and as a result over 90 percent of students are now admitted to universities.

In addition, since the mid-1990s, university funding has increased proportionally from 23.15 percent to 38.64 percent. University students cannot be excluded the additional fees that arise due the expansion of the university. Such fee increases have seemed to be an extra barrier for those students from disadvantaged families (Chu 2006).

According to the Educational Expenditure Proportion of GDP (MOE 2009), the budget for higher education has remained at 1.9 percent of GDP since 2002. The budget for expenses not related to higher education, however, fell from 3.3 percent to 2.9 percent of GDP between 2000 and 2008. This means that, other than higher education, the funding for any program or organization that comes from public sources has decreased due to the economic recession and governmental budget cuts. As a result, there has been fierce criticism against the MOE for their not-so-fair and unclear distribution of education expenditure, especially as higher education continues to comprise more than one-third of the total education budget, while spending for primary/secondary students and teacher education face cuts.

There obviously exists controversy regarding the priority placed on funding for higher education all over the world, and this includes Taiwan as well. The philosophy underlying funding policies prior to 1985 contrasted greatly with the philosophy that came after that year. Before 1985, amendments to the *Law of University* in 1972 and 1982 confirmed the leadership position of the government in the management of higher education. Since the number of HEIs was small, higher education was deemed a *public good*, and the government financed most public HEIs and a large percentage of the funding for private HEIs (Tang 2005). The amount of financial support was solely dependent on the number of students and staff at each university. HEIs unconditionally received sufficient funds from the government; therefore, all the universities and colleges were secure as long as they complied with the routine government budget.

During the 1970–1980s, there was no need and no motivation for HEIs to compete for external funding and student enrollment; concepts such as educational efficiency and accountability received no attention from either the government or the HEIs at that time (Gai 2004). However, since the early 1990s, higher education in Taiwan has experienced tremendous expansion in both the number of HEIs and the number of students, with the number of universities dramatically increasing, from 7 in 1950 to 164 in 2008. As the number of HEIs has risen, about 1 million Taiwanese students were enrolled in more than 160 universities during the academic year 2009–2010.

In order to reduce the financial burden on the government, the MOE has adopted a new policy to support all national universities in Taiwan by providing only 80 percent of the total budget, while leaving the remaining 20 percent to the financial resources of individual institutions. The proportion of government funding has shrunk more and more for some national universities, such as Taiwan University, which have seen their budgets reduced up to 50 percent. In addition, the Educational Funding System was introduced to ensure the efficient use of government funding, through which all revenue and expenditures are supervised and managed by the Board of Educational Budget Allocation established in 2001, with the aim of promoting more independence of HEIs and enhancing the efficiency of funding management (Tang 2005).

The development of higher education has an influence on the allocation of educational resources. Previously, resources were allocated equally without incorporating the mechanisms of competition and assessment. Yet while the population of students in higher education is growing rapidly, resources are unable to respond in kind. Insufficient financial support has led to the stagnation of teaching and research levels at universities, making improvement almost impossible. The main disadvantage of the ordinary funding method was an excessive dispersal of resources, which failed to encourage HEIs to engage in competition according to their specialties, and which led to the growth of academic competitiveness.

As previously mentioned, the force of worldwide neoliberal marketization since the mid-1980s became increasingly predominant in public funding policy in Taiwan. One main piece of evidence regarding this trend can be gleaned from the contractual relationship between the government and HEIs. In pursuit of educational excellence and global competitiveness, the MOE launched a series of competitive funding projects in 2000 in order to supplement the ordinary funding scheme. These included the Program for Promoting the Academic Excellence of Universities, the Program to Promote the International Competitiveness of Universities, the Research University Integration Project, the Program for Improving Research University Infrastructures, the Program for Expanding Overseas Student Recruitment; the Plan to Develop World-Class Universities, and the Program for Rewarding the Teaching Excellence of Universities, among others. Competitive funding was attached to each of these projects, and then funds were allocated under the philosophy of the *pursuit of excellence*. The competition is usually very stiff, and so the number of recipients is rather small, while the average amount of funding allocated to each recipient is conditional based on the degree of policy compliance. Among these projects, the Plan to Develop First-Class Universities and Top-Level Research Centers drew greater attention from both HEIs and the government starting in 2005. The total funding for that project was the largest ever, and only 12 or so top universities out of 162 institutions were chosen as recipients under this ambitious plan (MOE 2010b).

According to some critics, Taiwan's inadequate funding for education is a problem that has long been recognized (Wei 2007). The total annual national educational budget is about NT$430 billion (approx. US$14.2 billion), of which NT$140 billion comes from the central government. Compared with other developed countries, Taiwan has suffered from low investment in education. For example, Korea spends about 1.5 times (US$3,714:US$2,403) more than Taiwan for primary education, two times (US$5,159:US$2,531) more for secondary education, and 1.4 times (US$6,618:US$4,712) more at the university level. Even the funding of some Chinese universities, whose annual spending is as high as US$5,798, is much higher than the US$4,712 that Taiwan spends.

In addition, other funding for education, such as facility maintenance fees, runs short in Taiwan. Among these expenses are personnel costs, which account for 88 percent of the county and municipal government funding for education, while the rest is for other current expenses and investment capital. According to the Organisation for Economic Co-operation and Development (OECD) national standards, regular schooling operation fees often account for about 92 percent of education funding, of which personnel costs normally account for only about 81 percent (OECD 2009), much lower than that of Taiwan. An excessive proportion of staff costs necessitates a trade-off of other budget needs and results in poor teaching facilities and supplies, such as the failure to purchase library books, to contract for utility repairs, and so forth.

As for compulsory education, the management of these institutions belongs to local government. In addition to funding budgeted by local governments, there are also some grants offered by the central government. Owing to differences in regional income tax rates between rich and poor counties, local governments, however, still face the dilemma of insufficient funding to guarantee equal distribution of resources among schools and educational institutions, especially the major proportion that is spent on personnel expenses.

Why Does Educational Funding Run Short?

Regarding the statistics, in the OECD countries, the personnel cost is about 75 percent of educational expenditure (OECD 2009), while it reaches 83 percent to 93 percent in Taiwan. This is because the retirement pension funds of faculty and staff have long been calculated as part of educational expenditure in Taiwan. In the past few years, these pension funds have accounted for 10 percent to 17 percent of the government's educational expenditure, and this will increase to 20 percent to 25 percent in the near future when most of the Baby Boomer generation reaches retirement. The high personnel costs (including pensions) in Taiwan are one of the main reasons for the various features in the Taiwan education budget allocations.

The original scheme of Taiwan's teachers' pension system aimed to compensate teachers and other government employees for a below-average salary during the 1960–1980s in an attempt to recruit more talent to join the profession. In addition, teachers at the compulsory level had a lifetime tax exemption. Nevertheless, when the social context changed and teacher salaries became competitive, the old rule did not fit with current social needs and thus aroused social criticism, with such questions being repeatedly asked as, why should government employees and teachers be given security with a subsidized pension income plus 18 percent preferential interest? Why can teachers who reach their early fifties after working twenty-five years take early retirement and then collect their lifetime monthly retirement pension (around 75 percent of their salary before retirement)? Jealousy and tension between retired teachers/government retirees and the general public has continued to provoke disputes, especially during the recent economic recession (Bradberry 2011).

According to a former legislator, Chen-long Cheng, one of Taiwan's emerging educational crises can be attributed to the government's insufficient investment, partly due to the high demand from the teacher retirement pension system (udnjob 2004). In 2004, legislators, including Cheng, suggested that the government share the costs of teachers' retirement pension with the Ministry of Civil Service under the Executive Yuan in the same way that other public functionaries' pensions are managed. Yet, this proposal was rejected by the nation's Chief Statisticians and Accountants (DGBAS). The reason was that, if this action were taken, both the central government and local governments would have to spend extra billions of dollars on these costs, which would impair the government financial structure. A matter of great urgency is how to solve the problem of retirement pensions in order to break the deadlock that challenges Taiwan's education financing.

The emergence of mass teacher retirement accounted for 4 percent to 6 percent of total expenditure on education in the past few years, a great share of annual expenditure. To solve these budget-deficit problems caused by the uneven distribution of adequate funding, the law must be updated and other alternative formulas for calculating the budget must be initiated. In addition, Taiwan's universities also have to expand their financial resources by increasing their revenue from external contributions.

Additionally, some local governments have been accused of abusing grants from the central government for other purposes, which has undoubtedly struck local schools hard. For example, in FY2006, a total of NT$65.7 billion in funds were allotted, but NT$56.8 billion was used on noneducational affairs in the end. According to a report issued by the National Teachers' Association ROC (NTA) on December 25, 2006, concerning local governments' use of educational funding in FY2002–2004, the monies were designated for other purposes by overestimating personnel expenses (about 7 percent) and saving the balance of funds to reduce the debt or for other purposes.

The regulation in Article 13 of the Educational Funding Estimation and Management Act issued at the end of 2000 states that each county and city should set up an educational development fund. That is to say, educational funding should be estimated according to a subsidiary units budget model, which can accumulate funds over the years. It is expected that this strategy will ensure the sufficient return of balanced funding that is appropriately spent on educational affairs. In this case, once a budget is designated for equipment, utilities, hardware maintenance, and so on, one has to write off the amount accurately, and the balance of the budget should be recorded and returned to the educational development fund, because these accounts must be supervised. However, not every account receives oversight. For example, personnel cost is the exception. Most local governments have therefore taken advantage of this exception and used personnel cost to replace those accounts that required supervision when they budgeted funds. They may overestimate the amount of personnel cost until the end of the fiscal year, and took this estimated amount as their financial balance, which will be returned to the public treasury automatically and be used for noneducational purposes.

Any Way Out?

In the long battle line of fighting for a better educational environment, there are numerous impressive events left to discuss. The issue of "downsizing classes and schools" and "outcomes of education reform," for example, are noted below.

In August 2006, the Five-Year Refined Compulsory Education Development Program was announced by the MOE. This project stated that in academic year 2007, the size of elementary classes would be reduced to 32 students per class, and furthermore, in 2011 it would be lowered to 26.6 per class. Since the central government specified only policies but did not state where the money would be generated from, local governments could not help but criticize the policy as "the central government treats, while local governments pay the bill." Local governments addressed the difficulties of carrying out this policy and asked for grants from the central government to cover the expenditure of extra personnel, school properties, equipment, and so forth. The MOE finally pointed out that all the funding needs would be budgeted as general grants and would not cause overcrowding (Information Guide 2006). Consequently, in March

2009, several scholars expressed criticism at a press conference entitled "Let Children Know Education Is More Important Than Money" (不要讓教育窮得只剩下錢!!!), meaning that financial resources were impeding education for the less privileged. They were critical of the inconsistent and fragmented education policies that would eventually result in an insufficient usage of the unusual budget surplus of more than NT$80 billion over the next three golden years (udnjob 2009).

In addition, there have also been long discussions regarding the expansion of higher education in Taiwan and its consequent challenge of a shortage of students in the near future. According to a study on the unequal distribution of funding before and after the expansion of higher education in Taiwan since the mid-1990s, an increasing discrepancy exists between the rich and poor, and between the top-tier public and private universities in Taiwan (Wu and Wang 2008). Universities located in metropolitan areas with good reputations tend to be the ones that have higher rankings and more resources and donations from the private sector. As a result, the gap has widened between HEIs, and there are differences as well in the quality of education for students and the prospective job market for graduates.

Moreover, a very fast expansion has taken place in which the number of public universities and colleges grew from fifteen to fifty-one (MOE 2010a). A total of 120 schools have been established or restructured into universities and colleges since the period 1986 to 2010, which brings the total numbers of institutions of higher education to the present level of 163. Up until the mid-2000s, the transition from education for the elite to education for all seemed to be in a somewhat steady position towards a related or alternate path of the Taiwan education development (Trow 2006).

All of this data suggests that the expansion of higher education has been heavily dominated by private institutions in Taiwan since 1997. This growth has allowed all those who dream of pursuing a higher education to have more opportunities than in the past. This is not only good for those who, as previously mentioned, now have a chance to gain access to higher education, but also for those who studied in higher-education institutions in the past and now would like to enroll in the system again, whether to complete unfinished credits or to pursue a degree.

As the average expenditure data per university student from 1999 to 2007 shows, the amount is reduced according to a school's ranking, that is, the higher a school's ranking, the higher the expenditure per student. For instance, in the case of academic year 2007, most expenditure was located at the top research national universities, such as National Taiwan University (NTU), National Tsing Hua University (NTHU), and National Chiao

Tung University (NCTU). National and private universities are selected to join the Teaching Excellence Project. It turns out that the rest of the private universities have the lowest expenditure per student. The difference between the highest and lowest institutions can be more than 3 to 4 times if universities with departments of medicine are included. For example, the average expenditure per university student at NTU, NTHU, and NCTU was more than NT$250,000, with NTHU receiving more than NT$300,000 every year. In academic year 2004-2005, expenditure per student at NTHU was 2.05 times that at National Cheng-chi University (NCCU) (a comprehensive university renowned for social sciences), and 4.88 times that of the private Chung Yuan Christian University (CYCU). This means a year's expenditure per student at NTHU was more than 4 times the expenditure per student at CYCU.

The discrepancy outcome means Taiwan's universities focus investment on the fields of science and engineering, which forces the humanities-based HEIs to engage in relatively less research and produce fewer qualified graduates with fewer resources, as is the case with the top three universities mentioned above. As an example, National Taiwan Normal University (NTNU), one of the most prestigious HEIs in teacher education, has become another victim of this higher-education spending scheme. In the past, only normal schools, such as NTNU, were able to nurture teachers, and thus they received all related funding. With the expansion of universities, however, the ability to develop teachers has been opened up as well; therefore, the center for faculty development in universities now shares the investment, which used to belong exclusively to normal schools.

The financial situation also has an impact on the quality of secondary educational teachers. In other words, the allocation of Taiwan's higher-education resources is skewed for the sake of raising school numbers and subsidizing policies, and thus the focus on the nurturing of top research schools and the fields of science and engineering. Furthermore, research and teaching quality are deeply influenced by the differences in the amount of investment, with the former obviously emphasized much more than the latter.

The situation seems to be worsening every year in terms of university rankings when it comes to private universities in Taiwan. Universities' evaluation results ultimately determine whether institutions will continue to exist or not, as well as the resources they will be allocated by the government. Funding for universities includes tuition, grants from the government, donations from the private sector, and fund-raising activities. Yet, it is unconventional in Taiwan for the private sector to donate money to universities, especially to private universities, due to the need for the money flow to be transparent (there is a general belief in Taiwan that private institutions are established only for the purpose of earning money). As for universities independently raising financial resources, this is also hard to accomplish. Therefore, revenue from tuition and grants from the government constitute the major source of funding.

As for the differences in the budget allocations between higher education and compulsory education, the gap has narrowed from 5 times to 1.8 times over the last decade. More money is currently being spent on compulsory students than before. Nevertheless, class size is still quite large compared to class sizes in the other countries of the developed world. The average class in Taiwan was comprised of 41 students per class in 1992, and was reduced to 34.9 in 2002. Yet in 2002, there were still 30.1 students per class at the primary level, 35.7 in junior high, 41.5 in senior, 39.6 in vocational high school, and 51.8 per university class, the only level at which the student ratio per class increased (Directorate General of Budget 2004). Nevertheless, the national averages cannot overrule the fact that there is an increasing regional gap between rural and urban schools. Some suburban schools are packed with a few thousand students, while rural schools are suffering losses of student population. As the birth rate declined drastically over the past ten years (to 1.1 baby per couple in 2009), many remote primary and secondary schools were faced with the prospect of closing down or merging with other schools. The trend of closing has gradually moved up to higher education, especially for those private institutions located in less accessible areas.

The problem that compulsory education faces is a shortage of money. As mentioned above, most educational investment has been directed toward higher education. Furthermore, in reference to the average education funding per student in the funding allocation table above, we can compare Taiwan to the OECD countries and see that Taiwan's investment in both primary schools and junior high schools is far less than the average (2009).

References

Academia Sinica. n.d. *Education Reform Report* Taipei: Academia Sinica. Available online at: http://www.sinica.edu.tw.

Bradberry, Lily Chung. 2011. *Benefit with Humiliation 2011*. Austin, TX: i_love_taiwan Google Group. Available online at: http://groups.google.com/group/i_love_taiwan.

Chu, Yun-Peng. 2006. *Educational Expenditure and School Quality*. Taipei: Municipal Teacher's University.

Copper, John. 1988. *A Quiet Revolution: Political Development of the Republic of China*. New York: Praeger.

Directorate General of Budget. 2004. *Summary of Country Profile*. Taipei: Directorate General of Budget. Available online at: www.stat.gov.tw.
Education Yearbook. 2008. *Kindergarten Education 2008*. Taipei: National Academy for Educational Research. Available online at: http://192.192.169.230.
Gai, Che-Sheng. 2004. "An Analysis of the Perceived Need for Increasing Market Orientation in Taiwan's Policy on Higher Education." *Bulletin of Educational Research* 50 (2): 29–51.
Giroux, Henry A. 2002. "Neo-Liberalism, Corporate Culture, and the Promise of Higher Education: The University as a Democratic Public Sphere." *Harvard Educational Review* 72 (4): 1–31.
Huang, Jun-Jie. 2006. *The Pain of History 2006*. Taipei: Professor Huang Chun Chie Website. Available online at: http://huang.cc.ntu.edu.tw.
Information Guide. 2006. *Excellence Education: The 500 Million Project 2006*. Taipei: Mandarin Daily News. Available online at: http://www.mdnkids.org.tw.
Ministry of Education (MOE). 2000. *Educational Budget and Management Act, 2000*. Taipei: MOE. Available online at: http://www.edu.tw.
———. 2006. *Basic Educational Laws*. Taipei: MOE.
———. 2009. *Global Expenditure Comparison*. Taipei: MOE.
———. 2010a. *Summary of Education at All Levels SY2000–2010*. Taipei: MOE.
———. 2010b. *Educational Statistical Indicators*. Taipei: MOE.
National Policy Foundation. 2007. *Technical and Vocational Education Reform and Economic Development 2007*. Taipei: National Policy Foundation. Available online at: http://www.npf.org.tw.
Office of the President. 2011. *Constitution*. Taipei: Office of the President. Available online at: http://english.president.gov.tw.
Organization for Economic Co-Operation and Development (OECD). 2009. *Education at a Glance 2009*. Paris: OECD Indicators.
Tang, Yao. 2005. "A Study on the Transformation and Strategy on the University Finance Issues: The Example of Internal Control System." *Journal of Educational Research and Development* 1 (2): 61–81.
Trow, Martin A. 2006. "Reflections on the Transition from Elite to Mass to Aniversal Access: Forms and Phases of Higher Education in Modern Societies since WWII." In *International Handbook of Higher Education*, edited by Phillip G. Altbach, 18: 243–280, New York: Springer.
udnjob. 2004. *Teacher's Retirement Exempted 2004*. Taipei: United Daily News Group. http://pro.udnjob.com.
———. 2009. *Educational Change Committee 2009*. Taipei: United Daily News Group. Available online at: http://mag.udn.com.
Wei, Bo-Tao. 2007. *Lack of Educational Funding 2007*. Taipei: National Policy Foundation. Available online at: http://old.npf.org.tw.
Wu, Cong-Min. 1991. *Taiwan's GDP from 1910 to 1950*. Taipei: National Taiwan University. Available online at: http://homepage.ntu.edu.tw.
Wu, Hai-Yan, and Xun Wang. 2008. "Study of Game Scheme for Elementary Historical Education." Paper presented at the 3rd International Conference on E-learning and Games Edutainment, Nanjing, China, June 25–27.

Chapter 8

Structure of Preschool, Primary, and Secondary Education

Debate on School Days

According to Kosack (2011), governments usually require the support of employers in planning and prioritizing aspects of educational policy. Over the last few decades, in responding to the demand for qualified human resources to meet the need for economic development and political cohesion, Taiwan schools have encountered challenges, such as how to tailor the country's reform policies to improve learning and instruction, as well as how to revised the curriculum and examination system within the schools. The expansion of the required number of years of schooling and the annual number of school days also represents not only governmental efforts to upgrade educational quality but also the society's expectations for their younger generation in Taiwan.

As mentioned earlier, compulsory education was extended to junior high school beginning 1968 in Taiwan in the hope of upgrading the country's manpower for its economic development. Starting at that time, students received a public education up to Grade 9 based on their residential district, regardless of their different social and academic backgrounds. In the past, before 2001, Taiwanese schools had much longer school days, which contributed to students' high academic dedication and achievement. Understanding how a student spends a school day can be one of the best ways to comprehend how a people and a culture shape the younger generation in their formative years. Taiwan's education system is one of the most important socializing agents for Taiwanese youth. Like their many

Asian counterparts, Taiwanese students spend a large amount of time in school, generally from early childhood to their early twenties. It is also important to know what the "typical" school day is like and how external factors shape the school day.

A typical long school day represents the Asian educational philosophy that a lengthy school day and/or school year will provide more time dedicated to learning, and eventually result in higher academic achievement and test scores. Nevertheless, as research data shows, time spent on learning does not necessarily yield higher achievement unless a student studies out of self-motivation to strive for better-quality work. The schools' devoting more time to academic study is crucial to improving student achievement as long as the content is appropriately presented to students. Schools' using time wisely instead of allocating more hours to the school day is even more critical for achievement (American Educational Research Association 2007). In early 2010, U.S. President Obama proposed to extend the school day for American students in order that they might remain competitive with their international peers after completing their schooling. He indicated that one-third of the thirteen- and fourteen-year-olds in the United States have reading difficulties, and that the American curriculum in Grade 8 lags two years behind other competing nations. Therefore, he supported the idea of American school children spending more time in class, either through the lengthening of the school day or the shortening of the summer vacation period, so they would have more time to learn. From a comparative perspective, American school days are shorter than most of their counterparts.

In the United States, the typical school day lasts six hours, thirty-six hours per week (including lunch, recess, and other activities), and the school year is 180 days. Schools in England provide up to eight hours of instruction a day, 220 days a year. Australian students attend school 198 days, Israeli students 216 days, German students 220 days, Indonesian students 251 days, Romanian students 159 days, and Japanese students 243 days. Specifically, Japanese first graders spend 5.5 hours on average in school each day, while students in Grade 5 spend an average of seven hours in school. At the middle- and high school levels, Japanese students spend seven hours a day at school. The assumption underlying this philosophy is that more time in school increases student learning and results in better achievement.

And yet, the relationship between additional time on task and student achievement is less apparent than researchers expected. Many findings suggest (Aronson, Zimmerman and Carlos 1998; Massachusetts 2005) that the emphasis should be placed on the quality rather than the quantity of time, and that students should achieve out of self-motivation rather than external pressure. The relationship between time and learning achievement is also far more complex, and the effort to improve learning requires many more factors, such as staff, faculty, curriculum, instruction, assessment, peer group, and a comfortable environment that comes from parental support.

Despite these findings, Obama has been determined to prioritize education policy by encouraging students to spend more time in school, restructuring curriculum, increasing teacher salaries, improving school infrastructure, providing more advanced technologies to students, and even extending the school year to ensure that the younger American generation can not only keep up with their international counterparts, but also take the lead in the world professional environment of the coming era. Interestingly, in contrast, the number of school days in Taiwan was reduced starting in 2001 in the hope of alleviating pressure on students to study. This section attempted to portray what a school day looks like at each level of education and how this connects to the society at large.

Preschool Education

Historical Development

The first kindergarten was founded in Tainan, a southern city of Taiwan, in 1897, and was inspired by Japanese early childhood education. Early childhood education was uncommon in Taiwan in the 1950s, a time in which tight financial resources limited two-year preschool education to being only an optional part of the educational system (Government Information Office 2002). These circumstances had a direct impact on the enrollment rate in preschools. Not until the Preschool Education Act was promulgated in 1981, setting basic standards for preschools, did Taiwan's system of early childhood education enter a new stage of development. Since then, preschool education has expanded rapidly since the early 1990s. In 2010, the total number of preschool educational institutions was 3,283 kindergartens and 4,896 nursery schools (MOE 2010a), which is a great step forward, compared to the 570 kindergartens and fewer than 600 nursery schools in 1970.

According to the Ministry of Education (MOE), this relatively high number of preschools is due to the high expectations that most Taiwanese parents have for their children's intellectual development and capacity. It is also due to the needs of double-income nuclear families, which require help in nurturing and educating their young children at an early age. These institutions are expected to offer a study environment that helps children learn to interact with their peers within a group and enables them to receive a stable, rich, and guided learning experience. However, like most countries around the world, in Taiwan the majority of kindergartens and nurseries are privately owned and charge high tuition fees (in some cases ten times higher than the public schools), which can be a heavy financial burden for young families. The MOE has, therefore, encouraged elementary schools to set up public preschools. A total of 183,901 children attended 3,283 registered preschools in school year 2010–2011.

Educational Objectives

Early childhood education, broadly speaking, covers children's education from birth to six- or seven years old, and includes family values and basic knowledge. In a more specific sense, in the context of preschool, kindergarten, and nursery institutions, it refers to child care (Lu 2005).

The objective of early childhood education, according to the law in Taiwan, is to promote children's physical and mental integrity, to nurture them by educating them about health and the ethics of life, and to work closely with the family. In short, education at this early stage aims to, first, maintain children's physical and mental health. Second, it cultivates and develops children's good habits. Third, it enriches children's living experience, and, last, enhances children's life ethics (*Education Yearbook* 2008).

In recent decades, preschool has become a popular solution and a tool for preparing children to develop their social skills before they begin formal education. As a result, the role of preschools has become crucial to children's growth and development in a diverse country such as Taiwan. Starting about forty years ago, in the 1970s, cultural changes and the demographics in Taiwan created deep changes in Taiwanese families. Nowadays, more and more mothers are part of the work force, and consequently, more and more children are cared for at day-care centers and preschools. In a sense, the perceptions that the Chinese and Taiwanese have about preschool education have been greatly influenced by these changes.

In recent years, as Taiwan has felt the impact of the lower birthrate, more children with a parent who is non-Taiwanese have needed to adapt to the mainstream. Moreover, a widespread parental notion that a child should "not lose at the starting point" has come to have an influence on families and the choices they make for their children's education. As a result, more preschool institutions are now dedicated to offering knowledge and foreign language-learning activities for young children. This is how the ideals and practices of early childhood education are, in fact, affected by social values and expectations.

Types of Schools

There are two types of early childhood education institutions, which are based on the child's age and the agencies that govern the institution. Kindergartens and day cares are both part of Taiwan's early childhood educational system. Kindergartens that enroll four- to six-year-olds are part of the national education system, and are supervised directly by the MOE, and these institutions are permitted to enroll children for full- or half-day programs. On the other hand, day-care institutions, which enroll two- to six-year-olds, are overseen by the Ministry of Interior Affairs, which is in charge of social education institutions. These day-care facilities are responsible for the early development of children whose working parents are in pursuit of a good education for their children.

The divisions among governing agencies has caused some problems, such as double standards and conflicts in supervision and management. In addition, private kindergartens have come to outnumber public ones in Taiwan and most are independently operated, while the majority of public kindergartens are affiliated with public primary schools. In school year 2003, 240,926 children attended 3,306 registered kindergartens, among which 1,358 were public schools and 1,948 were private; there were 1.43 times as many private as public institutions. The percentage of public kindergartens has been increasing in the past few years, however. For example, according to records from school year 2006, the enrollment proportions of public and private kindergartens in this period rose from 32.03 percent to 67.97 percent, respectively, while the number of classes went to 29.47 percent at public kindergartens and 70.53 percent at private ones. With the increase in kindergartens affiliated with public elementary schools, there was a total of 3,283 registered kindergartens in school year 2010, of which only 1,723 are private (MOE, 2010a). In school year 2010–2011, 183,901 children were enrolled in 3,283 kindergartens, which comprised over 80 percent of preschoolers (MOE 2010b). In addition, all five-year-olds who attend public kindergarten are free of charge, whereas those attend private ones are eligible for tuition subsidy of NT$15,000 (US$508) per school term (MOE 2010a).

Part of the reason for the low preschool enrollment may be the significantly low birth rate in Taiwan (a 1.03 percent fertility rate in 2009), which has forced many private preschools to close. With Taiwan's dwindling birth rate, it is expected that even more kindergartens will be forced to shut down in the next few years.

When private kindergartens were still prevalent in mainstream preschool education, the following phenomena were observed, for example, an increasing student recruitment gap between urban and rural areas, between private and public schools, and between schools that taught Mandarin Chinese and those that taught English. Kindergartens, regardless of their public or private status in metropolitan areas, usually have fewer problems recruiting students, thanks to the highly competitive educational system and high population density. Outside the larger cities, private preschools are less affordable and competitive for average-income families (Government Information Office 2002).

Curriculum Reform

Early childhood education not only reflects the country's cultural heritage, family functions, parental expectations, and educational concepts, but also shapes socialization and affects social change. In this regard, many private preschools offer accelerated courses in various subject areas to meet public demand for a better head start for children, and such courses often encompass reading, writing, math/science, the arts, and physical education. Over the last decade, there has also been enormous growth in the number of English-immersion or bilingual preschools in order to meet parents' expectations for an English-immersion learning environment for the younger generation. This has been true even after the implementation of the nine-year integrated curriculum in 2001.

Didactic approaches and methods in educational institutions that have been adopted in Taiwan vary, from the well-known traditional Confucian philosophy to the Montessori, Froebel, Wardroff, and Dewey philosophies. Also, the thematic webbing approach, the project approach, and the Reggio Emilia approach have been introduced in many Taiwan preschools in recent years.

These early childhood educational institutions offer a task-oriented and skill-based curriculum in kindergarten. Although, the majority of teachers rely on material that has been already prepared, such as handbooks or guidance materials, they probably depend too much on these forms of teaching; many teachers put much emphasis on memorizing, recitation, and counting, and ignore children's own perspective and their physical and emotional development (inner and outer development). The contents of preschool curricula tend to be less and less tied to real-life experience and less applicable to real children's needs (Lin 2007).

Most kindergartens have a stipulated curriculum that focuses on health, language, play, tasks, music, and explorative education. In public kindergartens, English instruction is not strongly encouraged, whereas many of these private institutions use English as a recruitment tool and an incentive as well (Cross Straits News 2010).

A School Day

Kindergartens in Taiwan have a very flexible schedule. Schools usually open at around 7:30 a.m., with classes starting at around 8:00 a.m. Most classes end between 4:00 p.m. and 5:30 p.m., and if the parents are unable to pick up their children at this time, the children may have to stay at school until much later. Like many parents in the developed world, such long school days are designed for dual-income families, in which parents are occupied at work and less likely to take care of their children by themselves. Taiwanese kindergartens have a long lunch and nap time, with many short snack breaks. Class periods are also short, around half an hour per class, which makes the long school day less tiring for young students. The matter of children who stay at preschool beyond the regular school day reflects the parental dilemma of child-rearing responsibilities versus jobs.

Most children attend preschools, and the quality of each school varies to a great extent between public and private institutions, and rural and urban areas. Preschool education is not compulsory, so the prevalence of private kindergartens makes an evaluation of these institutions complicated. The objective of preschool education is unclear, and is influenced by parents' and society's expectations.

There has been heated debate on whether children in Taiwan should start foreign language learning (especially English) in early childhood, as there is concern that this may cause unnecessary stress for young children, or even harm children's' abilities to learn their mother tongue. Despite these debates, however, the current "English-learning fever" continues to boost every single level of education in Taiwan. Since there are numerous private kindergartens, and Taiwanese parents have high expectations for their children, most kindergartens offer English lessons in order to compete with other schools. Some kindergartens even hire a large number of foreign teachers without screening them carefully, with the aim of providing an English-only lesson plan.

Another emerging issue is due to the increasingly low birth rate in Taiwan, which not only has resulted in low preschool enrollments, but also in institutions shutting down and merging at the preschool and primary levels. The birthrate has been going down since 1997, and there was a decrease of about 114,000 newborn babies within a decade (2001–2010) (MOE 2010b).

Commentary

During the last decade, some of the most relevant policies on early childhood education were established, as follows:

- The voucher policy for early childhood education
- The plan to integrate nursery schools and kindergartens
- The plan to support impaired and disadvantaged five-year-old children in early childhood education
- The plan to integrate the teaching of English into the elementary curriculum
- The integration of creative education into the general curriculum
- Law enforcement for day cares and early childhood education
- The plan for a career development program
- The establishment of professional performance standards for teachers, as well as a teacher certification system

Above all, two major policies have taken place:

- To reduce the financial burden on parents, in the year 2010. As of September 1, 2010, the MOE and the Ministry of Interior enacted a program titled "Five-year-old children care programs free from tuition and education plans." This program grants tuition to five-year-old children, plus other school fees required after enrollment. Each year, the grant recipients receive a total child care annual amount of NT$60,000 (UD$ 2,000), and a total of one hundred children receive this benefit, which aims to reach a nationwide population children who are five years of age. Approximately 75 percent of all five-year-olds received the benefits. These programs have been created in order to accelerate the pace of system integration into kindergartens and nursery schools. According to the current preschool system, the practices of recruiting in preschool education and day-care institutions take place mainly in kindergartens and nurseries, placing a lot of responsibility on parents and care institutions. Administrative sharing and responsibility for education are important points in these relationships. The provision of early childhood education and care have become inseparable form one another, thanks to the changing family structure, which requires the mother to be employed. Children from four to six years old are experiencing a quality discrepancy, since there

are two different standards nowadays—the current system and the systems being developed for those who did not have access before. All of these issues have existed for many years already. Nevertheless, these efforts are meant to improve effective social integration in education.
• To accelerate the pace of children's integration into kindergartens and nursery schools. In addition, there are numerous issues related to teacher education, such as: an imbalance between supply and demand of teachers, too many unqualified teachers in kindergartens, a high turnover rate, low social status for teachers, and so on. Due to low wages, poor working conditions, and the overwhelming workload, the turnover ratio of teachers in kindergartens is alarmingly high. Not many teachers consider early childhood institutions as long-term career paths, as teachers leave in the early stages of their careers.

There are other issues that have an impact on early childhood education as well, such as the growing numbers of children of foreign brides (New Taiwanese Children), children reared by grandparents due to the increasing population of working females within the household, the high divorce rate, and single mothers facing financial responsibilities. Furthermore, disadvantaged children have generated the phenomenon of "one Taiwan, two worlds," where more than 90 percent of abused children are under age five and, among these, 50 percent are under age one. Another major issue is the extreme inequality in resource allocation for education (only 1 percent is spent on the early childhood education).

In sum, early childhood education is the foundation for all levels of schooling. As Taiwan has been experiencing a drastic decline in the birth rate since the 1990s, coupled with the transitional double-income family structure, preschools deserve more public funding and administrative support in order to have the ability to contribute to the betterment of the human being and social equity in Taiwan. The current attempt to implement an institutional integration between kindergarten and nursery school and to offer free tuition can serve as the milestones of reform in early childhood education.

Primary Education

Historical Development

Before 1945, when Taiwan was under the control of Japan, the education system was divided into two tracks, one for the Japanese, and the other for the local Taiwanese. Japanese was the official language, and it was later was replaced by Mandarin (the Chinese official language), which was foreign to most Taiwan residents during the transitional period in the 1940s. According to statistics, Taiwan's literacy rate was one of the highest in China and Asia before World War II. And yet, most people attended primary schools, except for some children from more privileged backgrounds who were admitted to a higher level of education, such as graduate education (Chou 2008). Many Taiwan senior citizens aged 70 and older, who went through the Japanese system and whose mother tongue was Chinese, can still speak fluent Japanese today. What was the experience of these people who experienced Japanese colonial education and later were forced to change to schools that had a Chinese curriculum and instruction? There were significant differences between the Sino and the Japanese traditions, knowledge, and values that were part of their cultural heritage in school, let alone their teachers, the means of assessment, self-identity, and so forth (Cheng 2008). The transition that took place in Taiwan's education system and the people involved before and after the Japanese occupation deserve more attention and research. The question of how students at all levels (though mostly at the elementary level) adapted to the new Chinese content and became united with the political regime of the Chinese Kuomintang (KMT) by 1949 remains unanswered.

Taiwan's primary education system has played a key role in the policy of assimilating the younger generation via a patriotic curriculum, as prescribed in legislation (based upon an orthodox ideology entitled "Three Principles of the People," derived from the concept of "for the people, by the people, and of the people," as coined by Sun Yat-Sen) and the mandated instruction of Chinese Mandarin, which replaced the Japanese and Chinese dialects after 1945 (Tsao 2008). The monolinguistic educational policy and culture that mandated one official language while forbidding other dialects was considered a success in China, although it occurred at the expense of sacrificing the local Taiwanese culture and identity (Lu 2011).

The policy continued its dominance until the mid-1990s, when the Taiwanese government introduced local features and dialects for the first time into school content at the primary level. For example, after aboriginal rights were incorporated into the Additional Articles of the Constitution, the Aboriginal Education Law was enacted in 1998, to address the development of education for aboriginal people (Heber 2009). All of these measures later became part of the official curriculum in 2001. From then on, not only Chinese and English but also the dialect/ethnic languages of aboriginal people were taught in primary schools.

According to Kosack (2011), the motivation of governments generally for launching universal education is due to pressure from employers who require more skilled workers when domestic and foreign labor markets cannot supply them, or else, when the domestic labor market is flexible and there is more personal demand for high-quality education. This need for skilled workers to drive Taiwan's economic development was the impetus for the universal nine-year education policy. Before the implementation of nine-year compulsory education in 1968, elementary students were under great pressure, and they depended on cram schools, secondary schools, or vocational junior high schools for added competencies and skills.

Corporal punishment administered by teachers to students was not uncommon on Taiwan's school campuses in both elementary and high school. In 1966, when Taiwan's gross national product (GNP) was US$3189 million, 40.96 percent of students sought jobs immediately after graduation, and most jobs were in labor-intensive industries (MOE 2011). The 1968 Compulsory Education Act represented a milestone in the upgrading of the human resources of Taiwan by offering equal educational opportunities to students regardless of their family background. Though it was based on a politically authoritarian decision by the late Chiang Kai-shek and his colleagues, and it resulted in a great shortage of teachers and a poor infrastructure in schools owing to a hasty decision-making process and strategies, the system has nevertheless served as a revolutionary plan for the enhancement of Taiwan's manpower over the last four decades.

The current Taiwanese National Education Act requires students to attend six years of elementary school and three years of junior high school between the ages of six and fifteen, with the exception of children with special needs or those who attend alternative education. The average class size of primary schools ranges from twenty and thirty-six students. In 2010, the government of Taiwan issued a policy to reduce the size of classes to twenty-eight students starting in 2011, with the goal of lowering class size to twenty-five by 2014. A homeroom teacher usually leads primary school classes, and students stay in their own classrooms for most lessons, with the exception of specialized courses such as science and music.

Educational Objective and Type of School

Compulsory education, pursuant to the national constitution, is intended to cultivate the well-rounded development of students in the moral, intellectual, physical aspects, in teamwork, and in the appreciation of aesthetics. In other words, the design of the curriculum is based on the life experiences of students, in addition to addressing mental and physical development, respect for individual differences, the stimulation of personal potential, and the development and enhancement of democratic ideas, it also implements the concept of multiculturalism and the learning of science for the purpose of a modern livelihood (National Academy for Educational Research 2011).

Curriculum Reform

Elementary schools consist of Grades 1–6, and instruction is held from Monday through Friday, from 7:30 a.m. to 4:00 p.m. (or noon on Wednesdays). Homeroom teachers and subject teachers share the instruction duties, with the former responsible for student conduct and discipline. The course subjects include:

- Mandarin (Chinese official language): the official language of instruction.
- Mathematics: Mathematics education covers the basics, including introductory algebra and geometry by Grade 6.
- Science: Comprehensive science classes cover basic biology, physics, and chemistry.
- English: English is a compulsory subject within the national mainstream school system starting from Grade 3 in elementary school on up.
- Native languages: Additional language classes are offered in Taiwanese and Hakka.
- Social science studies
- Music
- Art
- Physical education
- Flexible subjects and extracurricular activities during the vacation period (e.g., summer classes)
- Integrated lessons

In Taiwan, students at the compulsory level are assigned to the school closest to the school district in which they live and are registered. However, the quality as well as the focus of each public school can vary, so some parents register their children's home address at the residence of relatives or friends for the purpose of choosing the school they want their children to attend.

A School Day

As mentioned above, elementary school days usually last 8.5 hours, from 7:30 a.m. to 4:00 p.m. Most schools start their instruction around 8:40 a.m., followed by morning assembly or an activity. Major subjects such as Chinese and mathematics are generally offered in the morning session, due to the belief that the morning offers a fresh start and the best time for learning. A lunch break from around 12:00 p.m. to 1:30 p.m. separates the morning and afternoon sessions and encourages students to have a quiet naptime.

Classes in the lower grades (Grades 1–2) usually end at noon, except on one weekday, which depends on each school. Students in the upper grades usually stay in school until 4 p.m. four days a week, with one school day ending at noon (see Table 8.1).

According to a survey conducted among 2,174 students in forty-four primary schools nationwide, the majority of primary school students (84.3 percent of third to sixth graders) in Taiwan feel happy about their lives (Pan 2011). The annual report, conducted by *Better Life Monthly Magazine*, was released on February 22, 2011, and indicated that a total of three-quarters of school children attend a private tutoring center (安親班) or a cram school immediately after they leave regular school. In addition, 70 percent of children feel happy about going to school; however, 23 percent do not like school because they are afraid of a teacher's verbal abuse and too much required homework.

Even though elementary school students are less likely than older students to attend cram schools for academic reasons, under the recent multichannel school entrance plans, many parents encourage their children to take after-school talent classes or private tutoring lessons so as to have a better chance to gain admission to good schools in the future. Parents may require talent cram schools to provide report cards or certificates assessing their children's abilities so that their children will have more supporting evidencewhen they apply to schools down the road. Some of these cram schools overlook children's interests and aptitude, however, which also creates an additional burden on children and parents, in terms of receiving little in return for the tuition they pay. According to some surveys, families with poor financial resources cannot afford this extra option, so their children's academic performance may fall behind that of their peers, making it harder for them to compete for admission to higher-ranked schools (Chou 2008).

Commentary

In Taiwan, elementary school is considered the most carefree period of childhood, thanks to the policy of admitting children to junior high school as part of compulsory education without requiring them to take an admissions exam. Nevertheless, the recent reform includes twelve years of basic education, which takes into account the mental and physical prematurity

Table 8.1 A Sample Grade 6 Class Schedule in Primary School

Session	Period	Time	Duration	Monday	Tuesday	Wednesday	Thursday	Friday	
Morning		8:15 | 8:35	20 mins.	Morning Activity					
	1	8:40 | 9:20	40 mins.	Homeroom Teacher's Time					
				Chinese	Health Education	Chinese	Math	Chinese	
	2	9:30 | 10:10	40 mins.	Chinese	Math	Reading in Library	Chinese	Chinese	
			20 mins.	Interclass activity					
	3	10:30 | 11:10	40 mins.	English	Science & Technology	Sociology	Music	Sociology	
	4	11:20 | 12:00	40 mins.	Math	Science & Technology	Math	English	Math	
			80 mins.	Lunch Break (Lunch & Nap Time)					
Afternoon	5	13:30 | 14:10	40 mins.	Sociology	Chinese	Teacher's Training	Science & Technology	Visual & performing Arts	Computer
	6	14:20 | 15:00	40 mins.	Music	Physical Education		Physical Education		
			20 mins.	Clean-up			Clean-up		
	7	15:20 | 16:00	40 mins.	Integrative Activities	Integrative Activities		Integrative Activities	Dialects	
		16:00		Flag Lowering & Class Dismissal					

of sixth graders in Taiwan, and a more comprehensive integration of curriculum and exam-free entrance at the secondary level with the hope of reducing exam pressure of the junior high students.

In contrast, researchers like Harold W. Stevenson and his colleagues (the Stevenson group) often mention that the academic performance of American children is below that of their peers in Japan, Korea, and Taiwan. Unlike many American public schools, which are very much concerned with students' security, the Taiwanese put an extra burden on school teachers and students in terms of expectations for academic achievement. According to the Stevenson group, American schools are less effective in classroom management and instruction than those in Taiwan. The school year is longer and class time is also used much more effectively in Taiwan's schools. Taiwanese students spend more of their school day on academically oriented activities. In addition, parents play a crucial role in children's attitude toward schooling, with Taiwanese mothers much more likely to get involved in their children's school activities and parent-teacher associations (PTAs) than American mothers.

Elementary students are thus expected to endure more and more pressure from their school and family. The following example illustrates this obsessive, stressful phenomenon of schooling.

"School Assignments during Winter Vacation for Grade 5 students in Taiwan" –P.C. Chen

> The winter vacation is about to come to a close. Many children who have not yet finished their school assignments are striving to make the best of their remaining vacation time. A school in central Taiwan has required its fifth graders to complete the following homework, which can be divided into four major sections. First, the students have to write three essays, including a travel report on their winter holiday travel. Student are required to type the report, design a cover page, lay out the pictures, and scan photos to include in the composition, coupled with the tickets for the trip, so teacher can thereby certify that the essay is not fictionalized.
>
> The second assignment is for each student to make his or her own musical instrument based on the "musical instruments sound" unit studied in the previous semester. This instrument should be able to play songs such as "Little Bee." Prior to constructing the instrument, the student must develop a "plan," including creating a title for the topic, choosing the musical instrument, gathering the materials and tools, and following the procedures and methods for producing the instrument. In addition, a log sheet is required to detail the items used in the process of constructing the instrument, and the log must be checked and commented on every day during the winter holidays. This assignment requires turning in not only photos of the completed work but also musical arrangements and sketches, photos, and the descriptions of the musical instrument that one can play.

Third, a book review report is assigned that should contain a summary, preface, story background, character description (of the character whose behavior deserves the most analysis, from the student's personal viewpoint), story outline, and process, as well as an indication of the most impressive, inspirational paragraph in the book.

Last, online data clipping is assigned. The whole class is divided into several groups, and each group selects a topic, such as the Yangtze River and the Mongolian Plateau, or the Western region, depending on the "content" they find in network media, newspapers, books, magazines, collections, customs, environmental geography, climate change and development, and other related data. Students gather data on their topics from all of these sources. Students are asked to specify the sources in their final report, and then print it on A4 paper. Pictures, photos, and a cover page for the report are highly recommended.

The preceding homework maybe exceptional, but assignments of such can be overwhelmed for an adult. In Taiwan, the winter holiday (approx. three weeks) is too short for students to complete assignments like these. Needless to say, the complexity and labor-intensive nature of the work goes beyond the capacity of children in their early teens. In addition, in order for the students to be able to complete assignments, the family is expected to equip them with computers, scanners, digital cameras, and printers. Parental assistance was unavoidable owing to the high-level motor skills required for the completion of the musical instrument. Parents also needed to take children to the amusement park and keep the entrance tickets to serve as proof that the homework was completed during the school holidays. How does this homework for the winter break relate to family resources? How about children from disadvantaged backgrounds? (Chou 2003).

Elementary school in Taiwan is considered the most joyful period of schooling. Nevertheless, many school children attend shadow education after school for various reasons. Parental high expectation and long working hours, coupled with teacher's attitude may lead to child anxiety for academic success. Thus, some elementary children can be overloaded with outside study activities.

Secondary Education

Junior High School

Historical Development

Taiwan's system of middle school education began in the early twentieth century, when the Japanese first introduced it during the colonization period and it focused on vocational education (Wu 2002). After World War II, Taiwanese education expanded rapidly with the development of the society and the economy, and secondary education became an important link between primary and higher education. At the end of the twentieth century, Taiwanese education underwent a series of noticeable transformations, which affected not only the school system, school entrance guidelines, course structure, teacher training, and education theories but also policies related to secondary education (Huang 2004a).

Educational Objectives and School Type

Junior high school consists of Grades 7–9 and has been the second half of compulsory education since 1968. Attending secondary school is considered to be one of the most trying periods in a Taiwanese student's life, because although Taiwan has free nine-year compulsory education, students are required sit for qualifying examinations in order to be admitted to senior high schools or vocational high schools. This process is repeated again before entrance into universities or colleges. Preparation for entrance exams is the main source of pressure in schools.

In comparison to the assorted and multifaceted elementary schools, junior high schools are geared toward helping students pursuing a single educational goal, that is, achieving a high score on their senior high school entrance exams at the end of Grade 9. Consequently, the pressure on students from teachers and parents is intense. Though instruction officially ends around 5:00 p.m., students often stay at school until as late as 8:00 or 9:00 p.m. for "extra classes" (which typically consist of supplemental quizzes and review).

At the end of their third year, students participate in the national senior high school entrance exams and are assigned to senior high schools based upon their scores. Students may also take a separate national vocational school entrance exam if they wish to attend vocational school. In both cases, public schools are usually the most popular, while private schools have traditionally been viewed as a backup for those unable to score high enough to be admitted to public schools. Roughly 97.53 percent of junior high school students continued on to senior high or vocational school in 2009. Only 2.47 percent did not continue to senior high or vocational school (MOE 2010d).

Curriculum Reform

The subject matter covered in junior high school includes:

- Literature: Classical and modern Chinese literature and poetry, composition, and public speaking.
- Mathematics: Single- and two variable algebra, geometry, proofs, trigonometry, and precalculus.

- English: Essential English grammar
- Science and Technology
  - Biology: Taken during the first year, includes more in-depth study and lab work
  - Chemistry: Taken during the second year. More rigorous introduction to atoms, molecules, and chemical reactions, including lab work
  - Physics: Taken during the third year. More rigorous introduction to physical laws and equations, including lab work
  - Earth Science: Taken during the third year.
  - Technology: Taken during all three years. Introduction to some basic technology in daily life
- Social Studies
  - Civics: Basic democracy, politics, and economics
  - History: Focus on the history of Taiwan and China during the first two years, and world history during the third year
  - Geography: Introductory geography, accompanied by the geography of Taiwan during the first year, geography of China and East Asia during the second year, and the world geography during the third year.
- Home economics and crafts
- Art: Includes three independent parts: Fine Arts, Music, and Drama
- Physical Education
- Scout education: Outdoor survival skills

A School Day

Unlike many of their Western counterparts who attend school from 9:00 a.m. to 3:00 p.m., Taiwanese secondary students have a much longer school day, from 7:30 a.m. to 5:30 p.m., depending on the school. In most junior high schools, prior to the first period of the class, there is time for cleaning up the campus and for morning self-study in the homeroom, which allows students to review their lessons or take tests or examinations. A morning assembly follows, which altogether lasts from forty-five minutes to one hour. The campus clean-up and morning assemblies are not mandatory for all students at the same time. Students rotate participation in these activities every other week. Flag-raising ceremonies, the principal's talks about daily rules, and other routine assignments are announced at that time.

In junior high schools, most classes last 45 minutes. There is a lunch break, followed by nap time. Students may choose to remain seated and

Table 8.2 A Sample Grade 7 Class Schedule in Junior High School

Weekday / Period		Monday	Tuesday	Wednesday	Thursday	Friday
Morning		Morning Study Hall				
	1 8:10-9:00	English	English Corner	English	English Listening	Chinese Literature
	2 9:10-10:00	Chinese Literature	Chinese Literature	English	Chinese Literature	Chinese Literature
	3 10:10-11:00	Physical Education	Math	Math	Nature Biology	Math
	4 11:10-12:00	History Living	Visual Arts	Math	Cross-class Elective	Math
Lunch Break (Lunch & Nap Time)						
Afternoon	5 13:10-14:00	Nature Biology	Creative Writing	Home Economics	Civic	Counseling Activity
	6 14:10-15:00	Nature Biology	Health Education	Home Economics	Geography	Social Club Activity
Clean-up						
	7 15:20-16:10	Independent Study	Music	Information Technology Education	Physical Education	Class Meeting or School Assembly
	8 16:20-17:10	Performing Arts	Performing Arts s			Second Foreign Language
Class Dismissal						

read or study during that time. The philosophy behind this nap time is that it is not only a social tradition in Taiwan, but it also refreshes students' minds during hot weather. In the afternoon, most schools run from 1:20 p.m. until 4:10 p.m. The so-called "main subject" courses such as Chinese literature, science, English, and mathematics are offered in the morning session, when students have clearer minds for better concentration and more effective learning. Then, classes such as civic education, history, geography, integrated activities, music, health, and physical education are offered in the later hours of the day.

In the afternoon session, another tidying-up period for the classroom and the final campus cleaning time last about twenty-five minutes altogether. Afterwards, classes start again at 3:25 p.m. and last until 4:10 p.m. at which time most schools close, except for certain classes. For example, the ninth grade students may remain in their homeroom for extra tutorials in English, mathematics, Chinese, science, and so forth. Then the seventh period ends around 4:10 p.m. Many schools and parents ask students to attend an extra period for supplemental instruction or quizzes at their own expense that will, hopefully, enhance their academic performance. The evening self-study time on campus lasts from 8 p.m. to 9:30 p.m. for those ninth grade students who are preparing for high school entrance exams. Some attend cram schools for extra tutoring and test practice if they wish to at their own expense.

Despite the issues related to the extra study time that takes place in secondary education, very few studies have been conducted on school sites, let alone any sophisticated or in-depth classroom observations. Without first-hand data, it is impossible to identify the underlying causes for the instructional problems in junior high schools. According to G. Spindle (Hsieh 1988), classroom instruction is often regarded as a "black box," the process of which is rarely known to the outside world. According to the authors of a research project entitled "A Study of Secondary Teachers' Daily Activities in Taiwan," the findings about secondary classroom teaching in the 1990s indicated (Chou and Chen 2000):

1. As a result of the prevailing attitude about requiring credentials in Taiwan, instruction in secondary schools has been dominated by cramming and memorizing. Preparation for high school entrance exams has become the first priority of school teaching at the expense of the cultivation of students' well-balanced development.
2. A teacher's daily schedule in junior high schools is usually very busy. Teachers' weekly classroom teaching hours are relatively short, but they have many other duties to fulfill during the entire school day. In the study, 80 percent of the teachers stayed at school over eight

hours per day, working from 7:30 a.m. to 4:30 p.m. In addition to the required classroom instruction, 82 percent of them conduct a two-hour period of supplementary instruction after school every week. Though classroom teachers are released from a few hours of instruction, they are responsible for student counseling and classroom management.
3. Classroom instruction is very teacher oriented and teacher centered. Most of the instruction is related to content development and tests.
4. Teachers' daily routines after they finish their classroom instruction are very demanding with respect to correcting papers and grading examinations. The trade-off is that teachers become less likely to engage in class preparation and activities for professional growth.
5. Most teachers express that they have difficulty in dealing with a class of students with diverse learning backgrounds, especially under the current centralized educational policy, and with students' and parents' obsession with the students' acceptance to a good high school. Although class tracking is forbidden by law, in reality, this grouping system has come to exist on many campuses, especially in private schools and in suburban and rural areas.
6. Teachers take on various roles beyond instruction. Homeroom teachers, in particular, assume heavy student guidance duties. Dealing with student grades and behavioral problems has become a priority for teachers. The latter, for many teachers, is even more challenging than classroom instruction.

Classroom instruction in junior high schools is profoundly influenced by the required textbooks and supplemental materials, which are the key vehicle for the presentation of ideas and the bulk of information. Thus, examples of the instructional independence of textbooks and other materials are rare, because the great majority of teachers design their lectures with only the entrance examinations in mind.

Due to the prevailing attitudes among junior high school students toward passing the exam for a good high school, which then will lead to access to the university, instruction has become a process of testing rather than providing a well-rounded education. As a result, students in the second or third year of junior high school come to view their teachers merely as people whose job is to evaluate them by numerous exams rather than persons to help them grow and fulfill themselves. In the course of instruction, since the crucial aim is to prepare students for the entrance exam, teachers are required to disseminate information to students. Students are also expected to absorb the information for exams and remain passive in the classroom.

As a result of the great emphasis on examinations, educational problems, especially in junior high school, have come to the attention of Taiwanese society during the last few years. Issues related to education are a focal point, such as class tracking, the excessive number of study aids and paper exams, the endless practice exams, and student discipline problems (such as bullying). In other words, for the last few decades, preparation for high school entrance exams has become the only priority of school teaching, and this sacrifices students' mental and physical development. The debates over what causes the above-mentioned problems in junior high schools have been ongoing (Chou 2008).

Issues and Commentary

Effort versus Innate Ability

Though Taiwan is becoming a more democratic and multicultural society, it is still uncommon for Taiwanese parents to praise for their children, and they expect good behavior from their children (Hwang 2004). When asked, "What is the most important factor in determining a child's performance in the school?" Taiwanese parents usually respond "effort" rather than "innate ability," whereas American parents mostly cite the latter (Stevenson and Lee 1996). The home environment supports Taiwanese children in their academic performance rather than their extracurricular activities. In modern Taiwanese society, many young parents also support cultural activities for their children, so in addition to schoolwork, many students also take language and music classes after school. Nevertheless, the higher the level of schooling, the less likely students will continue these lessons due to the pressure of studying for future exams.

Smith (1997) described the competitive setting of the modern Taiwanese secondary schools as "academic Darwinism," which implies that only the most capable students will move on to higher levels of schooling. In Taiwan, secondary education emphasizes individual competitiveness, which requires students to compete aggressively to survive to the next educational level.

Going to School for What Reason?

According to the "Taiwan Education Panel Survey (TEPS)" of 2005, junior high school students spend more time with their parents every day than do senior high or college students (TEPS 2005a). In addition, junior high school students spend more time with their mothers than fathers. Nearly 58 percent reported spending four hours per day with their mothers compared with 36 percent with their fathers. Compared with those who spend less than one hour with their parents, those who spend more time with their parents have better parent-child relationships (Went 2010). Such situations have caused the parent-child/student relationship to change in Taiwan.

TEPS 2006 has shown that the more a student studies with his or her classmates, the more fulfilled the student will feel. TEPS also indicates that 84.4 percent of junior high school students regard school as a happy place, especially when the classroom climate is positive and teachers are dedicated to teaching. In other studies, it was concluded that peer groups also have an impact on secondary students' socialization. There is a positive relationship between the peer atmosphere and students' positive feelings about school (TEPS 2006).

If the teacher has an encouraging and positive attitude towards students, and assigns them more learning tasks or homework, the student will feel more positive toward the teacher. On the other hand, if teachers are indifferent, students will regard school as an unhappy place. Clearly, students are sensitive to the learning atmosphere at school. The more learning activities there are at school, the more satisfaction the students will experience. TEPS 2005 also points out that campus security is another source that contributes to students' happiness in school (TEPS 2005b). A supportive and secure campus environment will provide students with a better place to study

The Chinese examination system, which reinforces the value of scholarship and credentials as the preferred route to success, has continued to have a long-lasting influence on education in contemporary Taiwan. As Miyazaki and Schirokauer discussed in their book entitled *China's Examination Hell* (1981), the practice of giving examinations has been embedded in Chinese culture since ancient times. Studies show that the system of entrance examinations for high school exerts a pervasive influence over the whole nature of the school environment (Hsieh 1988). Classroom instruction has thus become the vehicle for passing high school entrance examinations, which then will lead to a better career path (Wang and Wang 1994). In this competitive school environment, achievement on tests is valued more than learning for the sake of learning.

Hidden Tracking

In Taiwan, many junior high school teachers feel frustrated and challenged in teaching a regular class of students due to the striking differences in students' motivation for learning and their abilities. Therefore, the tracking system, though prohibited by law, remains intact on some campuses in Taiwan (especially the private ones) and provides another solution to the problem described above. Tracking is a process whereby students are divided into categories according to ability, so that they can be assigned by groups to various kinds of classes. The most common method in Taiwan is to classify students as academic- or vocational oriented. Students, consequently, are placed into so-called "good" or "average" classes on the basis of their grades or scores on ability tests (achievement tests).

There are several reasons why teachers and parents support tracking and why it is widespread, though it is officially forbidden by the government. Many teachers and parents argue that students learn better when they are grouped with others at the same level of academic performance. They also contend that the placement process for tracking can accurately and fairly reflect past achievements and the native abilities of students, and that it is much easier for teachers to accommodate individual differences when students are in homogeneous groups. However, the vast majority of research on tracking comes to a similar conclusion: no group of students has been found to benefit consistently from being in a homogeneous group (Tieso 2003; Hallman and Ireson 2005; Oakes 2005). Students placed in average- and low-track classes do not develop positive attitudes later on. Instead, this arrangement usually impairs students' self-esteem among their peer group. In addition, students in a low track have been found to participate less in extracurricular activities at school, to misbehave more, and to become involved more often in delinquent behavior off campus. Taiwan's junior high schools also have encountered the consequences of tracking described here, and are struggling to come to terms with this dilemma.

According to Michel Foucault (1995), school has become a place where talents and status are differentiated, but it has also divided or individualized one person from another through comparison and hierarchy. Secondary schools in Taiwan today predominately motivate students through the hierarchical individuation of grade competition and exam performance (Jacobson 2010). As a result, many students become at-risk if they perform poorly in the competitive academic race. For example, some of them may sooner or later develop an inferiority complex and a severe sense of depression and failure (Mochizuki 1990).

Other students respond with a sense of resentment and hostility toward teachers and school. Student discipline problems have been increasing recently, for example, and can be attributed to teachers' ignorance of individual differences, experiences that alienate students in a class, and the text-oriented lecture format of instruction, which has much less utility for students who are not going to high school. The confusion and frustration increase with time, as do student problems. Moreover, the recent increase in incidents of violence against teachers and schools, as well as student bullying against peers is partly due to a much larger phenomenon that has its source in the process of academic competition (Juang 1984).

In the past, student discipline problems in Taiwan were not as serious as those in the United States. But in such a highly competitive academic environment today, many Taiwanese parents and teachers now find themselves confronted with the issues of bullying and school violence. Student bullying, such as an incident that occurred at Ba De Junior High School in December 2011, has aroused nationwide attention and great concern due to the overemphasis on academic achievement rather than seeking a constructive solution to student bullying and violence (China Post 2011).

A Voyage of Self-Identity in Learning

In Taiwan, schooling is still defined by the notion of a paternal, superior, and more knowledgeable teacher-centered culture that will cultivate or shape the younger generation into ideal citizens. Students' voices, creativity, and collaboration are absent or overlooked, thanks to strict academic practices of comparison and hierarchical standardization. Yet students nowadays are demanding more room for self-development, self-expression, and self-meaning. Nevertheless, Taiwan's schools still have a long way to go since the reform decade of the 1990s, as seen in the following portrait of a fifteen-year-old that illustrates his life in junior high school(Education Reform Forum 2009).

Portrait of a 15-Year-Old Student: Hao Chen

During the last three years, my life has been as if I were on a voyage without any direction, in the sea waiting to be carried along by the waves, with no goal, no direction or objective whatsoever. I am a 15-year-old student, and the mental exhaustion I have experienced at this stage of my life is overwhelming and hard to describe as either physical or spiritual. The side effect that every test brings is nothing but complete exhaustion.

In Grade 7, I went abroad and attended public school in the United States due to my parents' decision to leave our home to go abroad. As a result of their decision, I felt much sorrow, and other journeys began as well. My parents' decision to study abroad took me by surprise, and I was not thrilled at the time, since I was leaving my comfort zone. Later, I realized

I was going to spend a maximum of one year in high school. My experience abroad taught me to have the mindset that learning is fun, that studying is the same anywhere, wherever your interests are awakened; knowledge is there to be learned, and remains in a student's mind for a long time. Bottom line, you should have fun while understanding that learning is long-term over the span of your life, and not the rote memorizing techniques that I had learned before.

There was one class in particular that captured my attention; it made a huge impact on me due to the impression it left in my mind. In social studies class, the teaching takes different forms and different methods, such as storytelling, and discussions of opinion are a technique used to emphasize learning. Students' input is important and taken into account. I felt I was part of the class and in charge of my learning process; this is a very different approach than the one used in Taiwan's classrooms, where most students just sit and listen. I got to internalize knowledge for the long-term because I was able to share opinions and viewpoints, and it was fun! Plus it can be applied in real-life situations. That year made me realize and appreciate learning to the fullest. The whole experience made me put into perspective what learning really is, and which directions I should try to focus on.

A year later, I returned to Taiwan to attend Grade 8 and brought my high expectations, but it turned out that I saw school in a completely opposite way. There, I was expected solely to listen, memorize, and focus on test scores exclusively. My confusion and anxiety started to increase again, and I could not but wonder, why do I have to learn this and that? Therefore, I started to think about quitting school (if I had a choice) and doing nothing all day long except simply surfing online, where my stress could be at least slightly alleviated. The whole process of learning was full of crazy questions about learning and studying, and it lacked real motivation and objectives to strive for. Without a sense of self-control and heartfelt diligence, I totally went astray and felt like I would collapse.

Later, I came to realize that I was not alone in dealing with this frustrating situation. My friends around me were also trying to endure the same stressful exams that they had been taking since Grade 7 in Taiwan. I had a chance to observe them from a new enrollee's point of view, realizing that some of their manic behaviors were due to their mindset about the exams. The more pressure they felt, the more likely they would play basketball or video games as an escape. In particular, rushing to the basketball court became the top priority of their school day, and fooling around on the Internet took up all their free time under such tremendous pressure. Like me, many of my classmates became more and more hostile toward school and were at a stage of never surrendering to anyone. Some of them even attempted to rebel in other ways, but without success.

So, we all started to acquire the "test-passing mindset" in order to become "something" important. Many of us don't even perceive the pressure coming from this "test-passing mindset," although the impact is huge.

As mentioned above, hiding behind a computer while navigating online was almost the only thing that really put my mind on standby in order to relieve the pressure a little. Since looking for a different direction to take is not even an option, the overwhelming mental stress and pressure keep pushing us to the edge. A feeling of loneliness and tears often comes along. With no one in the family who really understands this situation, salvation appears to be nothing but a word. So, in seeking an escape, I have come to wonder, do I have a choice? How can I overcome or end this nightmare? What about the tests? We are required to pass the Basic Competence Test in order to continue on to senior high school, which will eventually lead to the university entrance exam. If not, I fail as a student.

This kind of life full of exam practice and drilling for standard answers went on for two years, and then came to an end as a nightmare soon to be forgotten. Upon my graduation after the exam, I found myself filled with uneasiness, clocked with scheduled work imprinted in my head, although sometimes I felt as lazy as a worm. Hence, the closer I get to graduating, the more pressure I feel, and the more anxiety arises in me. I have realized that it's been a while since I felt free of any burden or since the pressure was released from my shoulders and from my mind as well. Those are feelings that I can barely remember enjoying.

My experience in a Taiwan junior high school turned out to be a great disappointment for me, I wonder if there is a little something for me to have (given the "poor" results abroad), in a system where everything seems just impossible for me to follow through. (Education Reform Forum 2009)

The above essay from a 15-year-old demonstrates how junior high schools are full of drills and practices geared toward preparing students to pass the high school entrance exam at the expense of teenagers' social life and career exploration. It also shows how different Taiwan's secondary schooling is from the American system.

The Increasing Learning Gap

There is an increasing discrepancy between junior high school graduates in urban and rural regions in Taiwan on the Basic Competence Test (BCTEST), according to the statistical analysis conducted by the Basic Competence Test Center in 2008 (National Taiwan Normal University 2008). When the test scores in 2004 are examined, it becomes clear that family background rather than regional differences played a major role in student test performance at a time when the gap between students of average- and low-income families was increasing. Students from disadvantaged backgrounds, such as minorities and those with single parents, tend to earn lower test scores. To correct such a discrepancy in achievement among these students, the MOE launched an educational priority zone program to provide supplementary tutoring for those underachieving schools (one-fifth of the total seven hundred junior high schools nationwide). The results of this program are questionable due to the students' lack of proper family support and sufficient educational resources in these remote schools.

This is why the majority of Taiwanese parents have mixed feelings about education reform. In particular, many of their concerns have been related to the junior high schools as they have existed since the mid-1990s. Part of the reason for parents' attitude is that they are unfamiliar with many new education initiatives. Consequently, they have continued to pay for extra classes in cram schools or tutoring lessons for their children even after the entrance examinations for junior high school and university had been abolished. Ironically, the slogan that education reform will relieve children from carrying overloaded school bags has seemed to result in more and more different versions of textbooks and extra homework for students, especially for junior high students.

Senior High School (Upper Secondary Education)

Historical Development

Upon completing their compulsory education, junior high school graduates who wish to further their education attend senior high and vocational schools. Students who desire to gain admission to senior high schools and vocational high schools have been required to pass the Basic Competence Test for junior high school students (BCT) since 2001, which includes Mandarin, English, math, social studies, science, and writing (BCT 2010). Generally, each year of high school usually consists of two semesters, running from early September to late January and from mid-February to late June.

Taiwan's senior high schools underwent a rapid change during the last four decades. In 1994, the number of high schools started to increase in response to the social urge for expanding the number of high schools and universities in order to upgrade Taiwan's manpower and reduce exam pressure on students. Since then, the once-restricted access to senior high schools has been opened up, with the ratio of academic-track and vocational-track high schools transformed from 3:7 to 5:5.

Historically, there were only 177 high schools comprising 152,877 students in 1968, whereas in 2009, the student population increased to 403,183 students who attended 330 senior high schools; 354,608 who attended 156 vocational high schools; and 93,369 who studied at 139 comprehensive high schools (MOE 2010d). Attending high school nowadays is regarded as a universal practice, as almost 97.63 percent of junior high school graduates were admitted to the senior high level in 2009. The current high enrollment rate signifies that the idea of senior high school as a place for the elites is now in the past. Though in practice the total enrollment capacity for high schools of any type has exceeded the number of junior high school graduates since 1999 (109.4 percent), the pressure to attend higher rated schools is still severe for most junior high students (Yung 2010).

Educational Objective

In Taiwan, upper secondary education was, first, an attempt to fulfill student differentiation of aptitude and talent in response to the increasing number of higher education institutions. A significant role of secondary education is to try to classify the different type of students into their various areas of expertise. Second, it was meant to cultivate a common basic literacy in order to link the previous nine-year spiral course structure and content. Third, it was aimed at providing a curriculum development infrastructure with the hope of strengthening the capacity and ability of future generations (MOE 2010f). In addition, according to the conclusion of the MOE 2001 Review of Education Reform Conference, upper secondary education was intended to adapt to diverse student learning needs and talents by providing flexible programs in order to decrease the differences among various types of schools (Xu 2001). In accordance with current policy, each school should develop its own school-based curriculum and activities, not only to represent its own culture and heritage, but also to accommodate different needs of students for higher education or career development in the future.

Specifically, According to the Provisions of the *High School Act*

"High school is to educate healthy citizens by cultivating young bodies and minds, by establishing a specialized knowledge of academic research." It is also stated that: "A comprehensive high school consists of the integration of general subjects as well as vocational courses within one educational organization for the purpose of serving students' diverse needs in terms of abilities, aptitudes, and interests, with appropriate curriculum and instruction. "Whereas vocational high schools are generally designed to train young people in areas of basic skills, work ethics, and other areas necessary for entry-level technicians in the workforce (MOE 2010g)." Most students at the upper secondary level choose to continue on to higher education after graduation. In school year 2007, 97.03 percent of high school students went on to universities, 95.09 percent of comprehensive high schools students attended universities, and 76.46 percent of vocational high schools students went on to higher education instead of seeking employment. The high percentage of students admitted to higher education has generated great skepticism about the failure of vocational high schools, which were intended to cultivate basic vocational manpower but whose graduates instead choose to obtain a college degree.

Types of High Schools

Upper secondary education in Taiwan is a multifaceted system and one of great diversity, which is a result of the nine-year compulsory curriculum launched in 2001. Based on a range of factors, the majority of students are assigned to different types of schools. High school students are streamed into particular schools based on their entrance exam scores. Public or private senior high and vocational schools institutions are categorized into seven different types: senior high, senior vocational, comprehensive, single-discipline (i.e., arts and performance), experimental, the first three years of junior college, and combined junior high schools and senior high schools. Due to the diversity in the system, students have access to a wide variety of approaches to develop their intellectual interests as well as varied career possibilities, although many of these schools still run short of features that attract students to enroll. The most common types of upper secondary institutions are senior high and vocational high schools. The former mainly focuses on preparing students for university entrance tests, and it is usually the most demanding and requires students' meticulous effort and intense focus on practice examinations.

Among 625 high schools in 2009, senior high consisted of 330 schools, vocational high 156, and comprehensive high schools 139. The ratio of public and private high schools continues to be 56:44, while private vocational high schools have comprised between 32 percent and 35 percent since 2003, and the ratio has been around 5:5 for public and private comprehensive high schools. Up to 2009, the student population totaled 851,160, of whom 403,138 students were enrolled in high schools, 354,608 in vocational, and 93,369 in comprehensive schools. The statistics indicate that there are more public high schools than private ones, whereas private schools took the lead in the vocational track.

Some studies show that students from disadvantaged backgrounds tend to attend private vocational high schools owing to their lower entrance exam scores, while students from upper- and middle-class families tend to attend public high schools, especially the top ones (so-called "star high schools") that receive more resources and enjoy higher social prestige (Lin 1999). In order to provide students with more career options and delay high school tracking, many vocational high schools were converted to comprehensive high schools in the last decade, thanks to the MOE policy that encouraged the integration of an academic and a vocational curriculum within one institution in the mid-1990s. Another reason is the declining demand for the vocational track among high school students, especially for those private vocational high schools that are suffering from a shortage of students and resources.

Most junior high school graduates prefer senior high schools over vocational schools for academic reasons and to meet society's expectations. Nevertheless, since the implementation of the nine-year compulsory education in 1968, the numbers of students attending vocational high schools has increased and, in turn, provided much support for the development of Taiwanese industry. The changing ratio between senior high school and vocational high school students was around 6:4 in 1967, 3.8:6.2 in 1973, 3.2:6.8 in 1980, and 5:5 in 2007 (Huang 2004b).

The three-year senior high school is considered to be Taiwan's mainstream educational system, where students prepare for higher education, that is, where schools have primarily focused on preparing students to pass the Joint University Entrance Examination (JUEE) for the last five decades. Not until the government implemented multiple channels for entering universities in 2001, could students be granted admission to colleges or universities through a recommendation from a senior high school or by taking tests administered by different departments of universities. If students to do not receive satisfactory results on entrance exams, they may also sit for a JUEE for another university. The major difference between the old and new entrance system is that high school students now are encouraged to participate in more extracurricular activities and international competitions, which are crucial for admission to better universities, as more and more higher-education institutions (HEIs) are focusing on student global competitiveness.

Only in the mid-2000s did more junior high school graduates start to choose vocational schools, which provide them with practical instruction, and senior high schools, which mainly focus on academic development. In contrast, vocational high schools focus on career preparation, place more emphasis on vocational skills and tests, and are more result oriented than their counterparts.

According to the MOE, as of school year 2009–2010, the percentage of senior high school graduates advancing to postsecondary education was 95.56 percent, while the percentage of vocational high school graduates was 76.91 percent (MOE 2010d). Currently, the ratio of senior high schools to vocational high schools is around 5:5, and many argue that Taiwan should establish more comprehensive high schools, which were derived and copied from the U.S. educational system during the 1990s reform era. While senior high schools focus on academic advancement, and vocational high schools focus on career preparation, comprehensive high schools, first introduced to Taiwan in 1996, offer both academic and vocational courses in one high school. These institutions include junior high school graduates who want to focus on discovering what their career path might be.

Reform-Oriented Curricula

Unlike the new curriculum guideline (the nine-year integrated curriculum) launched for Grades 1–9 in 2001, temporary high school curriculum guidelines were passed and were intended to be integrated with the abovementioned curriculum in 2004 in the hope of broadening students' horizons by introducing more elective courses based on student interest and aptitude. The mandatory courses, covering twenty-two subjects, include integrated activities, the national language, English, mathematics, history, geography, civics and sociology, foundational physics, foundational chemistry, foundational biology, foundational earth science, physics, chemistry, biology, earth science, music, fine art, arts and life, life technology, home economics, physical education, health, national defense, information technology, and career planning. Specialized courses focus on career training (see Table 8.3).

The average number of courses offered each semester ranges from fifteen to sixteen subjects, which is relatively high compared to Western countries. In contrast, most vocational high schools specialize in areas such as agriculture, industry, business, maritime studies, marine products, medicine, nursing, home economics, drama, and art.

More than 90 percent of vocational students choose to attend college or a university of technology instead of seeking jobs, due to the expansion

Table 8.3 The Typical Senior High School Course and Credit Distribution Outline

Type	Field	Course	Credit	Grade 1		Grade 2		Grade 3	
				1st Term	2nd Term	1st Term	2nd Term	1st Term	2nd Term
Required	Integrated activities (w/o Credit)								
	Language	National Language	12	2	2	2	2	2	2
		English	24	4	4	4	4	4	4
	Mathematics		24	4	4	4	4	4	4
	Social studies	History	16	4	4	4	4		
		Geography	8	2	2	2	2		
		Civic Studies	8	2	2	2	2		
			8	2	2	2	2		
	Sciences	Foundational Physics	2	2					
		Foundational Chemistry	2	2					
		Foundational Biology	2	2					
		Foundational Earth Science	2	2					
		Physics	3			3			
		Chemistry	3			3			
		Biology	2			2			
		Earth Science	2			2			
	Arts	Music	2			2			
		Fine Art	2			2			
		Arts and Life	2			2			
	Life	Life Technology	2			2			
		Home Economics	2			2			
	Health and PE	Physical Education	12	2	2	2	2	2	2
		Health	4	1	1	1	1		
	National Defense		4	1	1	1	1		
	Total Credit		148						

Source: Available online at: http://tosaint.com/rewrite.php/read-321.html.

of vocational higher education, the current low level of salaries in the workplace, and parental expectations. As Taiwanese society becomes increasingly liberal and diverse, other dialects such as Taiwanese, Hakka, and indigenous languages are finding their way into the educational system, even though Mandarin Chinese is still the only official language in schools. The mixture of foreign languages and indigenous languages seems to represent Taiwan's ambition in terms of both globalization and localization.

As mentioned above, every high school student is expected to take fourteen to fifteen subjects every semester. Criticism has been expressed that Taiwanese senior high school students have to complete too many required courses and credits, compared to their Western counterparts, to be successful in gaining admittance to college (Chou 2008). Moreover, the course load is not only heavy but also lacks integration and focus, according to some critics.

A Regular School Day

In public senior high schools, a school day starts at around 7:30 a.m. (for morning assembly) and ends at 5 p.m. (see Table 8.4). As students advance, they may have to take supplementary courses in order to prepare for the university entrance exams. It is widely accepted as fact that attending secondary school is one of the most challenging periods in a Taiwanese student's life due to the examination pressure in school.

Unlike many of their Western counterparts whose school day lasts from 9 a.m. to 3 p.m., Taiwanese secondary students have a much longer school day, from 7:30 a.m. to 4:30 or 5:30 p.m., depending on the school. As noted earlier, in most junior and senior high schools, prior to the first period, there is time for cleaning up the campus and pursuing individual study in the homeroom, followed by a morning assembly that lasts from forty-five minutes to one hour. The campus clean-up and morning assemblies are not mandatory for all students, but are rotated depending on what year of study students are in. Seniors who are busy preparing for the university entrance exams are relieved of most of the campus cleaning and assembly duties.

The school assembly takes place where students gather—in the assembly hall or on the school field (by rotation among different classes)—for civic education. Flag-raising ceremonies take place and the principal's talks about daily rules and other routine assignments are announced at that time. The homeroom individual study time allows students to engage in self-review lessons or take quizzes that are required by their teachers.

Table 8.4 A Sample Grade 10 Class Schedule in Senior High School

Weekday / Time	Monday	Tuesday	Wednesday	Thursday	Friday
1st Period 08:10–09:00	History	Chinese Literature	Math Connection	Foundational Physics	Math
2nd Period 09:10–10:00	National Defense	Chinese Literature	History	Foundational Physics	Math
3rd Period 10:10–11:00	English	Civics and Sociology	English	Special Topic (See Note)	Geography
4th Period 11:10–12:00	English	Civics and Sociology	English	Special Topic (See Note)	Geography
5th Period 01:00–01:50	Home Economics	Physical Education	Music	Physical Education	Arts
6th Period 02:00–02:50	Home Economics	Math	Foundational Biology	Chinese Literature	Life Technology
7th Period 03:10–04:00	Group Activity	Math	Foundational Biology	Chinese Literature	Life Technology
8th Period 04:10–05:00	Class Meeting				

In senior high schools, each class lasts fifty minutes. Unlike many Western high school students who change classrooms according to their elective coursework, students in Taiwan stay in the same homeroom for most of their subjects all day long, except for subjects that require a special arrangement, such as physical education, home economics, music, science experiments, and so forth. There is one-hour lunch break followed by a rest period, when students may remain seated and read or study. Such a rest period is a social tradition in Taiwan as well as a way for students to refresh their minds during hot weather. In the afternoon, most schools start at 1:00 p.m. and run until 4:00 or 5:00 p.m. The so-called main subject courses such as Chinese literature, science, English, and mathematics are usually offered in the morning session. Then, classes such as civic education, history, geography, integrated activity, music, health, and physical education are offered in the later hours of the day.

The classroom and the final campus clean-up time lasts about twenty-five minutes during the afternoon session. Afterwards, classes start again at 3:10 p.m. and last until 4:00 p.m., by which time most schools close. In some cases, seniors remain in their homeroom for extra tutorials in English, mathematics, Chinese, science, and so on. Then the seventh period ends around 4:00 p.m. Many schools provide extracurricular activities for students after school, except for seniors who need to attend an extra period for supplemental instruction or tests, to prepare for the university exams. In senior high school, extracurricular activities take on a bigger role, especially for first two years of school, when many student clubs require meetings for participation or competition. School band, choir, sport teams, and debate clubs are common on high school campuses.

After School Education (Cram Schools)

As mentioned earlier, the globalizing wave is quickly penetrating Asian countries, and as it sweeps over Taiwan's society, youngsters are still behaving very much like their regional neighbors in other Asian countries. Some of them might perk up for cram school classes after school hours, others might simply pick up a phone to chat with friends, wander around, listen to mainstream music, shop for the newest fashion trends, or enjoy movies at theaters and on the computer. Nevertheless, some private educational institutions keep students in the classroom as late as 9:00 p.m. on weekdays (see Table 8.5). In order to make up for lost class time when there are holidays during the week, students are required to attend school on weekends to avoid missing a single day of school.

Table 8.5 A Weekly After-School Schedule of an Average High School Student

Schedule		Monday	Tuesday	Wednesday	Thursday	Friday	Saturday	Sunday
Morning	07:30–12:00			Attending School			Cram school of Physics (9:00–12:00)	Cram school of Math (9:00–12:00)
Afternoon	12:00–17:00						Piano Lesson (14:00–16:00)	Cram school of Composition (13:00–16:00)
Evening	18:00–21:00	Homework & Study (20:00–23:30)	Cram school of Chemistry (18:00–21:30)	Homework & Study (20:00–22:30)	Cram school of English (18:00–21:00)	Homework & Study (20:00–22:30)	Leisure Time	Homework & Study (20:00–22:30)
	21:00–24:00		Homework & Study (22:30–24:00)		Homework & Study (22:30–24:00)			
Rest		bedtime (24:00)	bedtime (24:30)	bedtime (23:00)	bedtime (24:30)	bedtime (23:00)	bedtime (23:30)	bedtime (23:30)

As shown in Table 8.5 above, about half of a student's after-school hours are spent at a cram school. An average high school student spends one-half of his or her day at regular school and at cram school, one-fourth sleeping, and the remaining time taking transportation and doing other activities. Most high school students engage in school-related (including exam preparation) activities rather than having fun and focusing in their personal life (Chou 2008). Moreover, many ninth and twelfth graders quit school before graduation and attend intensive cram schools for drilling (or so-called "devil training camp") so that they will eventually achieve higher scores on their entrance examinations.

Recent High School Reform

In order to enhance competition for recruiting better students, many high schools set up special classes for their gifted students in areas such as science, languages, social sciences, music, arts, and even sports. The selection criteria are based on tests and practical skills that are evaluated by observation. The rest of the students are grouped into classes based on normal distribution.

A reform was introduced starting in 1996 to implement a dual stream into high schools as a way to help students who were undecided about their career track. Several experimental dual-stream high schools were established as a result, and later became comprehensive high schools. These new schools offered academic content and vocational skills courses in one school, which allowed students to complete 160 credits in both the academic and vocational tracks, and then to continue their studies in four-year technical colleges, two-year junior colleges, or universities as they chose. In 2008, these comprehensive schools accounted for approximately 30.19 percent of schools, and 13.76 percent of students of the total high schools.

In 1999, to improve the international environment in the high schools, a five-year Senior High School Second Foreign Language Education Plan was launched to upgrade the training of qualified teachers, strengthen course design, and modernize teaching facilities for foreign languages. In addition, more foreign languages such as Korean, Vietnamese, Japanese, French, and Spanish were also added to language programs. Another Excellence in Senior Schools Project was also carried out in 2005, which granted subsidies to senior high schools and senior vocational schools.

In order to infuse the principles of global competitiveness into upper secondary education, the MOE in 2002 encouraged schools to set up a global learning environment that included well-structured English courses. As a result of this initiative, high school students with special talents and gifts are selected to participate in International Science and Math Olympiads. Two years later the MOE also helped to establish the Taiwan International Association for Education Tours to facilitate senior high students to visit other countries during school breaks. Up to 2009, it was estimated that more than 4,621 students from 115 schools in Taiwan joined education tours to Japan only, and that up to 5,500 Japanese students visited Taiwan. Such tours not only help broaden students' global horizons but also enhance mutual understanding between Taiwanese students and their overseas peers.

The government has funded student exchanges and visits with overseas sister schools each year since 2005. It is estimated that more than 12,800 international students studied in Taiwan's upper secondary education institutions by 2011. All of these exchanges with other overseas high schools have helped to enhance students' international competitiveness.

In order to develop Taiwan's human capital resources to meet the demand in the twenty-first century, another proposed program is underway to include upper secondary school as part of compulsory education, that is, to require twelve years of education. The MOE initiated a new scheme in 2007 targeting quality assurance as a way to encourage general high schools and vocational high schools to personalize and localize school features and traditions.

As previously noted, students who have a special interest in vocational training can attend senior vocational schools, junior colleges, and colleges and universities of technology. Vocational high school graduates are expected, in principle, to be equipped to start a business or to seek employment, and yet most of them nowadays pursue a degree at universities/colleges of technology. There are three levels of vocational training and education: (1) vocational skills and career aptitudes in high school, (2) more advanced vocational education based on theoretical principles at the college level, and (3) vocational skills for industry-related academic training.

The MOE, along with the Human Resources Programs passed by the Executive Yuan in 2005, expanded the industry-related content of school curricula into vocational schools to increase cooperation and partnerships between private firms and schools. Consequently, the Industry-Academia Partnership Program was created in 2006 in an attempt to enhance mutual cooperation through a series of bonuses in the "three-in-one" program (senior vocational schools plus colleges plus partner enterprises), the "three-plus-two" program (senior vocational schools plus two-year colleges), the "three-two-two" program (senior vocational schools plus two-year colleges plus two-year technological institutes), and the "three-plus-four" program (senior vocational schools plus four-year technological institutes) (Chen n.d.). All of these new policy initiatives were meant to strengthen student practical training experience coupled with vocational theory at school. These measured encouraged more firm-school/company-school temporary exchanges of employment and internships among students and faculty and, with the revision of the *Education Personnel Employment Law*, alleviated restrictions (Kuo 1994).

Senior high schools are currently still in a position in which they frequently stream students into different tracks of study and define their academic reputation based on their entrance test scores. The operation of high schools, in terms of educational goals and objectives, curriculum and instruction, administration and student guidance, and so forth is geared toward students passing university entrance exams. Consequently, high schools become a buffer for reproducing the society and its hierarchy; top high schools acquire more social resources and better reputations, whereas schools that are average or lower rated suffer from being labeled as "poor achievers."

According to Lin (2002), literature on the changing form of the division of labor in advanced industrial economies in the context of the global economic transformation indicated that the current high school curriculum characterized by the separation of academic from vocational studies can no longer provide the knowledge and skills that people need for the new era of a knowledge-based economy. By contrast, a unified curriculum based on the principle of converting specialization within comprehensive high schools has been proposed to overcome divisions between academic and vocational learning, and between different curriculum subject areas. Not only the United States but also European countries have reviewed the existing dimensions of connectivity that may vary separately in the upper secondary curriculum and all subject areas as well. In Taiwan, several revisions of new high school curricula were undertaken over the last two decades.

Taiwan's high schools have been highly influenced by the economic development and social change that have taken place in the country. In the 1970s, the government actively encouraged the development of vocational schools in order to meet Taiwan's rapidly changing demand for labor-intensive industry. The structure of the economy as well as the labor market was in the process of an early transformation to the information technology (IT) industry, which required more qualified personnel from secondary and higher vocational education in the late 1980s (Wu 2006). The ratio between high schools and vocational high schools remained at around 32:68. Up to the 1990s, Taiwan experienced a rise of employment-oriented vocational secondary education, coupled with the rapid expansion of higher education at the same time, and the ratio between high schools and vocational high schools was adjusted from 4:6 to 5:5. As well, comprehensive high schools were introduced that were expected to take the lead and become mainstream high schools for the twenty-first century.

Nevertheless, similar to many efforts that took place in Europe in the 1980s, the earlier reform plans of comprehensive high schools did not succeed in Taiwan due to the ambiguous self-identity of these schools, which was caught between an academic and a vocational orientation, and due to faculty resistance as well as conflicts for students, who had to mediate between these two systems on one single campus (Chou 2009). It is important that upper secondary education receive a more in-depth review of its vocational orientation and transitional issues, which have continued to arouse social debate and public criticism, especially with the implementation of twelve-year compulsory education in the near future.

Most high school graduates still choose to continue on to higher education, that is, a university or university/college of technology, regardless of their interests or aptitude. More than 90 percent of high school and comprehensive school students in Taiwan attend institutions of higher education, suggesting that the academic-vocational streaming of upper secondary education did not fulfill its original objectives. Moreover, those who are not academically qualified also seek to attend universities instead of taking the vocational track. Consequently, some universities admit students with the lowest entrance-exam grades (i.e., 18 out of a total score of 500), which creates great controversy and tension between the universities and society at large. The MOE was forced to step in and establish a minimal score for university admission nationwide to prevent any further decline in the quality of higher education in Taiwan after 2007.

On the other hand, three-quarters of vocational high school students seek admittance to a university of technology, which conflicts with the MOE's goal. Taiwan will encounter an enormous manpower shortage of an estimated 310,000–330,000 basic technical personnel by 2015, according to a government report (MOE 2010d). As the birth rate continues to decline (from 320,000 to 200,000 high school applicants within the next eight years), increasing numbers of vocational high schools will encounter a great shortages in student enrollment unless these schools can come up with constructive solutions to improve the quality of faculty, curricula, instruction, and programs. A recent policy that the MOE has proposed for upper secondary education is to subsidize tuition fees for private high schools and vocational schools so that the original discrepancy in educational expenses between public and private high schools can be offset, which will serve as the foundation for the implementation of the twelve-year basic education reform scheme (MOE 2010e).

However, other problems still remain, including the fact that senior high schools place too much emphasis on academic achievement but overlook other aspects of a student's development. Additionally, teachers continue to use single-dimension pen-pencil grading criteria, and there is a wide learning gap between junior and senior high school curricula. The subject areas in high schools, for instance, do not coincide with similar subject areas at the junior high school level. As examples, the English vocabulary capacity for senior high schools requires seven thousand to eight thousand words, much higher than the requirement of fourteen hundred at the junior high school level, and Chinese classical literature in high schools requires moderate literary training, which junior high school students lack (Huang 2008). Many students just beginning high school became frustrated due to their weak preparation for their study in upper secondary education.

Other than these issues, vocational high schools face the problems of an inability to keep up with current developments in technology, uneven distribution of educational resources among schools, a lack of a clear educational vision, and administrative issues that make it difficult for students to change majors. Comprehensive high schools are also encountering challenges, such as an undefined school vision and a self-identity that hinders their development, unstable public policies and funding resources, and many others.

High School Educational Expenditure

Compared with Organisation for Economic Co-operation and Development (OECD) countries on average, high schools in Taiwan, both in education expenditure as a share of gross domestic product (GDP) ratio and student-teacher ratio, are relatively low and account for about 77 percent of that of their OECD counterparts. Compared with other countries, the funding that Taiwan invests for its high school students on average each year is about US$5,000, only half of that of Germany and the United States, and less than a quarter of that of Japan and South Korea. If calculated at the rate according to the gross national product (GNP), the spending for senior high school and vocational high education in Taiwan is also low. It will take about a NT$60 billion (US$2 billion) investment in education to catch up with the average standard for education spending in OECD countries, let alone narrow the gap between public and private high schools, and between urban and rural areas in terms of funding and resources. For example, tuition fees for private schools (especially private vocational schools for students who are more well-off) are three times higher than those of public schools, which make them less competitive in keeping up with their public counterparts with respect to staff

Table 8.6 Regional Discrepancies in High School Students' Performance on PISA

PISA 2006		Remote Area		Small Town		Town		City		Big City	
		Average	Standard Error	Average	Standard Error	Average	Standard Error	Average	Standard Error	Average	Standard Error
Taiwan	Reading	447	45.7	446	9.9	483	6.5	500	7	522	5.3
	Math	486	50.3	482	15.7	537	7.3	554	8.3	579	7.7
	Science	489	37.6	472	13.3	520	6.7	538	7.1	559	6.9
OECD	Reading	461	3.2	480	1.8	493	1.4	501	1.8	512	2.7
	Math	471	2.9	488	1.5	499	1.2	505	1.7	507	2.6
	Science	478	2.3	491	1.5	501	1.2	508	1.7	509	2.8

Source: OECD (2006).

recruitment and facility maintenance fees. In addition, due to regional discrepancies in budget allocation between central and local governments, many county-affiliated high schools suffered from unstable funding and resource shortages.

Another example of the unequal distribution of resources has resulted in a regional discrepancy in high school students' performance on the Programme for International Student Assessment (PISA) 2006 (see Table 8.6).

The outcome of the PISA proves that grant funding is one of the key factors that contributes to the differences in student PISA performance according to regional location. Those from urban areas, which receive more funding, perform better on this international standardized test.

As for public and private senior high schools, the educational resources are uneven as well. The proportion of public and private funding goes to 6.6:3.4. Private schools face high personnel costs, shortages of teaching equipment, and the problem of retaining qualified teachers who receive less remuneration than teachers in public schools. Thus, though students enrolled at private schools pay three times more tuition than public students, no one can guarantee that they will receive a reasonable level of teaching quality.

Another new threat to high schools comes from the restructuring of government administrations in cities and counties that took place in the winter of 2010. Sixty-eight high schools, originally governed by the MOE Central Office, are now on the verge of surrendering control to local governments. They will in turn be vulnerable and subject to unstable educational funding due to regular political elections and tax shortages at the local level. As far as the administrations of these senior high schools are concerned, they fear not only that their schools' future development may be restricted or may feel the impact of the policies of local governments, but also that grant sources may become unstable.

References

American Educational Research Association. 2007. "Time to Learn." *Research Points* 5 (2): 1–4.
Aronson, Julie, Joy Zimmerman, and Lisa Carlos. 1998. *Improving Student Achievement by Extending School: Is It Just A Matter of Time?* San Francisco, CA: WestEd.
Chen, Zi-Wed. n.d. *Hand in Hand with University Industry Cooperation Program and Education Reform on Technical & Vocational Education*. Chiayi, Taiwan: Nanhua University. Available online at: http://www.nhu.edu.tw.

Cheng, Cheng-Chen. 2008. "Governing of Colony to Reassuringly Examine Taiwan History at Period of Japanese Occupation." Paper presented at the 2008–2009 Discussion of Taiwan Culture Research with Crossborder Scholars, National Tainan University, Taiwan.
China Post. 2011. "MOE to Reintroduce Anti-Bullying Exams." Taipei: *China Post.* Available online at: http://www.chinapost.com.tw.
Chou, Chuing Prudence and Wei-Ren Chen. 2000. *Learning from Others: Special Issues on Comparative Education.* Taipei: Wenjin.
———. 2003. *Taiwan's Educational Aspects.* 55–57 Tainan, Taiwan: Sher-Yi.
———. 2008. *Mr. President: How Are You Going to Deal with Education in Taiwan?* Taipei: Psychology.
———. 2009. "Academic Exchange between Taiwan and China: Preliminary Results of National Taiwan University." Paper presented at the Cross-Taiwan Strait Talk on Education Conference, National Cheng-Chi University, Taiwan, October 24, 2009.
The Committee of the Basic Competence Test for Junior High School Students. 2010. *2010 Basic Competence Test for Junior High Hchool Students.* Available online at: http://www.bctest.ntnu.edu.tw.
Cross Straits News. 2010. *Kindergarten Education and Cross-Strait Relations.* Beijing: Xue Er Si. Available online at: http://sz.youjiao.com.
Education Reform Forum. 2009.12.17. *Why A Pale Fifteen of Age?* Taipei: United Evening News. Available online at . http://mag.udn.com.
Education Yearbook. 2008. Kindergarten education. Taipei: National Academy for Educational Research. Available online at: http://192.192.169.230.
Foucault, Michael. 1995. *Ethics, Subjectivity and Truth.* New York: The New Press.
Government Information Office. 2002. *Taiwan Yearbook 2002—Mainstream Education.* Taipei: Government Information Office. Available online at: http://www.gio.gov.tw.
Hallman, Susan, and Judith Ireson. 2005. *Secondary School Teachers' Pedagogic Practices When Teaching Mixed and Structured Ability Classes. Research Papers in Education* 20: 3–24.
Heber, Robert W. 2009. *Comparisons in Aboriginal Education: Taiwan and Canada.* Regina, Canada: Saskatchewan Indian Federated College. http://www.arts.ualberta.ca/cms/heber.pdf.
Hsieh, Hsiao-Chin. 1988. "Schooling Ethnography in the United States." *American Monthly* 3 (5): 115–124.
Huang, Buo-Rui. 2004a . "Taiwanese Middle Education." *International Middle Education.* Kaohsiung, Taiwan: Fu-Wen Press.
———. 2004b. *Taiwanese Middle Education.* Kaohsiung: Fu-Wen Press.
Huang, Yi-Wen. 2008. "An Exploration of Basic-Test Records from Junior Middle Schools at Remote Districts." *School Administration Journal* 58: 60–76.
Hwang, Guang-Guo. 2004. "Life Goals and Role Responsibilities in Confucian Societies." *Indigenous Psychological Research in Chinese Societies* 22: 121–193.
Jacobson, R. B. 2010. "Narrating Characters: The Making of a School Bully." *Interchange* 41 (3): 255–283.

Juang, M. T. 1984. "The Relations between School Life Quality and Accommodation of Junior High School Students," MA thesis, National Taiwan Normal University.
Kosack, Stephen. 2011. "The Education of Nations: How Governments Decide to Provide Education, in Taiwan, Ghana, and Brazil." Paper presented at the Annual Meeting of the Midwest Political Science Association, Palmer House Hotel, Chicago, IL. April 12, 2007.
Kuo, Wei-Fan. 1994. *Crucial Topics of Education Reform.* Taipei: National Foundation of Educational Research. Available online at: http://w2.nioerar.edu.tw.
Lin, Da-Sen. 1999. "The Impact of Family Background in Taiwan on the Diversion of Upper Secondary Education: A Discussion on the Difference of 'Public/Private Senior High/Vocational School.'" *Soochow University Sociology Newspaper* 8: 35–77.
Lin, Nan. 2002. *Social Capital: A Theory of Social Structure and Action.* London: Cambridge University Press.
Lin, Yu-wei. 2007. "Current Critical Issues of Early Childhood Education in Taiwan: Reflections on the Social Phenomenon and Governmental Policies." Paper presented at the American Educational Research Association 2007 Annual Meeting: The World of Educational Quality, Seoul, Korea, April 9–13.
Lu, Mu-Lin. 2005. "Policies of Higher Education in Taiwan and the Development of Private Higher Education Institutions." Paper presented at the Seminar of Transformation in University Management, at National Tamkang University, Taipei, Taiwan, June 8, 2005.
Lu, Yi-Rong. 2011. *Mandarin Possessed a Strong Position after the Government's Withdrawing to Taiwan.* Taipei: Taiwan Lih Pao. Available online at: http://www.lihpao.com.
Massachusetts 2020. 2005. *Time for A Change: The Promise of Extended Time Schools for Promoting Student Achievement.* Research Report. Boston, MA: Author.
Ministry of Education (MOE). 2010a. *Education in Taiwan 2010–2011.* Taipei: MOE.
———. 2010b. *Taiwan's Number of Births and the Birthrate.* Taipei: MOE.
———. 2010c. *Educational Statistical Indicators.* Taipei: MOE.
———. 2010d. *Schools, Teachers, and Students by Years.* Taipei: MOE. Available online at: http://english.moe.gov.tw.
———. 2010e. *The Plan to Promote Twelve-Year Basic Education.* Taipei: MOE. Available online at: http://140.111.34.179.
———. 2010f. *Senior High School Act.* Taipei: MOE. Available online at: http://edu.law.moe.gov.tw.
———. 2010g. *Vocational School Law.* Taipei: MOE. Available online at: http://edu.law.moe.gov.tw.
———. 2011. *Statistics of Foreign Spouses Offspring in Compulsory Education.* Taipei: MOE. Available online at: http://www.edu.tw.
Miyazaki, I., and C. Schirokauer. 1981. *China's Examination Hell: The Civil Service Examinations of Imperial China.* New Haven, CT: Yale University Press.
Mochizuki, K. 1989. "The Present Climate in Japanese Junior High Schools." In *Japanese Schooling: Patterns of Socialization, Equality, and Political Control,*

edited by J. J. Shield, 139–157. University Park, PA: The Pennsylvania State University Press.
National Academy for Educational Research. 2011. *Comparison Between Historical Events*. Taipei: National Academy for Educational Research. Available online at: http://history.moe.gov.tw.
National Taiwan Normal University. 2008. *Research Results Show Socio-Economic Status of Individual Affects Grades*. Taipei: National Taiwan Normal University. Available online at: http://pr.ntnu.edu.tw.
Oakes, Jeannie. 2005. Keeping Track: How Schools Structure Inequality (2nd ed.). New Haven, CT: Yale University.
OECD. 2006. *The PISA International Database*. Paris: OECD. Available online at: http://pisa2006.acer.edu.au
Pan, Huan-ya, 2011.2.22. *Half of Children Are Worried about Being Bullyed*. Taipei: United Daily News. Available online at: http://mag.udn.com.
"Portrait of a 15-Year-Old." 2009. *United Evening News*, December 17, 2.
Smith, Douglas C. 1997. *Middle Education in the Middle Kingdom: The Chinese Junior High School in Modern Taiwan*. Westport, CT: Praeger.
Stevenson, H. W., and S.-Y. Lee. 1996. "The Academic Achievement of Chinese Students." In *The Handbook of Chinese Psychology*, edited by M. H. Bond, 263–279. New York: Oxford University Press.
Taipei Municipal Jianguo High School. 2006. *The Second Semester Schedule*. Taipei: Taipei Municipal Jianguo High School. Available online at: http://tosaint.com.
Taiwan Education Panel Survey (TEPS). 2005a. *A Comparison of Family Time During Secondary Education Period*. 34. Taipei: Academia Sinica. Available online at: http://www.teps.sinica.edu.tw.
Taiwan Education Panel Survey (TEPS). 2005b. *A Campus safety survey*. 29. Taipei: Academia Sinica. Available online at: http://www.teps.sinica.edu.tw.
Taiwan Education Panel Survey (TEPS). 2006. *Student Perception toward School Climate*. 69. Taipei: Academia Sinica. Available online at: http://www.teps.sinica.edu.tw.
Tieso, Carol.L. 2003. *Ability Grouping Is Not Just Tracking Any More. Roeper Review* 26 (1): 29–36.
Tsao, Feng-fu. 2008. "The Language Planning Situation in Taiwan with an Update." In *Language Planning and Policy in Asia, Vol. 1: Japan, Nepal and Taiwan and Chinese Characters*, edited by R. B. Kaplan and Richard B. Baldauf Jr., 237–300. Bristol, UK: Multilingual Matters.
Wang, Wen-ying, and Jenn-wu Wang. 1994. *The Limitation and Constraint of Education and School Reform in Taiwan*. 69. Taipei: Kuei-Gwong Company.
Went, Yue-Xian. 2010. "Relationship among Junior High School Students' Personal, Family, School Life and Feeling of Happiness." MA thesis, National Taipei University.
Wu, Ming-Ji. 2006. *Establishing a Governmental Agenda for e-Learning Development: A Case of Taiwan*. Taipei: Institute of Technology and Innovation Management, College of Commerce, National Chengchi University.

Wu, Wen-Hsing, Shu-Fen Chen, and Chen-Tsou Wu. 1989. "The Development of Higher Education in Taiwan." *Higher Education* 18 (1): 117–136.
Wu, Wen-Xing. 2002. "Education and Society During the Japanese Era." *The History of Taiwan*. Taipei: Wu-Nan Press.
Xu, Ming-Zhu. 2001. *How to Solve the Problems of Accommodating High Schools into Community* (in Chinese) Taipei: National Policy Foundation. Available online at: http://old.npf.org.tw.
Yung, Chaur-shin. 2010. "The Aftermath of 12-Year Compulsory Education: Secondary Education at the Crossroads." *Bulletin of National Institute of Educational Research* 46: 1–26.

Chapter 9

Higher Education

Teacher Education

In Taiwan, teacher-training programs are available in postsecondary institutions and usually require up to four years of study. These programs fall into two categories: programs for training secondary-education teachers, and programs for training primary-school and kindergarten teachers. Normal universities primarily offer the former programs, while education universities chiefly offer the latter. Both types accept senior high-school graduates for a four-year program, with an internship period of six months. To teach at colleges or universities, an advanced degree is required, preferably a doctorate (MOE 2005).

The 1994 amendments to the *Teacher Education Law* allowed all public and private universities to take part in teacher training, making it easier for students to obtain teaching certificates by taking related courses. This effort to provide a greater variety of channels for training teachers and education professionals was carried out to meet the demands of a diversified modern society. Second-year college students (sophomores) or graduate students are eligible to apply for teacher-training education programs. Full programs include general education courses, discipline courses (moral and ethics education), specialized courses in education, and a half-year teaching practicum. Those who complete the program obtain a certificate, but a student must also pass a qualification exam administered by the Ministry of Education (MOE) to qualify finally as a teacher. Of the 7,857 candidates who took the teacher-qualification examination in 2006, 58.48 percent passed. The in-service teacher education attainment distribution is as follows: college 1.31 percent, university 77.18 percent, master's degree 18.26 percent, and doctorate 0.18 percent (MOE 2006a).

In July 2002, the MOE amended and announced the *Teacher Cultivation Act*, which revised the teacher-certification system and methods. The original certification of credentials (inspection of documents) was changed to the certification of qualifications. The first teacher-certification examination was held in April 2005. Moreover, since 2006, the MOE has published the *Teacher Training Annual Statistics*. This is an assessment mechanism that provides complete data on the supply and demand of teacher training by reviewing the teacher-training conditions from the previous year in terms of statistics based on a teacher's age, district, and subject specialization.

On the other hand, one does not need to have graduated from a normal university or studied in an education-related department to work at the MOE. Since the MOE is part of the government, the basic requirement to become an employee is to pass the civil service examinations and be hired by general governmental administrative workers. This results in the problem of government administrators not knowing how to plan curricula effectively in different school districts and treating each educational policy as a standard administrative case.

If Taiwan sacrifices educational expertise to gain uniformity in the government structure, educational administration in the future will consist of only laws and orders, and will lack actual professionalism. Thus, schools may become blended due to a unitized evaluation system, and lose their individual uniqueness and depth (Lin 2010).

Shadow Education

Common in East Asia, shadow education or cram schools have become the de facto parallel education system because they are so prevalent in countries like Japan, Korea, China, Taiwan, Hong Kong, Vietnam, and many others. Cram schools are mostly privately owned, and are commonly called *buxiban* in mainland China and Taiwan. In 2001, Taiwan had only 5,891 registered cram schools, but the number has been growing rapidly since then. The number of cram schools has boomed unexpectedly, and has doubled across the country. More than 18,300 registered cram schools remain active in shadow education, with 15,248 schools centered on traditional school subjects like the Chinese and English languages and the sciences. Taipei city has the most cram schools in all of Taiwan (2,786 schools), with Taipei county coming in a close second (2,672 schools) (Government Information Office 2010a).

Elementary school and junior high school students are those most highly targeted by Taiwanese cram schools, and these two populations have made up almost 84 percent of the total cram-school enrollment from 2005 to now. Most junior high school students leave school after 5 p.m. Some of them go straight home for dinner, and others continue their studies at cram schools. Most of these schools are examination-oriented private institutions that focus on drills and practice. On average, parents pay approximately NT$2,640 (US$80) per subject per month for their children to attend one of these schools. If a student takes three subjects at a cram school, the fees may run up to NT$7,920 (US$240) per month. This is a great financial burden for the average family in Taiwan.

The term "cram school" comes from the root word "cram," which means to prepare hastily for an examination, or to study a subject intensively, especially for an imminent examination (Bray 2009; Chou and Yuan 2011). In other words, cram schools are specialized schools that teach their students to meet particular objectives or goals in a short period of time. Some typical objectives are to help students pass various entrance examinations for different levels of education (Huang 2004). As the name suggests, the aim of cram schools is to impart as much information to its students in the shortest possible period of time. The goal is to enable the students to memorize, which means to unthinkingly repeat back information that is deemed necessary for particular examinations or tasks. Cram schools are sometimes criticized, along with the countries in which they are prevalent, for the lack of training their students receive in critical thinking and analysis.

Cram schools, whose teaching materials are closely related to the subjects taught in regular schools, are generally separated into the traditional buxiban and the *anchinban* (安親班, commonly known as day cares). Buxibans are basically composed of one teacher who provides a group of students with materials and instruction for subjects taught in regular school. Some popular subjects include mathematics, English, and science (chemistry and physics). In contrast, anchinbans employ teachers or adults whose main duty is to look after a group of children and help them with their homework and assignments until their parents arrive to pick them up.

The academic schools include institutions that focus only on the main subjects that are related to high school and college entrance exams: Chinese, English, math, and the sciences. These buxibans are basically composed of one teacher who provides a group of students with materials and instruction for subjects taught in a regular school. Most academic-oriented cram schools require their teachers to hold at least a bachelor's degree. In fact, nowadays many of these teachers hold an advanced degree. Some cram school teachers may receive very high pay if their instruction is interesting and effective, and they usually teach for several cram schools.

Nonacademic-oriented buxibans are cram schools whose teaching programs are not directly related to a regular school curriculum. Some common types are the talent and skill class, in which a teacher provides a group of students with a program designed only for a specific subject or course, such as a foreign language, essay writing, calligraphy, music, art, dancing, sports, among others. In general, the numbers of cram schools are determined by market demand. Therefore, the higher the demand of the general public, the greater the opportunity for cram schools to flourish.

Some cram schools, especially those that concentrate on languages, are part of a direct chain or a joint chain of schools. Some large language cram schools might have a chain of schools nationwide, or they might have expanded into the mainland market. In general, the large language cram schools have their own administration system and training programs. In order to provide good, quality instruction, teachers at those language schools are required to take some training courses before they start teaching. Normally, the joint chains of schools are required to pay a premium salary to the head office of the cram school.

The Taiwanese government has been pushing for a curriculum change for the past few years, hoping to lessen students' stress and decrease the number of students attending cram schools. Moreover, a multitrack school entrance plan has been established so that students with other talents can still enroll in good schools even without studying for examinations. However, these changes have not only failed to lessen students' stress, but have also led to an increase in the number of students attending cram schools. Students are not only studying for courses that are covered in examinations but also subjects related to skills and talents, hoping to gain the qualifications to enter schools without taking the necessary examinations. As a result, cram schools in Taiwan are proliferating. That is to say, the plans that the Taiwanese government has been pushing have not at all changed parents' willingness to send their children to cram schools, and have resulted in even more students seeking help through these schools.

> If one stands in front of Taipei Main Station, it is possible to see many buxibans along the road. After dark, a large number of students flood into these buxibans for different reasons each day. If one looks at this overcrowded street scene, full of anxious students, teachers, and parents, one will understand how prevalent cram schools are in Taiwan.

Why are cram schools so common? Taiwan has the same heritage as other East Asian countries, which have great respect for academics and intellectual ability, as influenced by Chinese Confucianism. Most parents believe that if their children can enter a highly ranked high school or university, they will have a better career in the future. In order to achieve this goal, most parents feel no hesitation to send their children to cram schools for extra hours of instruction if they can afford the tuition. In attempting to relieve students of the pressure of exams and an overload of studying by rote memory, Taiwan's MOE launched a series of education-reform programs, including a new version of curriculum guidelines and textbooks. Moreover, a multitrack school-entrance plan has been established so that students with other talents can still enter good schools even if their test scores are not as high as required.

The number of students in a class depends on the size of the cram school. In a large cram school, some of its classes might have more than one hundred students. Sometimes, even several projectors are needed for teaching a large class. In the classroom, students take notes on the material the instructor is teaching, and should they have a question, they can either ask the instructor during or after class.

What are the reasons behind the success of Taiwan's cram schools? Students are attracted to these cram schools because:

1. They raise students' academic performance, especially their test scores. Therefore, students who fall behind academically in school may choose to attend cram schools in order to receive additional instruction (Xue, 2004).
2. Society's values and competitiveness are emphasized in school entrance exams. A study conducted by Chou and Yuan (2011) pointed out that the societal overvaluing of credentials and a college degree has created an enormous pressure on the exam-driven learning that students experience in schools. Such trends have indeed brought forth the pressure in providing school programs geared toward passing certificate (or credentials).
3. Parents who expect their children to be high achievers will never be content with their children's grades, and eventually, will send their children to cram schools to help them achieve an even better performance (Huang 2004).
4. Public schools cannot satisfy students' needs to increase their academic performance. Even though Taiwan has widespread public education, the quality of teachers is mixed (Huang1981). Some parents also worry about teachers' dedicationand teaching, and hence, they tend to send their children to cram schools (Hsu 2002). Another study further shows there is a gap between what students learn at

school and what is covered in the school entrance examinations, so students feel that they "must" attend exam-oriented cram schools in order to achieve the higher grades they desire (Xie 2004).
5. Students overestimate the value of cram schools and tend blindly to follow other students. Many Taiwanese students believe that cram schools provide better instruction than their regular schools, so they think that attending cram schools will help them understand course material better.

Even though cram schools are prevalent in Taiwan, some resulting problems deserve attention (Chou and Yuan 2011):

1. The learning process moves faster in cram schools than regular schools, causing students to potentially disrespect and disregard teachers' instruction at school.
2. Students do not work hard at regular school but instead rely on cram schools.
3. Students have to focus on regular school and cram school at the same time, which increases their stress levels.
4. Students tend to lose their ability to explore knowledge due to exam-driven education.
5. Teachers at cram schools do not have teaching certificates and are not qualified personnel, which may have a negative impact on students' learning process.

There is no doubt that cram schools have made a significant contribution to the supplementary education of Taiwan, both in the academic-oriented and the nonacademic-oriented aspects. Nevertheless, the prevalence of cram schools has also prompted some reflection on the part of education administrators and parents, who have expressed mixed feelings about cram schools. If cram schools are competitive enough to help students to improve academic performance, then what about the public schools? A buxiban is not a free ride; it charges lots of money and places a financial burden on parents. Poor families cannot afford to send their children to such schools. Can public schools provide a high-quality competitive education that meets the needs of students from more disadvantaged backgrounds? If the existence of cram schools in Taiwan is unavoidable, how can we improve the quality of public schools, lessen the pressure on student that comes from entrance exams, and convince parents to restrain themselves from overloading their children and to respect their talents in areas other than academic performance? These are questions yet to be answered.

Higher Education: Historical Development

The development of higher education in Taiwan over the last century represents a transition from the colonial system to the Chinese system prior to 1949, from a highly centralized administration to government-regulated and market-driven management after 1987, from restricted access for the elite to a more universal orientation, and from a single-facet standard to a more diverse operation. The impact of foreign influences and local heritage on the current system and the uniqueness of a system that combines Japanese, American, Chinese, and local features indicate the choices facing Taiwan in its pursuit of localization and globalization in higher education (MOE 2006b).

The Seed Stage (1895–1945)

Prior to 1919, the Japanese authorities did not establish any formal educational system in Taiwan and let the so-called "experimental period" in education die out. After 1919, the *Taiwan Education Decree*, based on a Western education model, was introduced, in which higher-education institutions (HEIs) consisted of three colleges, namely medical, agriculture and forestry, and business schools, coupled with an additional department in medical science and a senior business school. By 1920, the coeducational system was introduced to Taiwan for the first time, and all instruction at each level (primary through postsecondary) was in Japanese.

During the colonial assimilation period, educational policy was based on ethnic discrimination, and segregation between Japanese and Taiwanese existed throughout all levels of schools. Common schools (elementary schools) were the main educational institutions for all students, until later, when Taipei Imperial University was founded, which admitted sixty-six students in 1928. The majority of the university students were elite Japanese. The authorities did not permit the social sciences to be taught. Agriculture and medicine for epidemic diseases were the only two departments for which Taiwan students could compete for admission, and the latter led to a high-income and a secure life. The field of medicine still remains the first choice among top high school students today in Taiwan. In the past, many affluent Taiwanese went to Japan to pursue postsecondary degrees instead of attending a university in Taiwan due to the extremely limited quotas for local people.

Transition and Development Stage (1945–1987)

After World War II, with the restoration of Taiwan, China gained sovereignty over the island's territory and culture. At the postsecondary level, the Japanese influence was replaced by the Chinese model, a prototype of American higher education, after August 1946, as previously noted. Many aspects of higher education, such as the academic structure, administrative organization, curriculum and instruction, degree and graduation requirements, and so forth were reorganized according to the model of Chinese universities imported from the mainland.

During the 1950s–1960s, foreign aid and investment in Taiwan helped establish an export-oriented economy and labor-intensive industry on the island. Higher education felt the impact of and was aligned with this change in order to prepare manpower to export labor-intensive products. After the 1960s, Taiwan's higher-education system (particularly junior colleges) developed rapidly, thanks to the growth of secondary schools and the expansion of labor-intensive industries. Thus, the number of HEIs increased 15-times (from 7 in 1950 to 105 in 1986), while student enrollment increased 52-times (from 6,665 in 1950 to 345,736 in 1986) (MOE 2006b).

Up to the 1980s, Taiwan started to move toward becoming a society that produced more capital and technology-intensive goods for export and was shifting to the service industry. By that time, Taiwan had transformed from a recipient of foreign aid to a recipient of foreign investment, and the country's system of higher education had also reached a stage where many HEIs started to recruit international students instead of sending their own students abroad.

Concerning education administration, the government updated legislation to regulate higher education so that it could adapt to the new era. In the 1970s, applications to establish private schools were terminated. Following that time, technological-vocational education and general higher education coexisted with each other, later developing into two branches of higher education in Taiwan.

Expansion Stage (1988 to the present)

There was a period of time when the establishment of private HEIs was strictly controlled and banned before the mid-1980s. However, as Taiwan's economy progressed and the political process moved toward democratization in the late 1980s, universities began to promote the pursuit of academic freedom and autonomy that was inspired by their American counterparts. In addition, the higher-education system in Taiwan entered a stage of dramatic growth after the lifting of martial law in 1987. The revision to the *University Law* in 1994 further limited the authority of the MOE over universities and colleges, and campus operations have since become more flexible in appointing presidents, charging tuition fees, offering courses, and recruiting students.

Starting in the mid-1990s, universities of science and technology were established through the upgrading or reorganizing of institutions, which contributed to the great expansion of both the number of HEIs and the student population. Consequently, some programs were initiated to consolidate or transform universities by institutional merger, university evaluation, the competitive allocation of resources, and so forth. While public funding shrank, Taiwan's pursuit of a world-class university system continued, thanks to the increasing number of universities that were established. This initiative came in response to the global trend toward improving the quality of higher education, especially in the area of research (Chou 2008).

There are two categories of universities in Taiwan, general universities and universities of technology and vocation. The former, according to the *University Act* (2010), aims to "encourage academic research, cultivate talent, enhance culture, serve society and accelerate the development of the country, by guaranteeing academic freedom and thus, shall enjoy autonomy within the range of laws and regulations" (MOE 2011). In contrast, to keep up with a changing society in terms of its values and technology, the goals of technological and vocational education in Taiwan include (Lee 2010; MOE 2012):

1. Heavy emphasis on general learning while building a solid schooling system
2. Laying a foundation for career development through study that is applied to technology
3. Application of learning to project-directed work
4. Implementation of a system based on certification through dexterity and skills examinations
5. Technology development applied to vocational education to meet and fulfill students' needs
6. Fostering teaching strength through recruiting teachers from different industries, and developing and enhancing their practical skills

7. Combining theoretical and practical experience for a cooperative education
8. Contributing to community development through continuing education

Like many Asian countries, the system of higher education in Taiwan is made up of diverse perspectives defined by different educational purposes. Taiwan's HEIs are comprised of four-year colleges, universities, institutes of technology, and two- to five-year junior colleges. As previously noted, most programs at HEIs last four years except for those programs that train teachers, architects, lawyers, dentists, and physicians, which take an extra few years. Unlike the American professional schools that start after college graduation, law and medical schools start right from the first year of university in Taiwan. More and more universities offer nondeclared programs based on general foundation/education for the first two years at college with the hope of broadening the scope of student learning and the interdisciplinary capacity of students.

One major shift in the field of higher education is the merging of vocational and technological institutes into mainstream higher education. At present, junior colleges only account for a small proportion of schools that admit students directly from junior high schools into five-year programs. On the other hand, most students eligible for higher education are required to have graduated from a senior high school or senior vocational school. Two-year junior colleges, two-year technological colleges, and four-year technological colleges are designed for graduates to continue with advanced vocational programs. Those who wish to pursue academic career paths are more likely to choose a university education.

In academic year 2009–2010, undergraduates comprised more than three- quarters of the population, whereas about 15 percent were master's students, and the remaining were doctoral students (MOE 2010a). Channels for admission to colleges or universities are based on test scores from entrance examinations, and selection is based on individual applications and recommendations by high schools. The main goal of high school students is to achieve high scores on university entrance examinations in order to attend better universities (Pan and Yu 1999). However, students who have completed junior college programs may transfer to a four-year college or university as freshmen or second-year students after passing the required examinations.

There are at least two ways to be admitted to college. The first is through a recommendation and screening process. Third-year senior high school students may take the General Scholastic Ability Test (GSAT) in the winter, which assesses their high-school level competence in Chinese,

English, mathematics, and the natural and social sciences. Then, students, with their own portfolio of academic and social achievement, can apply to their targeted institution(s) of priority through their competitive school recommendations. The second way is by college entrance examination and placement. Every July, students who did not succeed in the GSAT can sit for a University Department Required Test (UDRT), consisting of three to five subjects from high school, and they will be assigned to a college based on their test scores.

Another way to gain entrance to college is to take an entrance exam for a vocational institution. In order to improve the traditional written entrance examination and to embrace more diversified entrance schemes, the government set up a Testing Center for Technological and Vocational Education (TCTE) to take charge of the recruitment policy and advancement for technological colleges and universities. Since the 2001 academic year, TCTE, a specialized institution of testing, has taken on a broad range of activities and tasks related to the development of and research into the Technological and Vocational Education (TVE) joint college-entrance examination. In the past decade, more than 150,000 examinees took the TVE entrance exam for the vocational track, outnumbering their counterparts for the GSAT (for academic orientation). Nevertheless, the GSAT has always attracted more attention in terms of news coverage and social resources, which represents the social favoritism shown to an academic degree over vocational training in Taiwan (Chou 2008).

Program and Curriculum

Higher education in Taiwan is usually broadly categorized into the following branches: the College of Humanities and Sciences, the College of Social Sciences, the College of Medical Sciences, the College of Engineering, the College of Professional Schools. Most universities and colleges are supervised by the MOE, except for the military academy and the police academy. Taking National Taiwan University (NTU) as an example, there are three streams of courses. First is general and liberal education. General education covers a wide range of required courses such as Chinese literature, foreign languages, physical education, and service learning, while liberal education consists of eight areas: literature and arts, historical thinking, world civilization, philosophy and moral reasoning, civic awareness and social analysis, quantitative analysis and mathematics, material science, and life science. These courses are designed to enhance a diverse dialogue and integration among different academic fields and old and new ways of thinking, and especially to cultivate students' cultural literacy as the country begins to embrace globalization and localization in a lifelong learning society.

Second, courses required by department/graduate institutions consist of half of the graduation credits, which normally range from 128 to 148 credits (one credit equals one hour of class per week, and there are eighteen weeks per semester). Third, students are free to choose elective courses and credits from a campus or through the intercampus system (NTU 2008a). One exception is that students who have passed the prerequisite test of the teacher education program are then qualified to take courses in the teacher education program, and will become teacher candidates upon completion (NTU 2008b).

Issues and Commentary

Higher Education Expansion and Increased Access

Like many other countries in the world since the 1980s, Taiwan's university system has undergone drastic change, including great expansion of its student population. Furthermore, with the unprecedented growth in the number of private universities and technological and vocational institutions that has occurred since 1994, higher education is becoming more accessible to Taiwan's younger generations aged between eighteen and twenty-two. The total number of citizens holding a diploma of higher education was 6.68 million in the year 2008, having risen by 4.24 percent from the previous year (Government Information Office 2010b).

In addition, there has been long-term growth in the number of HEIs over the decades. Regarding university expansion, as shown in Table 9.1 below, the total growth rate equals 1.75 times within a decade. As for the decrease in the number of junior colleges, they have been restructured to become universities or technological colleges rather than be shut down. The number of students enrolled in universities has increased 2.17 times, that is to say, twice as much the student population that has been admitted to universities in the last decade.

Alongside these changes, the growth in master's and doctoral education has also been remarkable. The number of students admitted to graduate schools in 2008 was 4.2 times greater than in 1998, and it rose to 3.03 times in the area of doctoral education (MOE 2010b). According to a *Commercial Times*' report published on February 20, 2011, it is anticipated that Taiwan will award one million master's degrees and PhDs by the end

Table 9.1 Higher Education Expansion in Taiwan

	SY	1998–1999	2008–2009
No. of Schools	Junior Colleges	53	15
	Colleges & Universities	84	147
No. of Students	Junior College	452,346	117,653
	College & University	463,575	1,006,102
	Master's Degree	43,025	180,809
	Doctorate	10,845	32,891

Source: Taiwan Government Entry Point (2010).

of 2011, and that the proportion of the population with advanced degrees will be one of the highest in the world. Compared to a decade earlier, a total share of 25.1 percent of the national population above fifteen years old, which is one of every four people, possesses an advanced degree, and merely ten years ago the proportion was lower than 10 percent.

In addition, Taiwan has nearly the highest university admission rate in Asia, with 68.1 out of 100 students aged eighteen being admitted to university, which is four times higher than the admission rate in Hong Kong and China. In terms of specific numbers, the university student population reached 1.02 million in 2010, up from 302,093 students in 1994. There are 163 universities and colleges, including 112 universities (45 public universities versus 67 private ones) (compared with 23 universities in 1994), 36 independent four-year colleges (35 in 1994), and 15 five-year junior colleges (72 in 1994).

The expansion of higher education in Taiwan can, therefore, be regarded as a restructuring of private institutions accomplished mainly by creating new institutions and upgrading existing ones, although other strategies, such as splitting, merging, and increasing the size of the existing institutions, were also used historically. However, public institutions remain more prestigious than private ones.

As a result of the expanded number of universities, more students nowadays can be admitted to institutions of higher education regardless of their social background, gender, ethnicity, and age. The once elite-oriented HEIs are accessible and responsive to Taiwanese society (Huang and Chen 2008). In spite of this accessibility, however, universities are experiencing greater pressures due to budget cuts and constraints on resources as the government moves toward a neoliberal ideology. Therefore, HEIs are now focused on competing for students and resources by generating marketing based on their research "products" and programs (Chou 2010).

Control over the quality of university teaching is threatened as more and more private universities are striving to recruit students, fearing the low birthrate that is occurring. In addition, the unemployment rate of university graduates increased from 2.7 percent in 1993 to 5.8 percent in 2009, which ranked the highest among their peer graduates at other educational levels. This situation has placed serious financial burdens on families. The statement, "Higher in terms of university degree, higher in terms of unemployment rates" has been disseminated among postsecondary institutions as employment opportunities for college students have become more scarce than before. At the same time, many corporations complain about the new employee fresh from the university who obviously lacks a work ethic, loyalty, and practical experience. Some employers have even experienced a personnel shortage due to the higher expectations of college students in terms of salary and their desire for convenience in commuting between home and the office (Chou 2008). Another issue is that increasing numbers of students cannot find a job related to their university degree. A survey indicated that only a quarter of university graduates in the last five years found a job connected to their college major, among whom 52.38 percent were arts majors, 50 percent mass communication majors, 48.21 percent medical science and public health majors, 46.43 percent natural sciences majors, and 46.15 percent architecture and urban design majors. (Cheng 2010).

Another negative impact has resulted from the loose connections and the increasing gap between university education and industry requirements. As mentioned earlier, education was very much influenced by economic development under the centralized government plan from the 1950s to the 1980s. Yet, as Taiwan approached the 1990s, an increasing discrepancy developed in the supply and demand between the educational and the economic sectors, especially after the expansion of the numbers of HEIs in the last decade. More companies criticized the inability of schools and universities to equip students with the competency and professionalism that correspond to the needs of the new technology workforce and the knowledge-based economy.

In 2007, the total number of HEIs was 163, which constituted 1.30 million students, with a 90 percent admission rate. Each year, approximately 300,000 students graduate from universities, of whom 130,000 become unemployed. On the other hand, among 91,490 research personnel, 87 percent come from universities and academic institutions rather than being employed in industry or the corporate sphere, which are in need of research and development staff. The application of academic research that originates in institutions of higher education comes up short in terms of better serving the needs of companies and industry in Taiwan. Most high-technology companies have fewer than one hundred thousand employees in the professions of semiconductor manufacturing, image display, digital life, biotechnology, communications, and the information service industry, but universities will only be able to supply two thousand in those six key industries in Taiwan for the next six years. The solution to how to deal with such a human resource shortage demands a more aggressive higher-education policy and strategy that will strengthen the collaboration between the university and the corporate world.

In addition, there is the issue of the increasing numbers of the "working" population among university graduates in Taiwan. The unemployment rate for these individuals was 4.67 percent in 2009. Those who are part of the working population phenomenon spent at least twenty-seven weeks as part of the labor force during the year, although their incomes were lower than incomes at the official poverty level in the United States in the same year. And in Taiwan, the average monthly income of local workers was NT$42,141 (US$1,451) in 2010, which was the average income back in 1998, thus showing no improvement in earning power whatsoever.

On average, a Taiwanese worker tallied 2,154 working hours in 2008, more than 50 percent higher than German workers, who totaled an average of 1,432 hours in the same year, although in terms of compensation, the salary that Taiwanese workers earn is only one-third that of their German counterparts. Many of these members of the "low income workforce" were unemployed university graduates, a total number of about one hundred thousand university graduates in Taiwan in the year 2009, and this number accounted for more than 45 percent of the total unemployed population in the country. These unemployment numbers indicate the need for change in regards to aligning the needs of both higher education and the labor market. Changes such as those currently occurring in the labor market might foster an urgency to revise policy (Wang 2010).

Institutional and Disciplinary Stratification

Higher education in Taiwan is becoming more and more stratified due to the uneven allocation of educational funding, as mentioned above. For example, the overall data on university expenditure per student showed a significant increase between 1999 and 2007, and average spending declined after that. In this period, most public universities benefited from the increase, especially HEIs such NTU and some other top universities that received the bulk of their funding from the MOE and donations from the private sector, while most second-tier public and private HEIs encountered more and more funding shortages. An increasing trend of stratification among HEIs has led to polarization in terms of educational resources and institutional prestige.

The gap has become increasingly wide not only among HEIs but also among disciplines. Regarding average spending per student in top public universities, science and technology majors receive twice as much government funding as their peers in the humanities and social sciences, which also accounts for four times more than that for students at private institutions. The gap between institutions and the disciplines continues to widen and accelerate as government funding allocation is increasingly based on accountability and competition. The saying that "the rich get richer, and the poor become poorer" is not uncommon in describing the stratification in Taiwan's system of higher education.

In this case, private universities that lack outstanding qualities and performance not only cannot obtain special grants from the government, but they also encounter more and more shortages in recruiting students. In 2009, university enrollment overall faced a shortage of a total of seven thousand students, among which were some national universities with acceptable reputations. It is forecast that a great number of private universities will be forced to close down in 2015 due to the low birthrate in Taiwan. The whole country will also face the immediate impact of a series of university closures and staff and faculty layoffs in academia in the near future if the reintegration and merger of existing universities and the recruitment of more foreign students, including the relaxing of restrictions on students from mainland China, do not come into effect. A possible solution is for the government to facilitate private universities in identifying and developing their unique and indispensable attributes.

Social Distance between the Public and Private Universities

Among the universities in Taiwan, in school year 2009, for example, 60 percent were private, consisting of 63 percent of the student population, whose tuition is twice as much as that of their peers at public institutions (Lin 2005). Research studies have shown that students admitted to public HEIs tend to come from upper- and middle-class family backgrounds, whereas students from more disadvantaged backgrounds tend to study at private universities. According to a survey of one of the national top universities of Taiwan, the average cost (including tuition, room, and board) of attending a public four-year university is around NT$1 million (US$33,000), and NT$1.2 million (US$40,000) for private institutions, of which more than 60 percent comes from family support (Chou 2007).

In a research project entitled "Who Are NTU's students?," Lo pointed out that 82 percent of NTU students graduated from twenty top national high schools between 1997 and 2000, of whom 57.6 percent of these students grew up in the Taipei metropolitan area, and had an admission rate sixteen times higher than those students from the most remote counties on the east coast (Luoh 2002). In terms of university majors, 42 percent of students in the law schools come from families in which 42 percent of fathers (17 percent higher than average students) and 27 percent of mothers (7 percent higher) have a university degree. These results suggest that there is a high correlation between admission to a top national university and family background, which includes parent education, family income, residence, and high schools. Nevertheless, students from public universities receive public subsidies totaling up to NT$800,000 (US$27,000) over four years, and outnumber to a great extent their private peers who pay twice as much university tuition.

Compared with its international competitors, Taiwan has had a relatively low tuition-fee policy since the 1950s, thanks to the belief that schooling should fulfill a mission as the main avenue for social mobility. However, the policy of providing low university tuition fees has been challenged since the 1960s due to the practice of supporting privileged groups and government employees whose offspring are more likely to be accepted into the highly subsidized public universities (Huang 1978). The studies of Lai and other researchers have justified this doubt and called for revision of the current discrepancy in tuition between public and private institutions, in order to rectify the issue of reproducing the lines of social class that higher education has created (Lai 2010).

REFERENCES

Bray, Mark. 2009. *Confronting the Shadow Education System*. Paris: UNESCO International Institute for Educational Planning.
Cheng, Yun-Shuan 2010. *Only A Quarter of University Graduates Found Jobs Related to Their Majors*. Taipei: Forum, April 5. Available online at: http://forum.doctorvoice.org.
Chou, C. P. and J. K. S. Yuan. 2011. "Buxiban in Taiwan." *IIAS Newsletter*, Spring.
Chou, Chuing Prudence. 2007. "Beyond University Tuition." *Journal of Education Research*, 154.
———. 2008. *Mr. President: How Are You Going to Deal with Education in Taiwan?* Taipei: Psychology.
———. 2010. *Expectations of Academicians and Academic Sinica 2010*. Hong Kong: The China Review News. August 5. Available online at:http://www.chinareviewnews.com.
Government Information Office. 2010a. *The Republic of China at a Glance*. Taipei: Government Information Office. Available online at: http://www.gio.gov.tw.

———. 2010b. *Mainstream Education 2010.* Taipei: Government Information Office. http://www.taiwan.gov.tw.
Hsu, Chi-ting. 2002. "Study of Grade Nine Students' View on Cram Schools and School Education." Unpublished master's thesis, Graduate Institute of Science Education, National Taiwan Normal University.
Huang, Guang-Guo. 1981. "Problems in Academics and Buxiban." *Chinese Forum* 11, no. 10: 8–24.
Huang, Hsing-mei E. 2004. "Effects of Cram Schools on Children's Mathematics Learning." In *How Chinese Learn Mathematics: Perspectives from Insiders. Series on Mathematics Education.* Vol. 1, edited by Liang-hou Fan, Ngai-ying Wong, Jianfei Cai, and Shiqiao Li, 282–306. Singapore: World Scientific.
Huang, Kung-hui. 1978. "An Investigative Analysis of the Family Socio-Economic Background of the Candidates and Passers of University Entrance Examination." *Bulletin Institute of Educational Research Taiwan Normal University,* 20: 149–319.
Huang, Yih-Jyh, and Chun-wei Chen. 2008. "Academic Cram Schooling, Academic Performance and Opportunity of Entering Public Universities." *Bulletin Institute of Educational Research* 54 (1): 117–149.
Lai, T. M. 2010. *It Is Hard to Justify from a Private University Perspective 2010.* Taipei: United Daily News Group. Available at: http://mag.udn.com.
Lee, Lung-Sheng Steven. 2010. *Technological Literacy Education and Technological and Vocational Education in Taiwan.* Paper presented at the Industrial Technology Education for Pakistan 2010, February 17, 2010, Aichi University of Education, Kariya, Japan. Available online at: http://www2.nuu.edu.tw.
Lin, Wen-Sheng. 2010. *Taiwan Needs an Education System That Is International.* Taipei: United Daily News Group. Available online at: http://mag.udn.com.
Lin, Zhao-Zhen. 2005. *Saving Our College.* Taipei: Common Wealth Magazine. Available online at: http://www.lcenter.com.tw.
Luoh, M. C. 2002. "Who Are Taiwan University Students? From Perspectives of Gender, Birth Origin, and Residence." *Taiwan Economic Review* 30 (1): 113–147
Ministry of Education (MOE). 2005. *Teacher Cultivation.* Taipei: MOE.
———. 2006a. *Matters Including Evaluation, Teacher Qualifications Certification Exams, Teacher In-service Education and Normal (Education) University Engineering.* Taipei: MOE.
———. 2006b. *The Excellent Development of University Education.* Taipei: MOE. Available online at: http://english.moe.gov.tw.
———. 2010a. *University Act 2010.* Taipei: MOE.
———. 2010b. *Education in Taiwan 2010–2011.* Taipei: MOE.
———. 2010c. *Educational Statistical Indicators.* Taipei: MOE.
———. 2011. *Educational Laws.* Taipei: MOE.
———. 2012. *Technological and Vocational Education Reform Project - Expertise Training.* Taipei: MOE. Available online at: http://english.moe.gov.tw.
National Taiwan University (NTU). 2008a. *Course Finder.* Taipei: NTU. Available online at: https://nol.ntu.edu.tw.

———. 2008b. *Curriculum Mapping*. Taipei: NTU. Available online at: http://coursemap.aca.ntu.edu.tw.

Pan, Hui-Ling, and Chien Yu. 1999. "Educational Reforms with Their Impact on School Effectiveness and School Improvement in Taiwan, R.O.C." *School Effectiveness and School Improvement* 10 (1): 72–85.

Taiwan Government Entry Point, 2010. *Mainstream Education*. Taipei: Taiwan Government Entry Point. Available online at: http://www.taiwan.gov.tw.

Wang, Chris. 2010. "'Working Poor' Phenomenon Worries Labor Rights Advocates 2010." Taipei: The Central News Agency. Available online at: http://focus taiwan.tw.

Xue, Jing-Zhang 2004. A Study on the High Academic Achievers without Attending Cram Schools. Unpublished Master's Thesis. National Chung-Cheng University, Jia-Yi, Taiwan.

Chapter 10

New University Funding, Flexible Salaries, and a Quality Assurance Scheme

The New University Funding Scheme

The revision of the 1994 *University Law* served as a milestone that transformed the traditionally centralized system of bureaucratic control exercised by the Ministry of Education (MOE) into an environment where higher-education institutions (HEIs) were more self-reliant and autonomous. The law also "reduced the power and responsibilities of the MOE over university academic and administrative operation in curriculum guidelines, student recruitment, staffing, tuition, and so on" (Tsai 1996). Under this new regulation, increasing numbers of universities and colleges were established in different forms and through different methods. In other words, from the perspective of neoliberal ideology, the 1994–1996 Education Reform Committee, along with the MOE, believed that universities and colleges in Taiwan lacked heterogeneous approaches in terms of functions and goals. In order for the MOE to best support HEIs in fostering diversity, the HEIs needed to modify their general institutional characteristics as well as their mission. This was even the case with the private sector, where the founding of new HEIs had formerly been banned by central regulation before the early 1990s.

Accordingly, an "Administrative Funding Scheme" was introduced into public universities to improve their accountability and provide them with more flexibility in spending their revenue from student tuition fees, college-enterprise cooperation research projects, fund-raising from alumni, and so on. No longer relying on government budgets alone, public (or so-called "national") universities were now required to designate partial funds for sharing their daily administrative costs. The MOE planned as well to reduce its authority over university internal operation, such as course requirements and budgeting, so that universities can compete for public funding based on merits and performances. Yet despite these changes, the MOE and other government budgeting offices still had the right to regulate various university practices.

The MOE started a trial program based on these principles with five universities in 1996, allowing them more autonomy in allocating their resources. Today, fifty-four out of seventy public universities participate in this program (Taiwan Assessment and Evaluation Association [TWAEA] n.d.). Under this revised system, public universities are required to assume the full responsibility for a certain proportion (such as 20 percent to 50 percent) of their annual operation. As a result, public universities currently must acquire external funding resources, through such as avenues as fund-raising and industry cooperation. This shift is seen in the proportion of financial support that HEIs receive from the MOE, which has decreased from 62.7 percent in 2000 to 49.2 percent in 2006, whereas the proportion of tuition income has increased from 12.83 percent to 21.59 percent. The introduction of market mechanisms into universities means the transformation of higher education from a public service to a system in which users pay for services.

In addition, responding to the demand for projects to upgrade the quality of higher education through the enhancement of its efficiency and accountability, in early 1999 the MOE launched the Project for Pursuing Excellence in Higher Education, followed by the setting in motion of a *White Paper Report on Higher Education in Taiwan* in the year 2003. This government document laid out the most up-to-date improvements in higher education in Taiwan and, consequently, it provided broad guidelines aimed at helping HEIs attain excellence.

In order to become more financially self-sufficient, leading universities have initiated unprecedented fund-raising campaigns, gathering donations from their alumni, the general public, and business enterprises. However, many institutions have been less than successful in obtaining significant support from these sources, due to their lack of a well-established alumni network. Universities of lower prestige and those without wealthy alumni face further challenges in raising funds.

The Quality Assurance Plan

The assessment of student learning has now become an important indicator for quality assurance in higher education since the implementation of university evaluation, the five-year-five-billion plan, the teaching for excellence plan, and department/graduate evaluation. Chen (2002) indicated that the change in university governance resulted from four factors, including (1) demographic change, (2) globalization, (3) a knowledge-based economy, (4) information technology, and (5) commercialization.

Specifically, the university student population in the developed world accounted for 15 percent of the age cohort in 1969 compared to 51 percent in 1996, while it was 7 percent to 14 percent in the developing world (Organisation for Economic Co-operation and Development [OECD] 2009). The university admission rate has decreased from the elite type (15 percent) to the mass type (between 15 percent and 50 percent), and reached the stage of the universal type (more than 50 percent) (Trow 2005). As greater numbers of students gain access to universities, the question of how to exert control over quality in higher education becomes a great concern, and international agencies such as OECD, UNESCO, and the World Trade Organization (WTO) have initiated programs to foster quality enhancement. Governments also face the need to reallocate limited educational finances, which have experienced constraints due to the expansion of higher education. Thus, university ranking based on prestige and research performance has come to serve as one of the major criteria for government funding (Fiske 2004).

As a result of the influence of neoliberal ideology and the expansion of higher education, Taiwan's universities and colleges are now experiencing increasing pressure from the market and the government to compete for resources, funding, and students. In order to meet the challenge of global competitiveness and enhance university effectiveness, universities have been required to carry out regular self-evaluation in all aspects of teaching, research, and service. Meritocracy, accountability, and networking among faculty and staff now count for considerably more than in the past (Chou 2008). Accordingly, Taiwan's *University Act*, revised in 2003, reiterated the amendment of university evaluation to serve as one of the major mechanisms for funding that will eventually assure the quality of higher education. Quality assurance policies have been introduced and reinforced since 2005 based on the law.

Historically, Taiwan's university evaluation can be traced back to the following phases:

1. 1975–1990: The MOE was in charge of university evaluation
2. 1991–1994: Professional evaluation associations were sponsored to carry out university evaluation based on the midterm institutional development plan of an individual university
3. 1995–2000: Evaluation was regulated by the University Act and the Private Education Act, which required the implementation of university evaluation
4. 2001–2004: The university was encouraged to establish its own self-evaluation plan. An evaluation committee was set up by the MOE to carry out regular university evaluation, the results of which would be used for governmental budget allocations. Under the new framework of evaluation, all universities needed to establish their own teaching review system and set up research criteria for faculty as important references for performance and promotion.
5. 2004–2005: A professional evaluation association was commissioned for university evaluation. General university affairs were targeted based on six components: teaching resources, extension services, student affairs, general education, administrative support, and degree of internationalization. The new indicator of internationalization stressed the importance of university globalization, which focused on the ratio of: international students, courses taught in English, students who pass the General English Proficiency Test, and foreign faculty.
6. 2005–2010: TWAEA took charge of the task of university evaluation and quality assurance, focusing more on a university administrative perspective coupled with accountability of faculty and staff, students, and alumni.
7. 2011–2016: The second round will rotate and focus more on student-based learning outcomes with a more comprehensive system. A strategic plan integrating self-study and the benchmarking of quality improvement will be introduced to strengthen the whole school evaluation approach.

Above all, two key evaluation institutions should be mentioned: TWAEA, founded in 2003, for a technology university track, and the Higher Education Evaluation and Accreditation Council of Taiwan (HEEACT), established in 2006 for general universities, as a quasi-governmental agency to conduct university evaluations on a regular basis. In addition to conducting university evaluation tasks on a regular basis, these professional institutions also take part in tasks such as evaluation indicator development, evaluation personnel in-service training, and quality assurance research. These two organizations are also required to provide constructive evaluation reports for institutional improvement and recommendations to the MOE. The *University Law* entitles the MOE to allocate public funding to universities based on the above-mentioned evaluation results as reference (HEEACT 2012; TWAEA 2012; Please see: http://www.twaea.org.tw; www.heeact.edu.tw).

The HEEACT carried out its first round of nationwide evaluation at the departmental, graduate institution, and university level between 2006 and 2010. A total of 1,908 departments and graduate institutions out of 79 universities went through this evaluation process, which focused on the quality of universities, departments, and graduates. Reports on the evaluation results were released, and they aroused great social controversy and complaints from members of faculties and university administrations who were not satisfied with the outcomes. In particular, the study outcomes were highly correlated with public funding, institutional prestige, and student recruitment, which led to student shortages in some departments and universities in the years that followed. The study called for further clarification of the relationship between classification, accreditation, quality assurance, and institutional ranking, more clarification of the role of the MOE and the evaluation agencies, and more justification on the part of universities in terms of their results (Wu 2009).

The second round of national evaluations will start in 2011 and last until 2016, and will focus on student learning outcomes, followed by another round of whole school evaluations that will examine departments, graduate institutions, and universities from more comprehensive perspectives as well as delineate the features of each individual HEI. A framework consisting of plan, do, check, act (PDCA) will be included in the new cycle of evaluations, which focuses on indicators such as: institutional self-positioning, university governance and management, teaching and learning resources, accountability and social responsibility, and sustainable self-improvement and quality assurance (Wang 2010a).

The HEEACT indicated that six key decisions in the program evaluation process include (Wang 2010a): (1) What is the purpose of the evaluation? (2) Who will evaluate? (3) What questions need to be answered? (4) What and how will data be gathered? (5) How will the data be interpreted? and (6) How will the evaluation results be reported?

In pursuit of quality assurance for universities that is comparable to the global standard, Taiwan has established a mechanism of university evaluation and attempted to reach out to its international peers through a continuing exchange of dialogues, visits, and collaboration. Universities currently have a clearer path for setting goals and establishing more specific criteria for institutional improvement. One private university was even accredited by the American Middle States Commission on Higher Education (MSCHE), the first institution in Taiwan and Asia to be accredited since 2010, and this took place after a long series of self-assessment, candidate status, and self-study procedures.

On the other hand, with respect to individual faculty members, the establishment of another internal and external evaluation system is intended to monitor faculty publication records in various domestic and international databases such as the SCI, the SSCI, the Engineering Index (EI), and so forth. All of these new indicators serve as an effort to be in accordance with international standards that will lead to awards, achievements, and contributions to scholarship. The following example of "National Taiwan University Faculty Evaluation Policies" (amended in academic year 2005–2006) will demonstrate how the current evaluation system requlates faculty performance in details (National Taiwan University 2006):

- The evaluation policies are established in accordance with Article 21 of the University Act for the purpose of improving instruction, research, and service standards.
- All full-time faculty members must be evaluated on the basis of their teaching, research, and service endeavors.
- Evaluation of faculty members at all levels is based on a three- to five-year term according to their rank, employment starting date, and so forth.
- Faculty who disagree with the results of the evaluation may submit an appeal to the Faculty Grievances Committee.
- Faculty must pass the evaluation process in order to qualify for promotion, sabbatical, a raise in salary, a part-time job, to teach at other institutions, and for administrative positions.

Associate professors or professors who satisfy one of the following conditions shall be exempt from evaluation:

- Holding a fellowship from the Academic Sinica
- Holding MOE's Academic Award or National Chair Professorship
- Holding the position of chair/professor of a nationally or internationally renowned university
- Receiving an Outstanding Teaching Award (twice), or the Good Teaching Award (fifteen times) (one Outstanding Teaching Award is equivalent to eight Good Teaching Awards)
- Receiving one of NSC's various awards or research projects, or other teaching, research, or service awards, and so forth.

Although some faculty members may have to postpone the evaluation process for reasons such as childbirth, child rearing, or other major life events, they are eligible for late consideration of awards during the required period. These faculties will still have to undergo evaluation when appropriate.

In other words, a university evaluation policy is a top-down policy administered by the MOE to individual faculty by law, which requires not only regular institutional evaluation by the above-mentioned professional associations but also departmental assessment of the individual faculty member. Moreover, the evaluation results influence a faculty member's qualifications for promotion, salary, sabbatical leave, and extra duties related to teaching and promotion to administration. Evaluation can be waived only for recipients of awards at the national or international level.

All of these policies are an attempt to enhance university quality; however, more and more faculty members are falling victim to such evaluation criteria, which emphasize research more than teaching and performance in social capacities. In fact, faculty members across Taiwan have lost their jobs due to the failure to satisfy requirements for research performance or refusal to submit to an evaluation. One of the most controversial cases in Taiwan concerns a professor from a prestigious national university who was forced to leave due to his refusal to apply for self-evaluation. He had received two outstanding teaching awards on campus, and was recognized by his students. Yet he could not succeed in academia because he had published very few research articles, as well as failed to fulfill the university's requirement for self-evaluation. Thus, his case was vetoed twice, by the university and the MOE grievance committee. Nevertheless, his termination of employment generated nationwide student support (Wang 2010b).

It is expected that the process of evaluation will help universities to come up with a more concise and detailed plan to improve their core competence, course design, and educational goals. Basic student ability and learning achievement are at the core of the institutional evaluation. All the evaluation criteria such as the university role, management, teaching and learning resources, achievement and social responsibility, as well as improvement and quality assurance should be interwoven with student learning performance and incorporated as the first priority of university educational objectives (Chang 2011). After all, the purpose of university evaluation is to improve and assure educational quality based on self-positioning. Therefore, a framework such as the strengths, weaknesses, opportunities, and threats (SWOT) analysis and the PDCA cycle is widely applied, partly due to the need to comply with the expectations of evaluation agencies (Yen 2011).

Nevertheless, the evaluation process has been very time-consuming, and the mobility of human resources and money is overwhelming, according to university and staff involved (Peng 2010). Questions can also arise regarding the qualifications of the reviewers and the duration of on-site visits. Disagreement between university and evaluation commissioners over evaluation results has been a major concern to the stakeholders.

New System of Flexible Salary for Public Universities

The current seniority- and degree-based salary scale came to be regarded as insufficient to promote the necessary competitive environment among faculty that might lead to better teaching and research quality. Therefore, in order to enhance competitiveness among faculty members in HEIs, the government set in motion a competitive reward system, replacing the one described previously. The MOE, in conjunction with the academic sector, launched in August 2010 a possible solution to facilitate accountability and competition among HEIs and faculty and avoid a further brain drain and recruitment shortage of top international research personnel: the adoption of a flexible salary structure entitled "Recruit and retain special talented personnel implementing a flexible merit-based salary plan." This new plan will reward academic excellence based on performance over the past few decades and replace the old fixed-salary system for public university faculty based on seniority and degree (*Taipei Times* 2010).

According to the MOE, the total fixed salary (including a 1.5 month annual award) for a professor at a public university is between NT$1,350,000 and NT$112,5000 before taxes (US$45,000–37,500 in 2011) regardless of discipline. Professors in Hong Kong receive a 3.5 times higher salary, and in Singapore a 2.5 times higher salary than their American and European counterparts (Wang 2009). A recent migration of university professors away from Taiwan has caused serious concern in that country. In the case of Hong Kong, which is initiating a new system of a four-year university program, has recruited some top faculty from Taiwan by offering as an incentive two to three times the salary Taiwanese institutions offer (NowNews 2009). During the last eight years, a total of 27 research fellows have left the Academia Sinica, the top research institution in Taiwan, and were recruited by research institutions in the United States, Europe, and Hong Kong, while some prominent faculty from top universities of Taiwan also relocated to China, Canada, and other competing countries for various reasons (*China Post* 2010).

In responding to the global talent hunt and the issue of brain drain, the MOE drafted a blueprint to replace the existing salary structure (with one's salary based on one's degree and seniority) for university and academic institutions, and this plan has been in effect since August 2010. It is hoped that the new reward system will lead to the recruitment of top new staff at salaries competitive with international academic standards. It is estimated that the new system will require additional funding between NT$4 billion (US$125 million) and NT$5 billion a year from the MOE and the National Science Council (NSC) to attract top teaching and research personnel to Taiwan, while also discouraging faculty from leaving for other international institutions. This new plan also allows professors' salaries to be subsidized by the MOE's five-year-five-billion plan and teaching for excellence plan.

However, in light of the new flexible salary plan put in place by the government, many critics have expressed concern about the trend of increasing polarization and stratification that might follow the introduction of faculty salaries and benefits based on quantitative indicators, such as journal articles. The system has revealed an unequal distribution of salary increases between faculty in science and the humanities/social sciences, between top and mediocre HEIs, between public and private institutions, and especially between the activities of teaching and research. Complaints about the plan have resulted from the current oversimplified indicators of performance and meritocracy, which emphasize publication based on pure quantity rather than the quality and essence of performance with respect to teaching and other intangible contributions as well as the social impact on society.

The underlying assumption that Taiwan faculty are underpaid compared to their international counterparts, and that raising flexible income based on research performance will retain the best faculty and attract more top international personnel lacks legitimacy, as this notion deviates from the local context and overlooks the quid pro quo of the current academic salary structure. For instance, in addition to their annual base salary for twelve months, university faculty in Taiwan are granted more opportunities to obtain external income as compensation, owing to Taiwan's cultural heritage, which pays high respect to intellectuals and professors. Thus, university faculty (especially those working at public HEIs) also receive more fringe benefits from their consulting services in the public and private sectors, coupled with lifetime medical care and a pension, which are less common among their international competitors (Chou 2010).

Another issue is that the flexible salary system has a lower value for faculty in the areas of the humanities and social sciences, who publish less in the Social Sciences Citation Index (SSCI) and the Science Citation Index (SCI) than their counterparts in the natural sciences. Faculty members from two prestigious national universities with comparable student populations in Taiwan are treated differently according to the current rules of the game, in which only half of the faculty from the humanities and social sciences are granted this award, which is 50 percent less than their competitors with a science background. An increasing cultural and reward gap has worsened the existing unequal distribution of resources between the sciences and the social sciences as a result of the government's new scheme.

Another issue related to the plan is that the academic incentive pay system makes it far more complex and difficult to evaluate performance and accountability than in the past. As is the case with other professions, economic incentive is not the only factor that motivates faculty to accomplish goals and excel. Differences in level of performance in academia are large and contingent on circumstances. According to research, any tangible reward in the form of recognition, coupled with monetary rewards and promotions, will possibly yield productivity but will also require a strong intuitive appeal, such as self-motivation and dignity in accomplishing the achievement. Many academic faculty prefer the idea of the university paying them indirectly by improving the whole academic structure and environment rather than setting a flexible salary that only rewards the top "star researchers" for excelling, while the majority of faculty are devalued, owing to their assuming more responsibility for teaching and community service (Lin 2009) .

Although the trend of globalization is currently motivating every country to recruit talent and prevent a brain drain in its own academy, governments and universities are required to go beyond the myth of "money can talk, and the market will prevail." This is especially the case with Taiwan, whose academic system is facing both competition from global talent and also the local need for social transformation. A further restructuring process of the system of higher education will not only deal with salaries, but also take into the consideration the academic culture; the dynamics among government, the university, and the market; the revision of the current relatively low tuition fee; and the cultural expectations of students and the general public. In Taiwan, the introduction of this new reward system has resulted in a "winner takes all" attitude that creates mixed reactions and scrutiny from academic. .

Another phenomenon that deserves attention is the "double-income" syndrome among those retired public faculty who are recruited by private HEIs and then enjoy a double income both from their monthly pension and the new institutional salary. For the private HEIs, the recruitment of these retired senior faculty members can help not only to meet the quota of the full professor rank so as to fulfill evaluation criteria, but also obtain more resources via their existing networks and social prestige. This is even the case for several retired former Ministers of Education who were first hired as distinguished professors and then became private university presidents. These retirees frequently tend to be more likely to obtain public funding from the MOE and other sources for their HEIs. The question of favoritism between the government and certain private universities is a hidden agenda that has resulted partly from the market-driven system and structure in the name of accountability and global competition. In sum, the issue of whether university quality has been improved or not and who benefits from these new reform policies remains an open question in Taiwan.

References

Chang, Flora Jia-Yi. 2011. "Long-Term Administrative Development Experiences." *Higher Education, Technological and Vocational Education Newsletter 05*, February 10. Available online at: http://120.96.85.10.
Chen, Wei-Jao. 2002. *The New Development of University Governance*. Taiwan University Alumni Monthly. 23: 39–43.
Chou, Chuing Prudence. 2003. *The Great Experiment of Taiwanese Education: 1987–2003*. Taipei: Psychology Publishing.
———. 2008. "The Impact of Neo-Liberalism on Taiwanese Higher Education." *International Perspectives on Education and Society* 9: 297–311.
———. 2010. *Expectation of Academicians and Academic Sinica*. Hong Kong: China Review News. http://www.chinareviewnews.com.
Fiske, Edward B. 2004. *The Fiske Guide to Colleges 2003* Naperville, IL: Sourcebooks.
"Gov't Mulls Professor Salary Raise." 2010. *The China Post*, January 24. Available online at: http://www.chinapost.com.tw.
Higher Education Evaluation and Accreditation Council of Taiwan (HEEACT). 2012. *HEEACT Website*. Taipei: HEEACT. Available online at: http://www.heeact.edu.tw.
Lin, Shu-Duan. 2009 *A Study on the Flexible Salary Compensation System for National University Professors in Taiwan*. Unpublished master's thesis. Chia-yi, Taiwan: National Chung Cheng University.
Ministry of Education (MOE). 2010. *University Act*. Available online at: http://english.moe.gov.tw/content.asp?CuItem=8173&mp=1.
NowNews. 2009. *High Salary in Hong Kong*. Taipei: NowNews Network. Available online at: http://www.nownews.com.
Organisation for Economic Co-operation and Development (OECD). 2009. *Education at a Glance*. Paris: OECD.

Peng, Samuel. 2010. "How to Promote Grading of Student Achievement in University." *Evaluation Bimonthly*, 24: 28–24.
Taipei Times. 2010. "Academic Sector Proposes Flexible Salary for Experts." *Taipei Times*, January 1. http://www.taipeitimes.com.
Taiwan Assessment and Evaluation Association (TWAEA). 2012. *TWAEA Website*. Taipei: TWAEA. Available online at: http://www.twaea.org.tw.
Trow, Martin A. 2005. "Reflections on the Transition from Elite to Mass to Universal Access: Forms and Phases of Higher Education in Modern Societies since WWII." In *International Handbook of Higher Education*, edited by P. G. Altbach, 243–280. New York: Springer.
Tsai, Ching-Hwa. 1996. *The Deregulation of Higher Education in Taiwan*. Chestnut Hill, MA: Boston College. Available online at: http://www.bc.edu.
Wang, Bao-jin. 2010a. "University Evaluation Based on the Whole School Evaluation Approach." *Bimonthly Evaluation*, 23.
Wang, Tsai-Li. 2009. *Salary of Assistant Professor Is Lower Than Those Who Teach in Primary/Junior High School*. Taipei: United Daily News Group. http://mag.udn.com.
Wu, Chris C. 2009. *Higher Education Expansion in Taiwan: The Problems Faced*. Taipei: National Taiwan Normal University. Available online at: http://cve.ntnu.edu.tw.
Wang, Wei-ling. 2010b *It Is about Time for University Faculty to Be Alert Thanks to the Strict Evaluation System*. Taipei: United News. Available online at: http://mag.udn.com.

Chapter 11

World-Class Research University Project

Higher-education institutions (HEIs) in Taiwan are, on the one hand, expected and obligated to represent the identity of the nation and the individuality of the institution. On the other hand, they exist in the market of global competition as a result of internationalization, globalization, and "marketization" in the Asia-Pacific region. Asian countries such as China, Hong Kong, Japan, Korea, and Singapore are establishing world-class universities. These countries are trying to improve their national and international profiles by recruiting more international students and faculty.

As noted, with the lifting of martial law in 1987 and the revision to the *University Law* in 1994, the traditionally government-dominated higher-education system was redesigned to reduce the power of the Ministry of Education (MOE) over HEIs, so that campus operations could be more flexible and autonomous. The relaxation of legal restrictions that had bound higher education in the past has helped to promote a more diversified system, allowing for greater autonomy in appointing presidents, charging tuition fees (to some extent), offering courses, and recruiting students. Since then, higher education in Taiwan has entered a new era.

Since Taiwan joined the World Trade Organization (WTO) in 2001, the increasing need to incorporate the globalization process into the system of higher education, such as through cross-cultural interactions, student exchanges, and university faculty international competition, has led to even greater pressure to take advantage of this irreversible trend in higher education. In an era of rapid advancements in science and technology and the revolution in information and communications technology, Taiwanese universities have been called on to play a central role in knowledge-based economic development. Taiwan's HEIs are expected to enter another stage of transformation in the near future, not only through meeting the government's and the market's external requirements to produce human resources, but also through competing with other institutions on the international stage.

The national government in Taiwan has made higher education a strategic priority as a way to reinforce its global competitiveness and knowledge-based economy, and has endeavored to build the capacity of top universities, particularly prestigious public institutions. In an attempt to provide universities with more incentives for pursuing excellence and to offset the declining quality of universities due to rapid expansion and public budget cuts, the MOE first promoted the World-Class Research University Project in 2003. Then, in 2005 the MOE launched another policy entitled the Higher Education for Excellence Plan, which provided NT$5 billion (approximately US$1.6 billion) to twelve Taiwanese HEIs over a span of five years, from 2005 to 2010, with the goal of creating a higher-education system of excellence, adapting to the changing trends of the future, and producing great leaders. In so doing, the MOE seeks to establish top universities in the hope of improving fundamental development; integrating human resources from different departments, disciplines, and universities; and establishing research centers for pioneering specialized interests. In the long run, the MOE has the goal of raising the national level of education, which will in turn increase national competitiveness. Follow-up evaluation programs have been implemented throughout the process to control outcomes.

Among its goals, the Higher Education for Excellence Plan seeks to make Taiwan one of the world's top-ten leaders in internationally published research papers, hire exceptional foreign instructors and researchers, increase the number of international students, increase the number of copyrights as well as the number of new natural species (plants or animals) created or discovered by Taiwanese universities and researchers, and so on. Schools that receive funding through the plan must make sufficient progress in these areas and pass various evaluations in order to remain a part of the plan. So far, the Higher Education for Excellence Plan seems to have made significant progress as shown in clear evidence of increased publication numbers, the number of foreign faculty members and students, and many other criteria.

Four years after the Higher Education for Excellence Plan was put into place, participating Taiwanese universities showed vast improvement (MOE 2009). In the QS World University Rankings of 2009, National Taiwan University (NTU) made it into the top-one hundred ranking for the first time at 95th place.

On the other hand, questions such as whether the Higher Education for Excellence Plan is actually beneficial for the Taiwanese people have also been raised (He 2008). Is the effort to transform Taiwanese colleges and universities into institutions worthy of international acclaim really being done with the intention to help every Taiwanese student, or is it only aimed at making Taiwan look better on the international stage? Does putting such a large amount of funding into a small number of elite schools sacrifice students who are attending other institutions? The Higher Education for Excellence Plan is clearly helping institutions to make progress, but to many observers, the benefits it is producing are still in doubt.

This project was renewed for the second round in 2011, and in addition to past requirements, universities are now mandated to establish an internal and external evaluation system employing diverse indicators such as the Science Citation Index (SCI), the Social Science Citation Index (SSCI), the Engineering Index (EI), and so forth, to be in accordance with standards that meet international recognition for awards, achievements, and contributions within researchers' field of expertise. To encourage more self-improvement in terms of accountability rather than comparison with international counterparts, the second round of the Higher Education for Excellence Plan has been revised somewhat to accommodate local needs and the university's goals.

The MOE is currently aiming for a minimum of ten world-class disciplines and research centers nationwide by 2016. Furthermore, it seeks to improve the applicable degree of value in university research to better assist the national development of industry and technology. Those new entrants and applicants must fulfill a minimum of three of the following criteria: (1) 85 percent full-time faculty personnel hold the rank of assistant professor and above, (2) the student-teacher ratio must remain under twenty-five, (3) research citations must rank in the top 1 percent in the world, at least during the last eleven years, and (4) departments and graduate institutions must have a 90 percent evaluation passing rate.

This five-year plan, called the Top University Plan, is the second phase of the five-year-fifty-billion plan, and will be carried out from January 1, 2011, to December 31, 2015 (MOE 2006).

Goals:

1. To accelerate the internationalization of top universities and expand the worldview of students
2. To improve the quality of universities' research and innovation, and strengthen the power of their international academic impact and the visibility of Taiwan's internationally published papers
3. To recruit and nurture talented personnel actively and enrich national human resources

4. To strengthen industry-university cooperation, promote industrial upgrading, and enhance national competitiveness
5. To respond to the needs of the society and industries, and cultivate top talented personnel in higher education

Selection Criteria:

1. At least ten world-class research centers or areas: the term "world-class" is defined as top-ten rated international papers published in leading journals worldwide or presented at international conferences. It can also be replaced by evaluation indicators selected by universities and approved by the Application Review Committee.
2. Total of 25 percent growth (annual 5 percent growth on average) in full-time faculties and research staffs recruited from overseas
3. Total of 100 percent growth (annual 20 percent growth on average) in number students pursuing degrees and in international exchange students
4. Total increase of two hundred academicians/fellows affiliated with domestic and worldwide academic institutions (annual forty persons on average) on full-time faculties
5. Total of 50 percent growth (annual 10 percent growth on average) in papers that have been HiCi (High Citation) in the last 10 years
6. Total of 100 percent growth (annual 20 percent growth on average) in number of faculty members and students engaged in short-term research, study exchanges, or pursuing a double degree (double major) overseas
7. Total of 100 percent growth (annual 20 percent growth on average) in all English programs
8. Total of 50 percent growth (annual 10 percent growth on average) in industry-university cooperative funding from nongovernment sectors
9. Total of 2,500 pieces (annual 500 pieces on average) of research and development (R&D) patents and new inventions
10. Total of 100 percent growth (annual 20 percent growth on average) in income from Copyright and Intelligence Property

Commentary on the Five-Year-Five-Billion Plan

It is obvious that the nation's higher-education policies and projects, for example, the five-year-five-billion plan, depend greatly on quantified indicators such as the SCI, the EI, and the SSCI. For example, the National Science Council (NSC) is one of the two most important funding-supplying and policy-promoting units in Taiwan. The indicators mentioned above were introduced by MOE in early 2000 to strengthen the objectives and efficiency of evaluation. However, the determination of the quality of academic papers should be fulfilled through practical evaluative mechanisms rather than these indicators, even if they are the SCI, the EI, or the SSCI. The MOE determined that an efficient and fair evaluating mechanism for allocating educational resources is required given the continuous expansion in the number of universities and the reduction in educational funds. In addition, even as it implemented deregulation and restricted HEIs' autonomy, the MOE continued to establish other allocation mechanisms for competitive funding in order to upgrade the quality of higher education. In so doing, the MOE largely included more quantifiable indicators and requested the total quantity of papers published yearly in indexes such as the SCI, the EI, and the SSCI as a basis of comparison and assessment.

In 2003, the MOE released an official intercollegiate ranking of papers published in international academic journals, which led to protests from universities/colleges of the humanities and social sciences headed by the National Cheng Chi University (NCCU). However, although the NSC and the MOE are unable to consider the overall value of academic achievements by adopting only quantifiable indicators, the method is now fairer and more accurate than previously, when there is no a standard for evaluation. Moreover, since the policy of adopting quantified indicators was implemented, the quantity of academic research at every university has indeed increased remarkably. To put it concretely, the current higher-education evaluating mechanism can be summed up in five phenomena (Wang et al. 2008):

1. Before adopting quantified indicators: There was not any reasonable standard for funding allocation, except for the general rules of public universities rather than private universities, and departments of science and technology rather than departments of humanities and social science. The adoption of quantified indicators, including the SCI, the EI, the SSCI, and the Taiwan Social Sciences Citation Index (TSSCI) helps insure orientation and a more thorough evaluation, and makes the decision process transparent.
2. Regarding academic research: Academic groups in all divisions face the same situation, which is that there are neither shared professional values nor a professional ethic. This situation also gave rise to the difficulty of professional examination; therefore, quantified

indicators were introduced to resolve disputes regarding academic appraisal.
3. Higher-education quality: Since the government promoted reform of higher education and implemented policies like the expansion and deregulation of universities/colleges, the number of universities has increased and the degree of intercollegiate competition has risen. Yet, higher education quality has not improved relative to expectations. The academic chaos mentioned in point 2 is thought to be one of the reasons for this.
4 .Educational administration: Though both the MOE and the NSC function as the administration for higher education and have the ability to establish relevant policies, they cannot so easily solve the problems of the quality of the nation's higher education and its academic research.
5. Attitude of universities and colleges: The MOE bases funding allocation on the quantity of international papers produced by faculty; therefore, universities and colleges encourage their faculties to have their published papers listed in prominent international indexes (such as SSCI, SCI, EI) by offering various incentives such as subsidies or a reduction of teaching hours. Thus, professors become paper-producing machines and are involved in complex relationships with different academic groups. In these circumstances, more attention is paid to the number of international publications rather than the quality of teaching, which as an impact not only on students' rights but also the goals of academic development.

In reference to point 5, the number of papers from Taiwan that are published in the SCI, the EI, and the SSCI has increased; however, the citation rate by international scholars is relatively low. According to a 1997 article in *Nature*, an international weekly journal of science, which examined the international impact of Taiwan's academic research, the country's Relative Citation Index (RCI) from 1981 to 1994 was 0.35, even lower than the Philippines (0.58), Thailand (0.52), Hong Kong (0.51), and Indonesia (0.47). Moreover, data from the International Statistical Institute (ISI) indicated that Taiwan's total published international papers ranked at number 21, but that the average citation rate ranked at number 96 out of a total of 149 countries. In the case of Finland, however, although its total published international papers ranked at number 24, lower than Taiwan, its average citation rate ranked at number 21, which is to say that Finland's academic papers possess a much greater impact than Taiwan's. Unfortunately, Taiwan's scholarship has not risen in the rankings even today.

According to the MOE's statistics during 2005–2009, Taiwan's SCI papers ranked at number seventeen, which was 10 ranks higher than Finland. However, Taiwan's and Finland's SCI impact was 3.37:6.21, which indicates that two-fifths of Taiwan's papers were not cited, while one-fifth of Finland's papers were not cited (MOE 2010). Taiwas has been long accustomed to the current situation, such as the repetitive nature of academic research studies, especially in the social science fields. It is clear that this is the main reason why Taiwan cannot upgrade its academic impact at the international level.

If we take Japan's situation as a reference point, we see that Japan, like the United States, does not depend on quantifiable indicators such as the SCI and the SSCI, but rather makes a professional evaluation on a practical basis, according to a researcher's various academic achievements. The quantity of published papers is only for reference, especially in the fields of economics, management, business, and so on. Furthermore, Japanese scholars cite publications from other fields and review these documents to enrich their own work in their subspecialties and make it more extensive, profound, and systematic. In the field of management, for example, there are many scholars in Japan who dedicate themselves to doing research in management history, economic history, the developing history of industry, and so forth. Though there are also traces of westernization in various types of Japanese research, compared to Taiwan, researchers in Japan also pay more attention to their own history and culture. In Japanese academic circles, related research and development keep attracting attention and accumulating continuously, and thus there is consistency in every field.

As many scholars have noted, upgrading Taiwan's international scholarship and the impact it has can be accomplished by focusing on subject matter that is related to the nation's identity and background, engaging in in-depth research over the long-term, and attempting to integrate Western theory with Taiwanese research. In this way, not only will Taiwan's international influence rise but a unified professional ethic and common views will also be developed.

As Hwang (2010) mentioned in his article "The Publication of Papers and a Country's Competitiveness in a Globalizing World," after the financial crisis in 2008, world capitalism could not help but adjust to becoming a multipolar world economic system. The question arises as to whether Taiwan will occupy a position in this newly formed world and survive. The key to achieving this goal is based on the possibility of local academic research studies (which are mostly based on university specializations) being conducted to help support local industries. Due to the expansion of higher education in the past ten years, the nation's institutions of higher learning have stepped onto the universal stage. In terms of the numbers of its institutions, Taiwan ranks among the top few worldwide, and its system absorbs almost all Taiwanese students between ages eighteen and twenty-two. The number of published papers listed in the SCI and the SSCI has been taken as a main indicator in evaluating the research achievements of faculty, and this has resulted in a formal recognition that "quantity talks" in Taiwan's academic research. If we take the total annual number of published papers of each country as an indicator of the "quantity" of its academic production, and the average number of index citations as a country's indicator of "quality," we find that Taiwan's "quantity" of published papers surpasses those of European countries such as Finland and Ireland, which are of a similar size to Taiwan. Yet the index citation rate of Taiwan's scholarly papers is at the same level as that of other Southeast Asian countries, including Thailand, the Philippines, and Indonesia.

Scientific research in countries with advanced technology is more original and innovative. The required experimental equipment or crucial scientific measuring instruments are usually designed or made by the researchers themselves. Taiwan's scientific research groups, however, lack the relevant training in the philosophy of science to accomplish this. Therefore, most researchers follow the research models of Western technologically advanced countries and pursue research of the "follow-up" type. They usually apply for a large amount of funding to purchase expensive instruments and set up costly labs in universities. Yet they use those expensive instruments rarely and produce few results in the end. Moreover the research topics that they investigate do not usually coincide with the nation's orientation toward technological development.

If Taiwan is to raise the status of its scholarly research, it is urgent that the country restructures the National Educational Research Preparatory Office into an independent institution of policy research and educational evaluation and, in coordination with the NSC, set up a multifaceted evaluation standard to satisfy the local universities, including in the fields of humanities, social sciences, and vocational education. By evaluating its institutions of higher education based on a technology assessment, strengthening cooperation among industries, and placing more value on the quality of research rather than the quantity of published papers, Taiwan will begin to solve the problems of its society.

The shift of more and more faculty jobs from private HEIs to public ones, and from general to top universities has resulted in ethical and loyalty issues in Taiwan. This trend has created some contradictions, because HEIs are supposed to work as a platform for the creation of new knowledge, serving the public as an intellectual agent of social criticism. Universities often take the lead or rise above the social rules, and their work is far more complex and unique than the mass production of standardized answers from lab experiments or the input-and-output model. They pride themselves on their capability to initiate new rules of the game rather than follow "the other" existing social norms.

Nevertheless, as a result of more rules and guidelines, such as the five-year-five-billion plan, the world-class university project, teaching for excellence, and university evaluation policies, which are issued top down from the central government, increasing numbers of faculty have surrendered their unique and critical outlooks to bureaucratic attitudes. In the name of accountability and standardized procedures, many faculty members are required to compete for research funds through their project applications. They are buried in the paperwork and data for budget applications and spend their time and money purchasing expensive scientific facilities for their research rather than being creative and thinking critically in their academic life (Yu Hui Liao 2010). This new mechanism of "perform and reward," though it encourages faculty to be more responsive to demands for public accountability, has also impaired potential scholars' freedom and autonomy. Most of the so-called top faculty nowadays are driven to write a research project for the sake of winning a grant, and are then forced to use their budget within a certain period of time. Faculty in the social sciences and humanities are especially constrained within this system, where old rules do not fit the new era of the dominant market–driven value (Yuan Hao Liao 2010).

References

He, Zhuo Fei. 2008. "A Study on the Strategic Management and Performance Evaluation of the 'Development Plan for World Class Universities and Research Centers for Excellence' in Taiwan." PhD diss., Tamkang University, Taipei, Taiwan.

Hwang, Guang Guo. 2010. *Paper Publications and Country's Competitiveness in a Globalizing World*. Taipei: National Central Library. Available online at: http://www.ncl.edu.tw.

Liao, Yu Hui. 2010. *Myth of Evaluation*. Taipei: My Formosa. Available online at: http://www.my-formosa.com.

Liao, Yuan Hao. 2010. "Top Universities Can Be Good at Neither Literature Nor Martial Arts." *Common Wealth Magazine* (June), 448. Available online at: http://mypaper.pchome.com.tw.

Ministry of Education (MOE). 2006. *Plan to Develop First-Class Universities and Top-Level Research Centers*. Taipei: MOE.

———. 2009. *Higher Education for Excellence Plan*. Taipei: MOE.

———. 2010. *Overview SCI*. Taipei: MOE. Available online at http://www.edu.tw.

Wang, Huei Huang, Su Ke Ye, and Zheng Zhao Li. 2008. "Evaluation Policy on Higher Education Reform." Unpublished research report. Taipei: MOE.

Chapter 12

Internationalization Efforts of Taiwan's Higher Education Institutions

Within the last decade, Taiwan's higher-education system has experienced transformation along the lines of decentralization and marketization (Mok 2000). Following the 1994 revision of the *University Act*, which prompted the restructuring of state-owned higher-education institutions (HEIs) into independent legal entities (Mok 2006), thereby reducing the control of the Ministry of Education (MOE) and making campus operations more flexible, Taiwan's government acknowledged that the state alone cannot satisfy the pressing demand for higher education and decided to create room for the expansion of private higher education (Mok 2000; Mok and James 2005). This step sparked growth in the number of HEIs over recent decades. This sudden increase in the numbers of HEIs not only generated competition among universities and colleges, but also hastened the internationalization of these institutions.

Formation of Taiwan's HEI Internationalization Indicators

"Internationalization" is a term being used more and more to discuss the international dimension of higher education. The word represents different meanings to different people, and is thus used in a variety of ways (Knight 2006b). While it is encouraging to see the term used more frequently and to realize more attention is being paid to the phenomenon of internationalization, it is also important to measure the performance of this process.[1]

It is difficult to make generalizations about the priorities, rationales, and trends in the internationalization process taking place in Taiwan's HEIs based on their websites. And yet, one can conclude that most Taiwan HEIs preferred to start with a successful internationalization plan (Rudzki 1995a). Currently, Taiwan's MOE has prioritized university internationalization, not only in terms of financial resources but also in the facilitation of educational reforms. Policies include calls for first-class universities and the subsequent start of the evaluation of HEIs by the Higher Education Evaluation and Accreditation Council of Taiwan (HEEACT). These efforts have subseque led to a debate on whether performance indicators overly emphasize global standards or whether international benchmarks are dominated by Western traditions and practices (Lo and Weng 2005; Mok 2006, 2007; Mok et al. 2008).

Although international students and faculties do play an important role in contributing to the internationalization of an institution, a firm administrative initiative and a strong curriculum program are also in great demand. While Taiwan's HEIs are recruiting more and more international students and faculties, and setting up more international programs, the majority of international faculties in Taiwan are still limited to language-related programs.

Several studies showed that indicators such as institutional leadership and organizational support systems are crucial in attaining the internationalization of an institution (Marden and Engerman 1992; Ellingboe 1998; Paige and Mestenhauser 1999; Mestenhauser 2002; Paige 2003). In addition, a focus was especially placed on curriculum programs that aim to provide learning opportunities that are intercultural, interdisciplinary, comparative, global, and integrative in nature (Paige 2005). Similarly, faculty and student involvement in international activities is highly regarded as an indicator that leads to a more international identity.

These findings also highlighted two global case studies written for UNESCO. Neave (1992a, 1992b) lays out two paradigmatic models of internationalization: one a leadership-driven model, and the other a base unit-driven model, which pinpoint the importance of administrative structures and strategic planning. Similarly, studies by the International Association of Universities (IAU) placed the main focus on the practices, priorities, issues, and trends related to the international dimension of higher education (Knight 2003, 2005). In the study, more than sixty-six countries in every region took part in the initial survey in 2003, and approximately ninety-five countries participated in the 2005 survey. The findings suggest that organizational support systems and institutional policies are important indicators in facilitating the internationalization of HEIs The results are similar to the case of Taiwan, where HEIs are gradually expanding their international support system into an independent division within the institution.

In the United States, the American Council for Education (ACE) has been very active in conducting studies pertaining to internationalization and has been one of the most influential higher-education organizations in this area (Paige 2005). These studies mentioned six key dimensions of internationalization that are used to measure and distinguish high activity in U.S. universities from other, less active institutions (Green and Olson 2003; Green 2005; Green et al. 2008). These were follow-up studies based on Siaya (2003) and Hayward (2000) that mapped U.S. students and reports on internationalization in higher education. The key dimensions include: articulated commitment, academic offerings, organizational infrastructure, external funding, institutional investment in faculty, and international students and student programs. In addition, Altbach and Knight (2007) reminded us of the importance of including mechanisms for accountability, monitoring, and the evaluation of internationalization efforts, which confirmed Mestenhauser's (2002) earlier suggestion.

The Association of Universities and Colleges of Canada (AUCC) (1995a, 1999, 2007) also identified institutional and academic policies, research and collaborative opportunities, and an international curriculum as some of the key dimensions in the internationalization of Canadian HEIs. The AUCC (1995b) further mentioned that performance indicators should be problem oriented and policy relevant so that decisions can be taken to improve university education. Progress and improvement in the delivery of education is the ultimate benchmark. Bartell (2003) also added as a key factor the importance of the existing culture within an institution, which emphasizes institutional commitments and strategic planning.

Internationalization Indicators of Taiwan's HEIs

According to the *Ministry of Education Award for University Faculty to Promote Internationalization Plan* (MOE 2009), Taiwan's HEIs are encouraged to recruit foreign (international) students, promote international exchanges, and upgrade universities' international competitiveness. The plan aims to facilitate university internationalization by identifying institutional strength and a strategic plan, increasing the enrollment ratio of foreign students, strengthening curriculum reform, and enhancing international cooperation and collaboration.

Beyond the MOE's policy plan, scholars have also tried to design indicators based on empirical grounds. The proposed higher-education internationalization index for Taiwan comprises twelve indicators (Chin and Ching 2009). These are the synthesized findings from the forty-six studies that were reviewed, combined with the interview results. The indicators are: institutional commitments, strategic planning, funding, institutional policy and guidelines, organizational infrastructure and resources, academic offerings and curriculum, Internet presence, faculty and staff development, international students and scholars, study abroad, campus life, and performance evaluation and accountability.

Institutional Commitments consist of articulated dedication to internationalization efforts, such as remarks included in the mission and vision statements and reiterated in the institution's prospectus or student recruitment literature (Green 2005; Green et al. 2008). This also includes support provided by top administrative leadership, which is critical to the success of the institution's work toward internationalization (Neave 1992a, 1992b; Davies 1995, 1997; Ellingboe 1998). In addition, the institution's efforts to join HEI organizations, whether locally or internationally, are also included.

Strategic Planning is the long- and short-term plans for internationalization of the institution, departments, faculty, and students. This includes an internationalization timeline, which highlights plans to establish branches and seek partnerships with both the academic community and private industry. A good strategic plan is an indispensable part of the process of internationalization (Paige 2005). Strategic plans should be based on the institution's mission, goals, or objectives, and should also serve as a rallying standard internally and indicate the institution's intentions to external constituencies (Davies 1995, 1997).

Funding represents the effort that institutions put forth to seek funds specifically earmarked for internationalization activities from organizations, government, and other private entities.

Institutional Policy and Guidelines include faculty policies and guidelines regarding hiring, rewards, sanctions, and codes of conduct. They also include student policies and guidelines related to admission, rewards, sanctions, and opportunities. The focus of institutional policy and guidelines is to ensure equality with regards to opportunity and benefits among local and international students and scholars.

Organizational Infrastructure and Resources indicate the availability of a support system for the process of internationalization. This includes physical facilities such as office space, human resources such as professionals and staff, and communication and technological resources. The presence of professional staff and personnel responsible for specific aspects of internationalization is considered as extremely important for achieving a more international academic culture. In many countries, international activities are now recognized as highly specialized activities that require professional staff with proper academic training and years of experience in international education (Paige 2005).

Academic Offerings and Curriculum are considered to be among the most important facets of an institution's efforts to become more international. Almost all of the studies reviewed here mentioned the importance of international academic programs. The availability of professional language courses and staff responsible for international curriculum development are key items in this indicator.

Internet Presence is the easy availability of important information on an institution's website. This includes links to international liaison or foreign-student admission offices, and bilingual information regarding important dates, fees, and news. Clear information on admission requirements, together with programs and course offerings, should be easy to find on the institution's Web page. This indicator is particularly important for East Asian nations, in which English is not spoken as a first language. In order to attract international students, it is imperative to have accessible bilingual information. This indicator serves as the window and gateway of HEIs in Taiwan to the rest of the world.

Faculty and Staff Development are the availability of support given to local personnel for collaboration, research, conferences, and other activities related to internationalization. Faculty involvement is the key to this process (Green 2005), as faculty members have the most direct contact with students and are responsible for the curriculum. In addition, the classroom remains the primary means by which to expose students to international issues, events, and cultures. This indicator measures the professional development opportunities available to faculty and staff members, opportunities that help them increase their international skills and knowledge.

International Students and Scholars relate to the availability of funds, scholarships, housing, office spaces, facilities, and other support systems. This category also includes student and language partners for international students, which helps newcomers settle in easily and helps promote intercultural activities.

Study Abroad is the availability of academic and nonacademic travel programs. In addition, it includes options for travel subsidies, orientation, and a campus facility at which international students and Taiwanese students planning to study abroad can share experiences.

Campus Life is the availability of academic and extracurricular activities geared towards international themes. This includes the presence of a campus-life office and officer and the availability of organizations or clubs with international themes. This indicator focuses on making the campus life of both local and international students and scholars more accessible and comfortable.

Performance Evaluation and Accountability is the availability of a monitoring system by which both internal and external performance evaluations are conducted. This includes a committee that reports on and makes recommendations for the improvement of the institution's efforts to become more international, and also identifies research and studies on internationalization. This indicator focuses on the importance of assessing and enhancing the quality of an HEI's international dimension, which is evaluated according to its stated aims and objectives.

Taiwan's HEI Internationalization Studies

Other studies that discuss the internationalization of Taiwan's HEIs were also noted. Huang and Chang (2004) explored the internationalization indicators of domestic college students extensively and chose Shu-Te University as a case study. The authors categorized efforts to become international into four types, namely: International Organization, International Business, International Experience, and International Media. Results show that students at Shu-Te University do indeed recognize these four types of indicators. In addition, the study also mentioned the importance of an international curriculum and foreign-language studies. Similarly, Wang, Hsiao, and Ping (2006) mentioned that the internationalization process in Taiwan is driven by increased international trade, the wider availability of capital, improvements in communication, a more international approach to education, and the transfer of technological and managerial skills. Indicators such as an international-oriented curriculum and the presence of international students and scholars are trends that are commonly found in Taiwan's HEIs.

Chen (2007) used the competing values framework in studying the internationalization of HEIs in Taiwan. Results show that quality assurance and accountability measures are needed to ensure a balance among these institutions. Indicators mentioned in this study are the presence of international students and scholars, institutional policies and guidelines, an international curriculum, and performance evaluation and accountability. Hsu (2007) observed that HEIs in Taiwan are experiencing the pressure of global competitiveness. In addition, efforts to make these institutions more international are mostly patterned and modeled on features that have been established according to the advantages of Western developed countries. With English being the predominant language, other indicators such as scientific research output, qualitative and quantitative academic indicators, or even the numbers of Nobel laureates produced are all favorable to Western countries.

Lu (2007) also mentioned that the major strengths generated by a more international approach to higher education in Taiwan depend on the vigorous support and drive of the administration. The major weakness of Taiwan's HEIs is due to its peripheral role in attracting international students, a less adaptive attitude to global changes, and lack of faculty incentives. Chiang (2008) did another comparative analysis between internationalization strategies and the actual implementation of such strategies. Results show that strategic planning is definitely an important indicator of internationalization. However, any progress after implementation is still in its early stages. Taiwan's HEIs should actively pursue efforts (with concrete actions) that will lead them to best meet the demands of internationalization.

Finally, Chen (2009) examined internationalization indicators in five public and private universities in Taiwan, among which six elements were identified, including: faculty, students, international research, international course programs, international visibility, and internationalization of the administration on campus. Additional results showed that the mechanism for evaluating the efforts to make Taiwan's HEIs more international is still not adequate. Furthermore, the current existing indicators lack an international vision directed toward students and courses, and therefore their accuracy and appropriateness are quite disputable (Chen 2009).

Internationalization Rationales of Taiwan's HEIs

More recently, the concept of internationalization has become a key element in shaping and challenging the higher-education sector in countries all over the world (Knight 2007; Mok 2000, 2006). During the last decade, internationalization has increased in importance, impact, and complexity (Altbach and Knight 2007; Knight 2007). Knight (2009) recently mentioned that there are new actors, new rationales, new programs, new regulations, and a new context of globalization. According to the results of the 2005 IAU survey, there is strong agreement (96 percent of responding institutions from 95 countries) that internationalization brings benefits to higher education (Knight 2005, 2006a). However, this consensus is qualified by the fact that 70 percent also believe there are substantial risks associated with the international dimension of higher education (Knight 2005, 2006a). Janez Potocnik, who is the European Union Commissioner for Science and Research, observed that progress in research and development (R&D) due to globalization and internationalization is only one side of the coin. There is also much risk, such as the unfair advantages that certain areas of the world have, and the disadvantages that others have. The brain drain of skilled European researchers is also perceived as a rising problem in academia (Potocnik 2005). Other issues that may arise, which have been widely acknowledged, include commercialization, foreign degree mills, and a growing elitism (Knight 2005, 2006a, 2008).

Efforts to internationalize higher education may pose many challenges in the future, with the trends of commercialization and commodification potentially seen as threats to human development, and research and national potential seen as benefits (Altbach and Knight 2007; Knight 2005, 2008). The risks seem to relate more to the cross-border aspects of internationalization than to campus-based activities. It is somewhat surprising that both developing and developed countries identified commercialization as a more important risk than brain drain (Knight 2005, 2006a).

In the 2005 IAU report mentioned above, it is also informative that the demise of cultural or national identity, the endangered quality of higher education, and the homogenization of curriculum were identified as the least important risks (Knight 2005, 2006a). These findings agree with Lobelle's (2008) case study of a Belgian university, which showed the risk of students leaving their home country and seeking employment or continuing their studies somewhere else. This sudden trend of student mobility had caused policies related to foreign students to shift from an aid approach to a trade rationale in many countries (Smart and Ang 1993), with such actions signaling that cross-border education is a commodity of free trade rather than a public responsibility (Kirp 2003).

The 2005 IAU report also noted some changes in the results since the previous survey, taken in 2003. In the new report, Asia replaced North America as Europe's second choice for international collaboration, and North America slipped to third. (Other European countries are the first choice.). Furthermore, in the same report, distance education ranks as one of the three least-active elements of internationalization, a change from 2003, when it was identified as one of the fastest-growing aspects. Given these shifts, the market for international students has become a dynamic growth industry sustained by universities, government agencies, private corporations, and entrepreneurs motivated by financial profit

(Altbach 2003). National governments are interested in sustaining active involvement through their ministries or departments of education or dedicated promotional agencies (Kemp 1995), which capitalize on the benefits of international student populations as linked to skills migration, economic growth, public diplomacy, and research associated with a knowledge society (Kishun 2007).

To internationalize an HEI is to implement university-wide reforms (Mok 2000, 2003, 2006; Altbach and Knight 2007). Comprehensive internationalization means a revamping of attitudes, resources, and policy (Aguilar 2002). However, most studies mentioned that an international approach is still not integrated into the mainstream of higher education (Knight 2003, 2005, 2006a). Presently, it is largely marginal to institutional plans of development, and it is often the first reform to be eliminated in a time of financial constraints. Moreover, the attitude of HEIs towards internationalization has proven to be the greatest barrier to its implementation, even more significant than financial restrictions. Aguilar (2002) mentioned that the absence of a concept for an international approach among the various stakeholders seems to be an obstacle that is intrinsic to the internationalization process. In addition, the lack of institutional policies, strategies, and priorities related to internationalization (incentives, financial resources, legislation), and the lack of national policies encouraging a more international outlook as a top priority for institutions of higher education are also deemed as barriers to such reform.

Many scholars would claim that in the last decade they have witnessed a dramatic movement of ideas supporting internationalization toward the notion of an income-production society. In other words, HEIs are more focused on the financial benefits of internationalization. While this trend might be true for a small group of countries, it is certainly not the case for the majority of institutions around the world. A more accurate description is that more diverse rationales are driving internationalization at institutional and national levels. The leading motivations for this approach still focus on enhancing the international knowledge and intercultural skills of students and professors, but other goals include the creation of an international profile or brand, improving quality, increasing national competitiveness, strengthening research capacity, developing human resources, and diversifying faculties and student populations.

The reasons for internationalizing higher education in general are numerous and varied. The rationales may be changing and at the same time closely linked to each other; they may be both complementary and contradictory, especially as they can differ according to the interests of diverse stakeholder groups (Knight 2004). An examination of the motivation for internationalizing the higher-education sector is a complex task;

however, the reasons for reforming HEIs to be more international in scope can be categorized into four groups: political, economic, academic, and sociocultural (de Wit 2002).

The rationale most relevant to Taiwan's efforts to internationalize its institutions of higher education is to raise academic standards and quality, followed by the desire to strengthen research collaboration, improve knowledge capacity and production, foster international and intercultural understanding, and encourage student exchanges and mobility. These results clearly indicate that the process of internationalizing the HEIs in Taiwan is mostly perceived as an academic approach, which is directly linked to enhancing the teaching and learning process and achieving excellence in research and scholarly activities (de Wit 2002). In addition, these results also suggest the importance of preparing internationally knowledgeable and interculturally competent students.

Among the perceived national rationales for pursuing internationalization in Taiwan, the most relevant items are: increased competitiveness (scientific, technological, and economic), global recognition, and to promote international solidarity and cooperation, all of which are closely related to an economic and political approach. The economic rationale has increasing importance and relevance in Taiwan and other developed countries around the world. Under the impact of globalization and the advancement of technology, countries are focusing on their economic, scientific, and technological competitiveness (Altbach 2005). Therefore, an effective way to improve and maintain a competitive edge is to develop a highly skilled and knowledgeable international work force and to invest in applied research (Knight 2003, 2004, 2005).

In addition, the political rationale is often considered more important at the national than at the institutional level, because the internationalization of higher education has historically been seen as a tool for foreign policy, especially with respect to national security and peace among nations (Knight and de Wit 1995; Knight 1997; de Wit 2002). Last, both the economic and political approaches involve the participation of the higher-education sector. Thus, at the national level, there is a clear connection between the internationalization of HEIs and the economic and technological development of the country.

Implications

In sum, during the last decade, university performance has drawn much attention from the public; hence, university ranking and international benchmarking are becoming more central in university governance. Governments in East Asia have, accordingly, initiated comprehensive reviews of their higher-education systems, which has prompted the internationalization of their HEIs. Therefore, it is not surprising that internationalization processes and strategies are becoming increasingly popular, while performance assessments of these initiatives are consistently emphasized.

Many scholars would claim that in the last decade they have witnessed a dramatic shift in the rationale for internationalization, which has led to the notion of revenue generation. While this trend might be true for a small number of countries, it is certainly not the case for the majority of institutions around the world. For Taiwan, its current motivations are still focused on enhancing international curriculum programs and encouraging international enrollments. In essence, Taiwan's efforts to make its institutions of higher learning more international in scope are still in the early stages. Further improvements are still needed to raise the overall level of the internationalization of HEIs in Taiwan.

NOTE

1. Research in this regard includes Neave (1992a, 1992b) and Knight (2003, 2005) for UNESCO; Hayward (2000), Green and Olson (2003), Siaya and Hayward (2003), Green (2005), and Green, Luu and Burris (2008) for ACE; Marden and Engerman (1992), Ellingboe (1998), Paige and Mestenhauser (1999), Mestenhauser (2002), Paige (2003), Whitaker (2004), Schwietz (2006), Shutina (2008), and Altbach and Knight (2007) for the United States; AUCC (1995a, 1999, 2007) and Bartell (2003) for Canada; Davies (1995, 1997), Knight (1997, 1999), and Knight and de Wit (1995, 1999) for OECD; Rudzki (1995a, 1995b, 1998) and Ayoubi and Massoud (2007) for the United Kingdom; Nilsson (2003) for Sweden; Teichler (2004) and Brandenburg and Federkeil (2007) for Germany; Kawaguchi and Lander (1997) and Paige (2005) for Japan; and Huang and Chang (2004), Wang, Hsiao, and Ping (2006), Chen (2007), Hsu (2007), Lu (2007), Mok (2006, 2007), Chiang (2008), and Chen (2009) for Taiwan.

REFERENCES

Aguilar, Martin P. 2002. "Barriers to Internationalisation: Attitudes, Resources, Policy." Paper presented at the IAU Lyon Conference on Internationalization of Higher Education, Claude Bernard University, April 12–13.

Altbach, Philip G. 2003. "Why the United States Will Not Be a Market for Foreign Higher Education Products: A Case Against GATS." *International Higher Education* 31: 5–7.

———. 2005. "Globalization and the University: Myths and Realities in an Unequal World." *The NEA 2005 Almanac of Higher Education*, edited by H. S. Wechsler, 63–74. Washington, DC: National Education Association.

Altbach, Philip G., and Jane Knight. 2007. "The Internationalization of Higher Education: Motivations and Realities." *Journal of Studies in International Education* 11 (3/4), 290–305.

Association of Universities and Colleges of Canada (AUCC). 1995a. *Internationalization and Canadian Universities*. Ottawa: AUCC.

———. 1995b. *A Primer on Performance Indicators. Research File*. Ottawa: AUCC. Available online at: http://www.aucc.ca.

———. 1999. *Towards a More Global Campus: Internationalization Initiatives of Canadian Universities*. Ottawa: AUCC.

———. 2007. *Internationalizing Canadian Campuses*. Ottawa: AUCC.

Ayoubi, Rami M., and Hiba K. Massoud. 2007. "The Strategy of Internationalization in Universities—A Quantitative Evaluation of the Intent and Implementation in UK Universities." *International Journal of Educational Management* 21 (4): 329–349.

Bartell, Marvin. 2003. "Internationalization of Universities: A University Culture-Based Framework." *Higher Education* 45: 43–70.

Brandenburg, Uwe, and Gero Federkeil. 2007. *How to Measure Internationality and Internationalisation of Higher Education Institutions: Indicators and Key Figures*. Berlin: Centre for Higher Education Development.

Chen, Chin Li. 2009. "A Study of the Construction of Measurement Indicators and the Internationalized Strategies for Higher Education in Taiwan [In Chinese]." PhD diss., National Sun Yat-Sen University, Kaohsiung, Taiwan.

Chen, Li Yu. 2007. "Implications of Competing Values Framework for Developing Internationalization Indicators in Higher Education Evaluation Plan [In Chinese]." *Journal of Educational Administration and Evaluation* 3: 1–18.

Chiang, Li Chuan. 2008. "Rethinking the State of the Art of Internationalization of Higher Education in Taiwan from the Nature of Strategy and Execution" [in Chinese]. *Educational Resources and Research Bimonthly* 8 (83): 47–70.

Chin, Joseph Mung-Chin, and Gregory S. Ching. 2009. "Trends and Indicators of Taiwan's Higher Education Internationalization." *The Asia-Pacific Education Researcher* 18 (2): 185–203.

Davies, John L. 1995. "University Strategies for Internationalisation in Different Institutional and Cultural Settings: A Conceptual Framework." In *Policy and Policy Implementation in Internationalisation of Higher Education*, edited by P. Blok, 3–18. Amsterdam: European Association for International Education.

———. 1997. "A European Agenda for Change for Higher Education in the XXIst Century: Comparative Analysis of Twenty Institutional Case Studies." *CRE-action* 111: 47–92.

de Wit, Hans. 2002. *Internationalization of Higher Education in the United States of America and Europe*. Westport, CT: Greenwood.

Ellingboe, Brenda. J. 1998. "Divisional Strategies to Internationalize a Campus Portrait: Results, Resistance, and Recommendations from a Case Study at a U.S. University." In *Reforming the Higher Education Curriculum: Internationalizing the Campus*, edited by J. A. Mestenhauser, and B. J. Ellingboe, 198–228. Washington, DC: American Council on Education.
Green, Madeleine. F. 2005. *Measuring Internationalization at Research Universities*. Washington, DC: American Council on Education.
Green, Madeleine. F., Dao T. Luu, and Beth Burris. 2008. *Mapping Internationalization on U.S. Campuses: 2008 Edition*. Washington, DC: American Council on Education.
Green, Madeleine F., and Christa Olson. 2003. *Internationalizing the Campus: A User's guide*. Washington, DC: American Council on Education.
Hayward, Fred M. 2000. *Internationalization of U.S. Higher Education: Preliminary Status Report 2000*. Washington, DC: American Council of Education.
Hsu, Yuan Hsiang. 2007. "The Feasibility of Internationalizing Taiwan's Higher Education System from the Perspective of Globalization" [in Chinese]. PhD diss., National Sun Yat-Sen University, Kaohsiung, Taiwan.
Huang, Ching Yuan, and Ying Ru Chang. 2004. "The Study of the Internationalization Index of Undergraduate Students in Taiwan: A Case of Shu- Te University" [in Chinese]. *Commerce and Management Quarterly* 5 (4): 417–433.
Kawaguchi, Akiyoshi, and Denis Lander. 1997. "Internationalization in Practice in Japanese Universities." *Higher Education Policy* 10: 103–110.
Kemp, Stephen. 1995. *The Global Market for Foreign Students*. Adelaide, Australia: University of Adelaide.
Kirp, David L. 2003. *Shakespeare, Einstein, and the Bottom Line: The Marketing of Higher Education*. Cambridge, MA: Harvard University Press.
Kishun, Roshen. 2007. "The Internationalisation of Higher Education in South Africa: Progress and Challenges." *Journal of Studies in International Education* 11 (3/4): 455–469.
Knight, Jane. 1997. "Internationalisation of Higher Education: A Conceptual Framework." In *Internationalisation of Higher Education in Asia Pacific Countries*, edited by J. Knight and H. de Wit, 5–19. Amsterdam: European Association of International Education.
———. 1999. "Internationalisation of Higher Education." In *Quality and Internationalisation in Higher Education*, edited by J. Knight and H. de Wit, 13–23. Paris: IMHE/OECD.
———. 2003. *Internationalization of Higher Education Practices and Priorities: 2003 IAU Survey Report*. Paris, France: International Association of Universities.
———. 2004. "Internationalization Remodeled: Definition, Approaches, and Rationales." *Journal of Studies in International Education* 8 (1): 5–31.
———. 2005. *Internationalization of Higher Education: New Directions, New Challenges. The 2005 IAU Global Survey Report*. Paris: International Association of Universities.
———. 2006a. *IAU 2005 Internationalization Survey: Preliminary Findings Report*. Paris: International Association of Universities.

———. 2006b. "Internationalization: Concepts, Complexities and Challenges." In *International Handbook of Higher Education*, edited by J. Forest and P. G. Altbach, 207–227. Dordrecht, The Netherlands: Springer.

———. 2007. "Internationalization: A Decade of Changes and Challenges." International Higher Education 50 (Winter): 6–7.

———. 2009. *The Internationalization of Higher Education: Are We on the Right Track?* Toronto: Ontario Confederation of University Faculty Associations. Available online at: http://www.academicmatters.ca.

Knight, Jane, and Hans de Wit. 1995. "Strategies for Internationalisation of Higher Education: Historical and Conceptual Perspectives." In *Strategies for Internationalisation of Higher Education: A Comparative Study of Australia, Canada, Europe and the United States of America*, edited by Hans de Wit, 5–32. Amsterdam: European Association for International Education.

Knight, Jane, and Hans de Wit, eds. 1999. *Quality and Internationalization in Higher Education*. Paris: OECD.

Lo, Y. William, and Fwu Yuan Weng. 2005. "Taiwan's Responses to Globalization: Internationalization of Higher Education." In *Globalization and Higher Education in East Asia*, edited by K. H. Mok and R. James, 137–156. Singapore: Marshall Cavendish Academic.

Lobelle, Marc. 2008. "Bologna and the Internationalization of Higher Education: Risks and Opportunities for the Louvain School of Engineering." Paper presented at the Bologna Conference on Student Mobility, Brussels, Belgium, May 29–30.

Lu, Hung Ling. 2007. "The Impact of Organizational Strategy on Internationalization of University [In Chinese]." PhD diss., Soochow University, Taipei, Taiwan.

Marden, Parker G., and David C. Engerman. 1992. "International Interest: Liberal Arts Colleges Take the High Road." *Educational Record* 73 (2): 42–46.

Mestenhauser, Josef A. 2002. "In Search of a Comprehensive Approach to International Education: A Systems Perspective." In *Rocking in Red Square: Critical Approaches to International Education in the Age of Cyberculture*, edited by W. Grünzweig and N. Rinehart. Muenster, 165–202. New Brunswick, NJ: Transaction Publishers.

Ministry of Educaton (MOE). 2009. *Award for University to Promote Internationalization Plan*. Taipei: MOE. Available online at: http://edu.law.moe.gov.tw.

———. 2010. *Summary of Education at All Levels SY2000-2010*. Taipei: MOE.

Mok, Ka Ho. 2000. "Reflecting Globalization Effects on Local Policy: Higher Education Reform in Taiwan." *Journal of Education Policy* 15 (6): 637–660.

———. 2003. "Similar Trends, Diverse Agendas: Higher Education Reforms in East Asia." *Globalisation, Societies and Education* 1 (2): 201–221.

———. 2006. "Questing for Internationalization of Universities in East Asia: Critical Reflections." Paper presented at the International symposium, Osaka, Japan, January 13–14, 2006.

———. 2007. "Internationalizing and International-benchmarking of Universities in East Asia: Producing World Class University or Reproducing

Neo-Imperialism in Education?" Paper presented at the Realizing the Global University: Critical Perspectives Workshop, London, November 14.

Mok, Ka Ho, Rosemary Deem, and Lisa Lucas. 2008. "Transforming Higher Education in Whose Image? Exploring the Concept of the "World-Cass" University in Europe and Asia." Paper presented at the CERC Annual Conference, Hong Kong, February 23.

Mok, Ka Ho, and Richard James, eds. 2005. *Globalization and Higher Education in East Asia.* Singapore: Marshall Cavendish Academic.

Neave, Guy. 1992a. "Institutional Management of Higher Education: Trends, Needs and Strategies for Co-operation." Paris: International Association of Universities.

———. 1992b. "Managing Higher Education International Co-operation: Strategies and Solutions." Paris: Unpublished Reference document for UNESCO.

Nilsson, Bengt. 2003. "Internationalisation at Home from a Swedish Perspective: The Case of Malmö." *Journal of Studies in International Education* 7: 27–40.

Paige, Michael R. 2005. "Internationalization of Higher Education: Performance Assessment and Indicators." *Nagoya Journal of Higher Education* 5: 99–122.

———. 2003. "The American Case: The University of Minnesota." *Journal of Studies in International Education* 7: 52–63.

Paige, Michael R., and Josef A. Mestenhauser. 1999. "Internationalizing Educational Administration." *Education Administration Quarterly* 35: 500–517.

Potocnik, Janez. 2005. *Internationalisation of R & D.* London: *Times Higher Education.* Available online at: http://www.timeshighereducation.co.uk.

Rudzki, Romuald. 1995a. "The Application of a Strategic Management Model to the Internationalization of Higher Education Institutions." *Higher Education* 29 (4): 421–441.

———. 1995b. "Internationalisation of UK Business Schools: Findings of a National Survey." In *Policy and Policy Implementation in Internationalisation of Higher Education,* edited by P. Blok, 3–18. Amsterdam: European Association for International Education.

———. 1998. "The Strategic Management of Internationalization: Towards a Model of Theory and Practice." PhD diss., University of Newcastle upon Tyne, UK.

Schwietz, Michele S. 2006. "Internationalization of the Academic Profession: An Exploratory Study of Faculty Attitudes, Beliefs and Involvement at Public Universities in Pennsylvania. PhD diss., University of Pittsburgh, Pittsburgh, USA.

Shutina, Reti. 2008. "An Investigation of the Role that the Nation's Six Major Higher Education Associations Have Played in the Internationalization of American Higher Education during the Last Decade (1996–2006)." PhD diss., University of Toledo, Toledo, Canada.

Siaya, Laura, and Fred M. Hayward. 2003. *Mapping Internationalization on U.S. Campuses.* Washington, DC: American Council on Education.

Smart, Don, and Grace Ang. 1993. "The Origins and Evolution of the Commonwealth Full-fee Paying Overseas Student Policy 1975–1992." In *Case Studies in Public Policy,* edited by W. J. Peachment and J. Williamson, 111–128. Perth, Australia: Public Sector Research Unit.

Teichler, Ulrich. 2004. "The Changing Debate on Internationalisation of Higher Education." *Higher Education* 48: 5–26.
Wang, Shih Ying, Lin Hsiao, and Feng Ying Ping. 2006. *Internationalization of University in Taiwan and the Tendency of the World* [In Chinese]. Taipei: NIOERAR.
Whitaker, Aliana Marie. 2004. "The Internationalization of Higher Education: A U.S. Perspective." MA thesis, Virginia Polytechnic Institute, Blacksburg, VA.

Chapter 13

Globalization and the Issue of Academic Publishing (the SSCI and the SCI)

In 2003, the Ministry of Education (MOE) in Taiwan adopted international publication indicators such as the Social Science Citation Index (SSCI), the Science Citation Index (SCI), and the Engineering Index (EI) as the standards for evaluating the performance of academics. The SSCI, the SCI, and the EI are citation index databases owned by Thomson Reuters, a for-profit private company in the United States. These standards have long been recognized by major Western English-speaking universities such as in Australia, Canada, the United States, the United Kingdom, and New Zealand. It was hoped that by promoting these standards, the overall competitiveness of higher-education institutions (HEIs) in Taiwan would be enhanced. The primary performance evaluation process involves counting the actual number of faculty publications in these three databases to determine the final rankings of each college and university. The academic faculties in higher-education institutions in Taiwan receive pressure to publish internationally in order to acquire SSCI, SCI and EI points.

In 2005, the MOE launched a Creating Top-Notch Universities with NT$50 Billion over 5 Years program (five-year-five-billion plan) (approximately US$1.56 billion; first named, a Plan to Develop First-Class Universities and Top-level Research Centers [PDFURC]) with the goal of enhancing the competitiveness of universities, and it has continued its sponsorship of the program for the second round that begins in 2011 (Central News Agency 2010). This program, based on a highly competitive scheme, allocates funds and resources to National Taiwan University

(NTU), National Tsing Hua University (NTHU), National Chiao Tung University (NCTU), National Cheng Kung University (NCKU), National Cheng-chi University (NCCU), and other key national universities, with a greater focus on the natural sciences such as engineering and medical science. In effect, these universities (except the only one focused on the social sciences, NCCU, which received the least amount of funding) have rich research facilities, receive financial assistance, and have equipment resources. In addition, in order to increase the effectiveness of domestic universities and bring them into the global academic network, through competition for resources based on objective academic outputs such as appraisal methods, a published paper in the SSCI, the SCI, the Arts and Humanities Citation Index (A&HCI) is the standard assessment criteria for academic research.

At the same time, since 2005, the MOE has initiated both the Program for Promoting Academic Excellence in Universities (PPAE) and the Aiming for the Top University and Elite Research Center Development Plan (ATU Plan), and also established a formal university evaluation policy, with a view to improving the competitive strength and international visibility of Taiwan's universities. Evaluation has thus taken on a highly quantitative dimension. Research performance is chiefly assessed in terms of the number of articles that scholars publish in SCI-, SSCI- and A&HCI-indexed journals, citation rates, and the associated impact factors, as the basis for a variety of programs that support and fund scholarly research.

These assessment standards have led Taiwan's scholars to focus on publishing in international journals. Academics prefer journals that are published in English instead of Chinese, and they choose subjects in line with what international journals prefer (Chen and Qian 2004). In 2008, as a direct response to these new policies, NCCU, in Taipei, set up an ATU office fully devoted to the development of certain selected key subject areas and the promotion of quality research. Yet despite the best efforts of all concerned to encourage academic excellence, the highly quantitative evaluation indicators have had some negative effects. Publication expectations are not uniform across all disciplines, for instance. Moreover, the distinctive characteristics of particular academic subjects have been largely ignored, and there have been instances of bitterness in certain departments whose staff felt they had been subjected to unfair competition. It has also been pointed out that the goal for such evaluation is to improve the quality of research; however, the nature of the subject and the impact of the social and cultural context must also be taken into account. In evaluating scholarship based on SSCI and SCI academic publication evaluative criteria, more than a single set of standards should be applied to highlight the strengths and weakness of published scholarly work.

Globalization and the Changing Publication Norm

Globalization has meant an increased demand from students, employers, and academics for indicators that show the international standing of universities (Williams and Dyke 2004). According to the widely cited ranking published by Shanghai Jiao Tong University (SJTU), indicators used for research quality evaluation and their data indicate that each article published in the fields of nature and the sciences, and articles in SCI-expanded (SCI-E) and the SSCI has a weight of 20 percent (Academic Ranking of World Universities 2007). In other words, when it comes to what constitutes the best research, scholars tend to assess it according to studies published in the fields of nature and the sciences, and indexed in the SCI and the SSCI, which are products of Thomson Reuters. Similarly, in *Asia's Best Universities*, published by Asia Week, one important indicator for research performance is citations in academic journals as tracked by the Journal Citation Index (*Asia Week* n.d.). The citation data that come from Thomson Reuter's Essential Science Indicators were also used in the world university ranking system conducted by the *Times Higher Education Supplement*.

Florida State University (FSU) (2007) noted that citation indexes are bibliographic indexes that allow the user to trace research from an article by searching for subsequent articles that have cited that original article. These databases are mostly employed in bibliometrics, a type of research method used in library and information science. Researchers primarily use bibliometric methods to evaluate and determine the influence and reputation of a single author, or the relationship between two or more authors based on publications within a given field or body of literature. The SCI, the SSCI, and the A&HCI are some of the most commonly used bibliometric tools for researchers (Palmquist 2001). While most authors and researchers think that citation indexes are mere tools to recover information, in fact there are actually numerous important, productive, and unique uses for such indexes (Garfield 1994a). For example, in addition to producing valid estimates of research quality, the SSCI and other such indexes can also be used to rank and evaluate journals (Garfield 1972).

Another important purpose of such indexes is to reveal the connections between ideas or concepts (Garfield 1994b). At the same time, it is also possible to map research and studies with respect to the year published and the field (Garfield 1993). These indexes also serve other functions, such as to reveal who is citing a particular researcher and the impact that his or her work is currently having on the global research community by determining whether a theory has been confirmed, changed, or improved, and by locating information on how a basic concept is being applied. These indexes also allow a scholar to track a topic through years of research literature and verify the accuracy of references (Thomson 2008).

University administrators have shown an increasing tendency to use these citation indexes in making a decision to appoint a faculty member to a position, in determining tenure and/or promotion (Kokko and Sutherland 1999), or even making funding decisions (Bauer and Bakkalbasi 2005). Nevertheless, there exists much criticism about the use of these tools to evaluate research performance (Ackermann 2001). Garfield (1994b) mentioned that a better evaluation system would involve actually reading each article for its quality, but then the problem would arise of reconciling the judgments of peer reviewers. Evidence does show there is validity to employing citation criteria as a measure for assessing the impact of scientific scholarship (Lawani and Bayer 1983). However, some scholars still claim that International Statistical Institute (ISI) citation indexes are far from objective, that the impact its journals have is a bit illusory, and that the word "global" stretches the truth about the master journal list (Cruz 2007). The use of the English language as the medium for academic writing has also raised many problems for non-English first language countries (Paasi 2005), issues that also exist in the fields of the social sciences and the humanities (Archambault et al. 2006).

Bauer and Bakkalbasi (2005) mentioned that the ISI citation indexes do indeed offer the most comprehensive coverage for past research, but for some subject areas, specialized databases may offer the best citation coverage, and for yet other areas Google Scholar may be an indispensable tool. However, with the continued changes brought forth by the advancement of information technology, in addition to the corresponding proliferation of resources that offer both citation indexing and the tracking of researchers, authors will indeed have more and more tools to aid their academic endeavors.

English Language Hegemony in Academic Publications

English is the world's language for communication; therefore, scholars must publish their research articles in English in order to gain international visibility. For scholars in the humanities and the social sciences, however, their research subjects are more concerned with local culture and social context, and therefore, they typically use the language that is most appropriate to address the topic. Journal articles included in the SSCI, SCI-E, A&HCI, and EI databases are mostly written in English. In general terms, research has indicated that out of the ninety-six articles listed in the sociology section of the SSCI, the United States accounted for forty-five publications, and the United Kingdom twenty-seven, while Germany and France were four and two respectively; wherein all articles are written in English instead of local Asian languages (e.g., Chinese, Malay, Japanese, etc.). Such statistics have led fewer Asian researchers in the humanities and the social sciences to submit their articles to the SSCI, the SCI-E, the A&HCI, and the EI.

In addition, Ye (2004) also noted that many social science scholars are mostly concerned with local or national issues. These are historical- and cultural-based research fields, for which articles are difficult to translate into English. Even if these works are translated into English, due to the contextual content, it is still rather difficult for foreign researchers to fully grasp the issues being discussed.

Ripples in the Scholarly Publication Landscape in Taiwan

With the MOE's adoption of the SSCI, the SCI, and the EI as the gold standard for evaluating the quality of research at Taiwan's 145 colleges and universities, the primary evaluation process came to consist of tallying the actual number of faculty publications in these three citation index databases to determine the final ranking of each and every college and university.

Upon the release of the first-round results in 2005, the media reported that some traditionally renowned public research universities had been "left behind." NCCU, for example, had spearheaded the training of the nation's leaders and top researchers across the social science disciplines over the years, but was now ranked forty-eighth (48/145), according to the Thomson Reuters SSCI standard. Likewise, most teacher colleges had long been stores of rich cultural knowledge, expertise, and resources necessary for the training of the nation's K–12 teachers, but they now received rankings near the bottom of the scale.

Critics across Taiwanese academia and society immediately expressed their dissent, arguing that the citation index databases are not appropriate and fail to serve as an effective evaluation mechanism of the diversified knowledge production and dissemination that are so valuable in the social sciences and humanities curricula. The three databases designed by Thomson Reuters can only serve as a reference to understand STEM (science-, technology-, engineering-, and mathematics-related) journals that are being published mostly in the United States. What has been left out, however, includes a broad spectrum of disciplinary knowledge that addresses cultural issues, education equity and social justice, multicultural education, local democracy, human rights, and education policy studies, just to name to few, that are equally valued in U.S. academia. The citation numbers and impact factors in these three U.S.-based databases cannot at all reflect the research quality and social impact of Taiwanese scholars, researchers, and activists who are deeply devoted to investigating knowledge across the disciplinary spectrum of the social sciences and the humanities.

Even in "industrialized" nations, colleges and universities have seldom used the number of publications listed in these citation databases as the baseline criterion for the tenure-review process and/or for program evaluation. In most cases, the tenure-review process has been comprehensive in both its nature and scope, and the review committees also take into account the candidate's local contributions to the college/university, diversified approaches to program initiatives, both the quantitative and qualitative aspects of student evaluations, and his or her scholarly contributions to the social services of the university, professional associations, and the local community. In other words, the number of publications in these databases has never been the norm of reference for these institutions, let alone for those who have a high regard for the development of well-rounded scholarship and a more holistic, democratic public life. In fact, the "one-size-fits-all" approach to basing a nation's academic evaluations on the number of publications in the Thomson Reuters databases nevertheless has the potential to highly skew the substance of contributions from local public intellectuals (and their institutions) who have dedicated themselves to pushing the disciplinary boundaries for new knowledge that can best address local conditions.

Moreover, it is highly problematic that the SSCI does not yet include most U.S. and Taiwanese top-tier research and scholarly journals in, for instance, such fields as public administration, public policy, law, or science education, which are equally important to fostering academic learning and a cross-cultural exchange of knowledge necessary to advance democratic public life.[1] Scholars have continued to assert that the number of scholarly publications in these databases can serve only as a piecemeal approach to understanding how scholars have contributed to academic discourse in those journals listed in the Thomson Reuters databases. It is, then, deeply problematic when a nation's governing class bases its evaluation and funding mechanisms on these three databases as a means of judging the quality of multifaceted disciplinary knowledge that is as pivotal to informing and enriching the production of knowledge as are the sciences.

According to the operations book of the MOE (2007), the numbers of publications in the SCI, the SSCI, and the A&HCI are the data that the Higher Education Evaluation and Accreditation Council of Taiwan (HEEACT) requests for its evaluation process. Universities tend to provide these publication numbers in order to convince evaluation commissioners of their institutions' achievements in research. In addition, the HEEACT also publishes the publication numbers of each university on their Web site, which tends to establish a certain kind of benchmark regarding the institution's performance. Parents and students also utilize this information in making their school choices. However, there is no clear regulation (policy) outlining the use of such publication numbers of the SSCI, the SCI, and the A&HCI in the evaluation of higher education.

Lai (2004) noted that the emphasis on the SSCI, the SCI, and A&HCI publication numbers has led to two negative effects. First, colleges and universities compete in recruiting scholars who have a large number of publications, thereby creating a false appearance of high academic achievement. Second, universities create policies to encourage colleagues to contribute to English-language journals; hence, professors who publish in Chinese seem to become second-tier scholars. Huang (2004) noted that the creation of a Taiwanese SSCI is a good way to solve this problem that has been created by the emphasis on the English-language SSCI in the social science arena. Furthermore, publication numbers should not be the only standard by which to evaluate higher education.

Chen and Qian (2004) noted that the use of such publication numbers as a kind of global academic standard has cause some unintended consequences in Taiwan, namely, that publications in the English language have become more important than those in the local Chinese language; mainstream international issues come to center stage in research, rather than local regional contextual issues; and publishing in a foreign English-language journal has become a more prestigious accomplishment than publishing in a local regional journal, which suggests that the language being used (English) has become more important than the quality of the scholarly paper. These reservations have generated serious debate in the academy about the validity of such global academic standards, with the opinions of both supporters and nonsupporters alike being biased.

Influence on Individuals

It is a fact that, as the SSCI and the SCI are employed as one of the evaluation criteria in academia, scholars would prefer to publish in SSCI- and

SCI-indexed journals. The responses of individuals to this issue can be grouped into 3 categories:

- **Extreme Antagonists**—these individuals tend to strongly criticize the adaptation of the SSCI and SCI standard
- **Mainstream Followers**—most individuals tend to feel uncomfortable with this norm, but they accept it without much reflection. They follow the administrative policy, just for the sake of receiving a reward or promotion.
- **Supporters**—those individuals who are good at using English as a medium for writing papers, or those individuals who come from specific fields.

Influence on Academic Fields

From an individual perspective, the SSCI- and SCI-based standard has more or less influenced researchers' approach to academic publishing. However, if scholars are grouped into two fields, namely the social sciences and the sciences, this standard reflects an obvious disparity in the influence it has on scholarship. Moreover, the SSCI- and SCI-based standard has an even greater impact on institutions. Recognizing that research and development (R&D) is important for economic growth and global competitiveness, governments around the world have increased their role in funding R&D activities. International surveys of universities, such as the recent the *Times Higher World University Rankings 2006*, have taken ISI data as crucial determinants of the quality of faculty and research. In order to be ranked internationally and thus to attract both students and funding, universities urge their researchers to publish in Thomson ISI-indexed journals and to have their work cited by scholars writing in such journals. Intellectually and financially, therefore, the ISI wields tremendous power over faculty, administrators, publishers, and funding agencies.

Influence on Academic Institutions

After the MOI released the first round of higher-education evaluations in 2005, the Taiwan government's managerial class further promoted the SSCI as the standard for "gate-keeping knowledge" that determines what constitutes valid forms of academic knowledge. Influenced by league tables and the "top-down pressure" to comply with the MOE's unprecedented, grand project of PDFURC, the new generation of scholars was forced to generate "SSCI-, SCI-, and EI-only" publications.

The good intentions behind such a large-scale investment in higher education, as many scholars have pointed out, may push Taiwan to enhance the quality of its postsecondary institutions and better prepare its education work force, and a well-rounded evaluation could serve as a golden opportunity to decolonize Taiwanese academe in the postcolonial, post–martial law era. However, the current national trend on evaluation, spearheaded by the MOE, has nearly brought Taiwanese academic research into a decade of recolonization. The overt emphasis on imported, U.S.-based, Anglo-American, English-oriented "official knowledge," rather than on grassroots knowledge that pays due recognition to the needs of local communities, has had a damaging effect on Taiwanese academe. In particular, the culture-based research production that has been at the heart of democratic participation and public life has been significantly degraded.

The controversy over the SSCI "heat wave" intensified in a tilt toward the "English-only" policy when English became the predominant lingua franca that dictates the formats of academic presentation and writing for a variety of cultural groups that comprise a majority of the non-English speaking and English as the second language (ESL) Chinese/Taiwanese audience. The blind pursuit of "objectified" knowledge, with the uncritical reception of the announced "objective standards" (which lump together the sciences, the social sciences, and the humanities) in the alignment with the "world-class rankings" has discouraged or even marginalized local endeavors by teachers, parents, scholars, researchers, and activists who have had a long-time commitment to local democracy and human rights issues, such as education equity and social justice, crossborder knowledge, and intercultural understanding.

The top-down pressure to comply with the SSCI, the SCI, and the EI standards soon became the best practice mandated by the MOE, when it began using the first-round SSCI evaluation as the major source upon which to base funding decisions in higher education. Later, the National Science Council (NSC) and some foundations jumped on the bandwagon, pushing for the SSCI, the SCI, and the EI to be used as key standards and aligning the objectives of knowledge production with the MOE's push for the nation's major project of PDFURC, its follow-up "alphabetical soup" initiatives, and the resulting funding competition guideposts. The major initiatives include Producing World-Class Universities in Five Years with Fifty Billion NTD, the Nationwide Assessment on Postsecondary Institutions and Key Guidelines on Higher Education Funding, the National Academy Annual Brown Bag Lectures and Academy Awards, and the National Science Foundation (NSF) Knowledge Projects. The government's wild pursuit of world-class university rankings was characterized by the ontological, epistemological, and methodological standardization of knowledge production across the many spectrums of Taiwan's academic communities.

The PDFURC project has resulted in a large-scale restructuring of higher education's key dimensions of development and knowledge production, and has threatened faculty tenure reviews, performance evaluations, institutional support of research, and pay rate flexibility. The policy's hegemonic nature and the political economy of restructuring have led the nation's HEIs nowhere. Hence, quantifiable numbers rooted in the U.S.-based and STEM-oriented institutions support the assessment criteria of the MOE. The SSCI, SCI, and EI databases have had the effect of completely sabotaging and "brain-draining" a generation of professors and researchers in the fields of education, the social sciences, and the humanities, as institutional priorities and college teaching have suffered in the quest to meet these number-crunching mandates.

Moreover, the overprivileging of the STEM and medical fields, and the forceful co-opting of the knowledge-review standards for the social sciences and the humanities into the same ontological, epistemological, and methodological criteria have produced a "thin" scientific knowledge that fails to address the cutting-edge of the nation's uniqueness and prestige, a culturally responsive system of operation that should help a nation to fare well in global competition. Such dead-end pursuits continue to be reflected in the latest release of the MOE's proposal on the second-stage PDFURC, which highlights the Essential Science Indicators (ESI) as one of the four key standards to evaluate, rank, and fund academic programs across the disciplines. According to the MOE, the newly invented ESI standards incorporate the SSCI and the SCI, and downplay the significance of the SSCI in the composition of the ESI in assessing what constitutes a "valuable" scholarly contribution. The traditionally understood dimensions, such as book publications and international recognition, have been cast aside and assigned an even lower point value.

Financial Consequences Due to Changes in Publication Norms

The MOE's recent higher-education reform efforts have led to a dramatic growth in SSCI-, SCI-, and EI-indexed publications. National Taiwan University (NTU), for example, "officially" ascended into the ranks of the top 100 world-class universities. Many departments and schools nationwide have gone to great lengths to refurbish themselves with new assistive technologies and hardware. Policy entrepreneurs are celebrating the following achievements: (1) Taiwanese students have continued to rank near the top in international comparison assessments on STEM subjects, (2) the field of STEM education has brought Taiwan into the top five in the world in terms of the annual production of scientific papers, and (3) the citation of Taiwanese STEM papers is now also among the top five in the world.

However, below the radar, much front-page news has never been reported: when college teaching fell in importance to a secondary position, giving way to the higher-valued indexing of published research in the SSCI, the SCI, and the EI, there followed a gradual loss of interest in the overall education development as a sustainable, long-time investment for students at the level of both K–12 and higher education. Teacher-education programs have long been many nations' critical bases for ensuring the quality of pre- and in-service teachers. However, when the nation is driven to pursue SSCI, SCI, and EI standards, teacher preparation is no longer the first priority among STEM faculty. In the context of Taiwanese education, instructors on average previously devoted more than 70 percent of their weekly duty hours to making sure they were bringing out the best of their students' potential, but now they face severe challenges in fulfilling this promise, as the tenure review process is almost solely dependent upon the number their publications indexed in the SSCI, the SCI, and the EI.

The severity of this situation has recently intensified with the emergence of a vicious circle related to research productivity, teacher-education preparation, and the overall quality of K–12 STEM instruction. The "academic work" for professors, pre- and in-service teachers, and K–12 students has been reduced to a competition to play the "points" game. Studies have shown that the philosophy of trickle-down excellence recklessly endangers the academic achievement of K–12 students in STEM subjects when the curriculum becomes a highly standardized chore of teaching to tests. As a consequence, students' low academic interest has manifested itself in a gradual decline in achievement in recent years. Taken together, these front-page stories should alarm both the academic and policy communities, nationally and internationally, because a nation's world-renowned STEM research production is not actually sparking its local students' interest, or at least ensuring the above-average development of local scholars.

There is also a need for a critical assessment of the actual contributions being made by this new wave of SSCI-, SCI-, and EI-indexed publications in terms of the improvement of local economies and communities. If the goal of the PDFURC projects is to boost national competitiveness, it becomes a matter of concern when the visibility of cultural intellectuals from the social sciences and the humanities drops dramatically in the Asian-Pacific region of academic public life. Within the current wave of "international cooperation," ironically, these intellectuals have almost stopped publishing books that were once admired and widely circulated within the Asia-Pacific region and beyond.

A Call for Collective Action (The Manifesto)

In order to stop government agencies and academic research associations from using the SSCI, the SCI, and the EI as the best practice for evaluating academic research and public policy, a group of Taiwan professors initiated a collective action and initiated a petition concerning the following issues (www.bgo.tw):

- **Stop Using the SSCI as the Best Practice for Evaluation and Funding Purposes**
  We urge both the MOE and the NSC to stop using the SSCI, or any other index citation databases, as the best practice for evaluating the quality of academic research in the social sciences and the humanities in higher education institutions; nor should the SSCI, or any other imported index citation database, serve as the baseline criterion for making major funding decisions related to academic research in the social sciences and the humanities.

- **Recognize the Rich Variety of Academic Research Practices in the Social Sciences and the Humanities**
  We urge the MOE and the NSF to include book publications and other formats of scholarly contributions in the evaluation criteria for the social sciences and the humanities, and to stop using the SSCI, the SCI, and the EI to oversimplify the academic and social impact of scholars in the social sciences and humanities.

- **Establish Institutional Profiles That Recognize the Local Visions and Development of Academic Disciplines**
  We urge the MOE to recognize both the horizontal and vertical diversities among Taiwanese higher education institutions and the epistemological diversity within and among the sciences, the social sciences, and the humanities. Institution profiles and evaluation criteria should address the ecological complexities of these differences, and especially the seemingly divergent intellectual development between research universities and technology-focused colleges and universities.

- **Foster a Culture of Social Responsibility and Academic Professionalism**
  We urge the MOE to recognize the intellectual responsibility in producing culturally responsive research and academic practice. Accordingly, the evaluation process should encompass, at the least, mentoring programs

and peer-review mechanisms that encourage the local-based knowledge production that connects academic research to various local communities (i.e., local schools, cities, townships, etc.).

- **Create Culturally Responsive Evaluation Criteria for the Social Sciences and the Humanities**
We urge the MOE and the NSC to reassess the validity and reliability of the current evaluation criteria (which have appeared scientifically thin and socially irresponsible) and to expand the dimensionalities of citation indexes, as shown in the following section, as an alternative means of administering comprehensive evaluations of programs in the social sciences and the humanities: (1) journals, (2) books, (3) conference papers, (4) research projects, (5) reviews, (6) prestige scores for serving on national and/or international professional committees, (7) online publications/ citations, and (8) other professional experience.

Since the petition was started in December 2010, it has been signed by more than seventeen hundred academic faculty, staff, and students in various fields of the social sciences. Surprisingly, around 10 percent of the petitioners who disagree with the SSCI- and SCI-driven policy are from the field of natural science. Currently, the group is continuing its lobbying efforts by holding press conferences, sending appeal e-mails to government officials and lawmakers, and visiting key decision-makers in the MOE and the NSC to request a change.

Implications

In Taiwan, even after negotiations between the MOE and experts from all academic fields, the criteria used in the 2005 university evaluation still included papers published in journals listed in the SSCI and the SCI as important indicators of research quality. Later, the MOE launched the ATU competitive funding plan, amounting to NT$50 billion that was to be distributed over a five-year period. The vice minister of education, Lu Mu-lin (2003), made the following announcement: "The Ministry would like at least one of its universities to be ranked among the top 100 leading international institutions of higher education within the next ten years and to have at least one university ranked as number one within Asia by the next five years."

Academics all over the world find it prestigious to have their articles published in journals included in the Master Journal List of Thomson Reuter's ISI. Publishers of non-ISI-indexed journals often make it their objective to have their journals listed in ISI, not only because of its prestige, but also because librarians usually make decisions on subscriptions based on the ISI. Scholars in countries like the Netherlands have improved their quality of research by encouraging scholars to have ISI publications (Nederhof 2008). Still, numerous institutions in various fields have adopted these bibliometric tools as a criterion in evaluating a researcher's productivity (Davis 1998).

Thomson Reuter's journal list does not list all journals (Cruz 2007). Sometimes even the most well-known journal in certain fields is not included (Eaton 2007). The fact is that almost 90 percent of these journals are of Anglo-American origin, with English as the main medium of writing (Paasi 2005; Zitt, Perrot, and Barre 1998). The use of these bibliometrics as a macro indicator of studies and at the same an analysis of a country's publication output per institutional sector would be helpful (Moed, Bruin, and Van Leeuwen 1995), but some findings show that, due to rankings and evaluations, publications tend to shift from *quality* to *quantity* (Moed 2008), suggesting to some extent that the focus tends to shift slightly shift towards the number of publications rather than their relevance.

It is really still a question of the feasibility of using Thomson Reuter's ISI as the de facto *global* academic standard, but due to the increased commodification of knowledge (Lincoln 1998), even these indexes are strongly biased against the culture and language of some Anglo-American countries in certain fields (Decker, Beutel, and Brähler 2004). With the continuous changes brought forth by the advancement of information technology, in addition to the corresponding proliferation of resources that offer both citation indexing and the tracking of researchers, authors will indeed have more tools to aid their academic endeavors. In essence, technological advancements in bibliometric studies, which help both scholars and evaluators to understand different genres, discourses, and texts, will not only provide a clearer picture of the historical trends in science and technology publications, but the results will also aid future scholarly publications in determining current directions in the field.

Taiwan's Current Publication Performance

Within the last decade, the academy in Taiwan has shown evidence of increased publication in scholarly journals. However, the number of citations failed to increase. The evidence shows the decreasing average citations per publication from the years 1996 to 2009 in Taiwan. Data gathered from the two most widely used citation databases, Thomson Reuter's ISI Web of Science (WOS), and the Elsevier Scopus (SCImago 2007; Thomson Reuters 2010) show the cumulative total number of publications and citations from the years 1996 to 2009. Bibliometric data gathered from the Thomson Reuter's ISI WOS and the SCI Journal & Country Ranking Web sites suggest that both databases show similar trends, as there is an obvious increase in the number of publications but a decrease in the average number of citations per publication. This phenomenon signifies that recent publications are not adequately used. As a fact worth noting, Taiwan remains one of the world's most prolific innovators, achieving the highest number of utility patents per million population (279.25) in the world (Dutta and Mia 2010); therefore, it should follow that its scientific publications are highly cited.

Such facts suggest that great importance must be placed on publications in subject areas such as science and technology. However, this perspective seems unfair to academic fields such as the social sciences, the publications of which would take a much longer time to develop as compared to those in the natural sciences. In reality, both the government and academia itself should not rely on the mere numbers of publications indexed in well-known international indices, but should also take into account local or regional publications.

In sum, Taiwanese higher education is heavily influenced by the Western (especially American) model in terms of structure and content. This is especially the case with academic research, which is often full of the borrowing of paradigms and replication, not only in the sciences but also the social sciences. For example, one of the National Chair Professors in Taiwan, Kwang-Kuo Hwang, has endeavored to promote the indigenization movement of psychology and social science in Chinese society since the early 1980s. In reviewing the limitations of mainstream Western psychology, Hwang argued that in the context of promoting the social awareness of multiculturalism, it is necessary to focus on indigenous/local issues (such as in the field of psychology) to better understand the global community. It is obvious that various types of value conflicts have been found to exist between Confucian cultural heritage and Western individualism in this age of globalization. Moreover, the cultural traditions of Confucianism, Taoism, and Buddhism among the Chinese have clearly had a great impact on the psychometric approach for handling collective conflict. The call for scholars to endeavor to shift the paradigm by introducing local theories and models that are accordance with Taiwan's features is underway. Another effort is being made to establish a library citation database in the Chinese language to reduce the hegemony of the English databases.

Call for a Paradigm Shift in National Academia

The call for the academy to endeavor to shift the paradigm by introducing local and autochthonous theories as well as modeling epitomes in accordance to the known Taiwan features is already underway. Anchoring on such a concept, the only solution is a plan to establish a library citation database in the Chinese (Mandarin) language to reduce the hegemony of the Western English-language citation scheme.

There is a heated debate over the meaning, purpose, and current use of the SSCI in Taiwan's system of higher education, and the discussion has already gone on for quite a long time (Yu 2010). These issues are in fact part of a high-profile case, because these talks between supporters and critics of the SSCI have already reached the local media. For instance, in the year 1994, Forrester and Watson (1994) surveyed journal editors and editorial boards of directors in order to ask them to rank the top ten journals in the field of public administration, including the subfields of policy analysis, budgeting and finance, personnel administration, and organization studies.

Sixteen years later, in 2010, Bernick and Krueger repeated the Forrester and Watson study almost step by step, and the research on these newer journal rankings can be found in the columns labeled "B&K (2010)" (Bernick and Krueger 2010). All the journals listed in the study were ranked in the top ten in one or more subfields, by either F&W in 1994 or B&K in 2010, although, as the SSCI column shows, ten of the top twenty-eight journals are excluded from the complete SSCI database. This lack of accuracy in presenting the information indicates that the SSCI database remains incomplete. Hence, the SSCI's total results are not comprehensive as a whole. These findings reveal a situation in which there could be cause for concern due to the lack of maneuverability to revise a tenure decision based on information that is considered to come from the best journals available, although they are not listed in the SSCI, which may leave room for doubt.

As surprising as this is, if we examine this situation in more detail, we find that the SSCI also indexes journals whose overall quality may be questionable at best. It is actually a troublesome situation to consider a case in which a researcher decides to publish in a SSCI journal only because that particular journal is indexed. As a result, a marked institutional pressure exists to "publish or perish," and this is underway in Taiwan's academy. This pressure exists, perhaps, because as scholars, we are supposed to make sense of the world and the society in which we live. Yet increasingly, university professors are working under the reality of "publish and perish." That is, unless faculty publish in the "right" places and in the "right" journals, they can still perish in any field even though they have properly conducted their research or produced a significant number of high-quality scholarly papers, which, as could just be the case, might fall outside of the scope of the SSCI. A system that relies on indexes such as the SSCI as the only evaluative criterion for faculty productivity is at the moment neither fair nor advisable if faculty care about improving the overall quality of and respect for Taiwan's academic research.

More than fifty years ago, Eugene Garfield created the SSCI and the SCI as a way to provide academic researchers, faculty, and students ease of access to the so-called most effective bibliographic and citation information. Nowadays, the SSCI and the SCI bear the same responsibility, although over time, these academic institutions appear to have lost sight of that original fundamental objective. The outcome is yet to be known of what might happen when Taiwan and other Asian countries misuse the SSCI as the sole criterion for assessing research quality in terms of matching a global standard as well as raising standards to a world-class scholarly level.

The SSCI Syndrome

United Kingdom scientist Snow (1959), in his book *The Two Cultures*, claimed in 1959, claimed that a devision exists between the Arts and Sciences. Hence, during a university faculty dinner, science professors and arts professors may talk about their research specialties without any intersection between them whatsoever. Up until now, two barriers have existed in Taiwan's society: the University of Arts and the Departments of Science are still entirely dissimilar, although the Department of Science and Technology has traditionally received more resources due to its direct link with development.

In recent years in East Asia, including Taiwan, the aspects of globalization, standardization and marketing effects have pointed the bandwagon of scientific measurement, to represent the domain, institution, or even a faculty's effectiveness and productivity. On the other hand, the university evaluation system uses and misuses its own system, regardless of whether it is the arts or the sciences, measuring every faculty member according to the SSCI, the SCI, the A&HCI and the number of articles listed in international periodical databases, or intellectual property and technology transfer certificates. These evaluative measures might be as good as they can be to assess universities. The MOE, the NSC, and other government departments have aligned with the "pursuit of excellence program," the "top universities" program, and the policies of research grants in order to accelerate internal synchronization with the global academic community of universities.

All of these factors are working to promote the wave of publications in international journals oriented to research, resulting in the following trends: (1) the need to write papers in English is reinforced, (2) international issues are emphasized as the mainstream focus of publications and often at the expense of neglecting local problems, (3) there is an overemphasis on over publishing and contributing only to English periodicals, and (4) there is an unequal allocation of resources between science and the humanities, thanks to their traditional differences in research productivity.

These trends raise many questions and highlight the misleading belief that it is effective to in create so-called global academic standards as a whole. For instance, if research papers published in an international database are the evaluation criterion, does this really enhance academic quality? As noted previously, significant differences exist between the arts and sciences models and approaches, and most of the academic community in science and engineering support evaluation according to the system described here. On average, nearly 50 percent of the natural science journals are included in ISI citation databases, but the ratio is less than 20 percent that of the social sciences and humanities. Furthermore, many studies have shown that conducting research in the science and humanities are not compatible. Therefore the rule of evaluation used for academic performance needs to be conditional. Hence, the predominance of the international journal articles again handicaps research in the humanities and the social sciences. Thus, a fair and effective research-evaluation paradigm is in great demand in Taiwan so that the SSCI and SCI syndrome can be resolved.

NOTE

1. According to the Washington and Lee Law Review Rankings (http://lawlib.wlu.edu/lj), the SSCI only includes twenty of the top fifty law-review journals. The database contains only a limited selection of legal journals and law reviews. Prestigious journals such as the *Harvard Journal of Law and Technology* and those from Yale University, Columbia University, and UC-Berkeley are not yet included in the SSCI.

REFERENCES

Ackermann, Eric George. 2001. *Developing Comparative Bibliometric Indicators for Evaluating the Research Performance of Four Academic Nutrition Departments, 1992–1996: An Exploratory Study.* Knoxville, TN: University of Tennessee.
Archambault, Éric, Étienne Vignola-Gagné, Grégoire Côté, Vincent Larivire, and Yves Gingrasb. 2006. "Benchmarking Scientific Output in the Social Sciences and Humanities: The Limits of Existing Databases." *Scientometrics* 68 (3): 329–342.
Asia Week. n.d. "Asia's Best Universities 2000." *Asia Week.* Available online at: http://www.asiaweek.com.
Bauer, Kathleen, and Nisa Bakkalbasi. 2005. "An Examination of Citation Counts in a New Scholarly Communication Environment." *D-Lib Magazine* September, 11. Available online at: http://www.dlib.org.
Bernick, Ethan, and Skip Krueger. 2010. "An Assessment of Journal Quality in Public Administration." *International Journal of Public Administration* 33 (2): 98–106.
Central News Agency. 2010. "'Creating Top-Notch Universities' Drive to Continue: President." August 5, 2010. Taipei: Focus Taiwan News Channel. Available online at: http://focustaiwan.tw.
Chen, Kuang-Shing, and Yong Xiang Qian. 2004. *Academic Production under the Neo-liberalism Globalization [in Chinese].* Paper presented at the Reflecting on Taiwan's Higher Education Academic Evaluation Conference, International Plenary Hall, National Library, Taipei, Taiwan, September 25–26.
Cruz, Isagani. 2007. *Challenging ISI Thomson Scientifics' Journal Citation Reports: Deconstructing "Objective," "Impact," and "Global."* Vancouver, Canada: PKP Scholarly Publishing. Available online at: http://scholarlypublishing.blogspot.com.
Davis, John B. 1998. "Problems in Using the Social Sciences Citation Index to Rank Economics Journals." *American Economist* 42 (2): 59–64.
Decker, Oliver, Manfred E. Beutel, and Elmar Brähler. 2004. "Deep Impact—Evaluation in the Sciences." *Social and Preventive Medicine* 49 (1): 10–14.
Dutta, Soumitra, and Irene Mia. 2010. *Global Information Technology Report 2009–2010.* Geneva, Switzerland: World Economic Forum and INSEAD.
Eaton, Jonathan. 2007. *Fine Tuning English Writing Workshop—September 14–15, 2007.* Taipei: National Taiwan University of Science and Technology; Taiwan Assessment and Evaluation Association.
Florida State University. 2007. *Library Terms.* Tallahassee, FL: Florida State University. Available online at: http://www.lib.fsu.edu.
Forrester, John P., and Sheilah S. Watson. 1994. "An Assessment of Public Administration Journals: The Perspective of Editors and Editorial Board Members." *Public Administration Review* 54 (5): 474–482.

Garfield, Eugene. 1972. "Citation Analysis as a Tool in Journal Evaluation: Journals Can Be Ranked by Frequency and Impact of Citations for Science Policy Studies." *Science* 178 (4060): 471–479.

———. 1993. "What Citations Tell Us about Canadian Research." *Canadian Journal of Information and Library Science* 18 (4): 14–35.

———. 1994a. *The Concept of Citation Indexing: A Unique and Innovative Tool for Navigating the Research Literature.* New York: Thomson Reuter. http://scientific.thomson.com.

———. 1994b. *Linking Literatures: An Intriguing Use of the Citation Index.* New York: Thomson Reuter. http://scientific.thomson.com.

Huang, Hou Ming. 2004. "SSCI, TSSCI and Taiwan Social Science Evaluation System [in Chinese]." Paper presented at the Reflecting on Taiwan's Higher Education Academic Evaluation Conference, International Plenary Hall, National Library, Taipei, Taiwan, September 25–26.

Hwang, Guang-Guo. 2009. "The Development of Indigenous Counseling in Contemporary Confucian Communities." *The Counseling Psychologist* 37: 930–943.

Kokko, Hanna, and William J. Sutherland. 1999. "What Do Impact Factors Tell Us? *Trends in Ecology & Evolution* 14 (10): 382–384.

Lai, Ding Ming. 2004. "Quantitative Indexes Are Not the Panacea of Academic Evaluation [in Chinese]." Paper presented at the Reflecting on Taiwan's Higher Education Academic Evaluation Conference, International Plenary Hall, National Library, Taipei, Taiwan, September 25–26.

Lawani, Stephen M., and Alan E. Bayer. 1983. "Validity of Citation Criteria for Assessing the Influence of Scientific Publications: New Evidence with Peer Assessment." *Journal of the American Society for Information Science* 34 (1): 59–66.

Lincoln, Yvonna S. 1998. "Commodification and Contradiction in Academic Research." *Studies in Cultures, Organizations, and Societies* 4: 263–278.

Lu, Mu-Lin. 2003. *The Making of World-class Research Universities in an Age of Globalization—Components & Challenges.* Taipei: Ministry of Education (MOE). Available online at: http://www.edu.tw.

Ministry of Education (MOE). 2007. *University's Research Achievement.* Taipei: MOE. Available online at: http://rd.shu.edu.tw.

Moed, Henk F. 2008. "UK Research Assessment Exercises: Informed Judgments on Research Quality or Quantity?" *Scientometrics* 74 (1): 153–161.

Moed, Henk F., R. E. De Bruin, and Thed N. Van Leeuwen. 1995. "New Bibliometric Tools for the Assessment of National Research Performance: Database Description, Overview of Indicators and First Applications." *Scientometrics* 33 (3): 381–422.

Nederhof, Anton J. 2008. "Policy Impact of Bibliometric Rankings of Research Performance of Departments and Individuals in Economics." *Scientometrics* 74 (1): 163–174.

Paasi, Anssi. 2005. "Globalization, Academic Capitalism, and the Uneven Geographies of International Journal Publishing Spaces." *Environment and Planning A* 37 (5): 769–789.

Palmquist, Ruth A. 2001. *Bibliometrics*. Austin, TX: University of Texas Austin. Available online at: http://www.gslis.utexas.edu.
SCImago. 2007. *SJR-SCImago Journal and Country Rank*. New York: Elsevier.
Snow, Charles Percy. 1959. *The Rede Lecture*. Available online at: http://s-f-walker.org.uk.
Thomson. 2008. *Web of Science*. New York: Thomson Reuter. Available online at: http://scientific.thomson.com/products/wos/.
Thomson Reuters. 2010. *ISI Web of Knowledge*. New York: Thomson Reuter. Available online at: http://www.isiwebofknowledge.com/.
Williams, R., and N. V. Dyke. 2004. *The International Standing of Australian Universities*. Melbourne, Australia: University of Melbourne. Abailable online at: http://www.melbourneinstitute.com.
Ye, Qi Zheng. 2004. "The Lack of the Sense of Social Practice: The Myth of Criterion-Based Evaluation [in Chinese]." Paper presented at the Reflecting on Taiwan's Higher Education Academic Evaluation Conference, International Plenary Hall, National Library, Taipei, Taiwan, September 25–26.
Yu, Chi-Lik. 2010. "A Statement on SSCI." Taipei: National Cheng Chi University, Forum of Public Administration.
Zitt, Michel, Francois Perrot, and Remi Barre. 1998. "The Transition from 'National' to 'Transnational' Model and Related Measures to Countries Performance." *Journal of the American Society for Information Science (1986-1998)* 49 (1), 30–42.

Chapter 14

Influx of International Students into Taiwan

In recent decades, student mobility patterns have shifted from the previous elitist experience characterized by scholarship of the wealthy few to the current mass movement of average individuals and groups (Teichler and Jahr 2001). In the twenty-first century, a select number of students define themselves as members of elite groups enrolled in high-quality degree programs in popular host destinations; the majority, however, leave their home nations to obtain degrees at personal financial expense. Others are motivated to acquire international experiences that complement concurrent academic programs in their home nations. Traditionally, international students immigrated to study with world-renowned scholars or to further their disciplinary knowledge in nations such as the United States or Britain. In the contemporary era, university students are more likely to study in the global arena in newly established host destinations to obtain advanced degrees, diplomas, or professional certification (Williams 1981).

In recent decades, many nations have shifted their foreign-student policies from an aid approach to a trade rationale (Smart and Ang 1993). This shift signals that cross-border education is now a commodity of free trade rather than a public responsibility (Kirp 2003). Given this new outlook, the market for international students has become a dynamic growth industry sustained by universities, government agencies, private corporations, and entrepreneurs motivated by financial profit (Altbach 2003). National governments are eager to be involved in attracting foreign students to study in their countries, and they stay connected to this trend through their departments or ministries of education, or dedicated promotional agencies (Kemp 1995) that capitalize on the benefits from international-student populations, such as skill migration, economic growth, public diplomacy, and research associated with a knowledge society (Kishun 2007).

Contemporary patterns of cross-border mobility encompass a complex, contradictory, and expansive discourse shaped by the discussions, policy issues, and mission statements of individual universities as well as the themes of education policy and global trade within the General Agreement on Trade in Services (GATS) and the World Trade Organization (WTO) (van der Wende 2001). This discourse has an impact on newly established competitor nations that are expanding their enrollment of international student, as well as the United States and Western Europe as leading yet declining host-nation destinations (Zachrisson 2001). The case of China exemplifies this position. In 2004, China was a leading country in terms of the numbers of students it sent overseas, with 343,126 university degree-seeking students who studied abroad annually (UNESCO 2006). In recent years, China has also emerged as a popular host nation, as demonstrated by its expanding numbers of international students, from less than 45,000 in 1999 to more than 141,000 in 2005 (McCormack 2007). Similar trends are occurring in Japan, South Korea, India, Malaysia, Thailand, and Taiwan.

Trends in Taiwan reflect traditional East Asian patterns. In the past decades, substantial numbers of university students from Taiwan studied in the United States and Britain, while very few international students chose the island nation as a host destination. Foreign students form the bridge from a nation to international society. The number of international students currently studying in Taiwan indicates the extent to which the country's system of higher education has become more international and competitive, as well as represents its ability to attract foreigners. In 2007, the total number of students (including degree-level students, exchange students, and students studying languages) reached 17,742, which is an increase of 3,263, compared to the total of 14,479 in 2006 (Ko 2008). Between 2001 and 2005, the enrollment of incoming international students from Central and South America rose by 208 percent, and from European nations by 95 percent. Students from Vietnam comprise the largest group, followed by those from Malaysia, Indonesia, Japan, and the United States. Scholars attribute the rising population of international students in Taiwan to the global popularity of Mandarin studies, the growing reputation of the country's universities as world-class institutions, and the availability of scholarships offered by the Taiwan Ministry of Education (MOE) (Ko 2008).

The Concept of Push and Pull

The examination of international student mobility trends and patterns is well established by a body of research identified with the "push-pull framework" (Fry 1984; Agarwal and Winkler 1985; Sirowy and Inkeles 1985; Cummings 1993; Altbach 1997). This research suggests that an international student's progress through developmental stages of decision making begins with a firm commitment to study internationally and ends with the selection of a host institution(s). Researchers have defined research push factors as conditions in home nations that engender interest in university education beyond national borders. Pull factors are attributes of a host nation that attract international students and affect the decision-making process for students who might study at particular institutions (Mazzarol 1998).

Agarwal and Winkler (1985) quantified pull factors for the United States as a host destination among students from fifteen developing nations. The authors noted that the percentage of international students enrolling in universities of the United States has declined in recent years. This shift was attributed to the rising cost of postsecondary education in the United States and the multitude of university program options currently available in students' home nations. This trend also involves nations that traditionally sent large numbers of students abroad; in recent years, these rising nations that offer quality postsecondary education have also become successful international centers by offering degree programs in English at a lower cost than those in the United States (Chan and Ng 2008).

In a related study, McMahon (1992) used a push-pull model to examine statistically the mobility patterns of international students from eighteen developing countries. Findings suggested that student flow was dependent on the level of economic wealth, the degree of involvement of the destination country in the world economy, and the priority placed on education by the home nation government. McMahon noted a negative correlation between economic prosperity in home countries and the volume of international student flow. Significant pull factors included the size of host-nation economies and their political interests as evidenced by foreign assistance, transnational cultural links, and the availability of international student scholarships.

In a summative study, Massarol (1998) surmised that six pull factors consistently influence students' selection of host nations and institutions. Students' overall level of knowledge about the institutions, access to information, and awareness of the destination nation represented a critical pull factor. Host institutions' reputation for quality and the recognition of their degrees in students' home nations were significant attributes of this factor. A second pull factor was the number of personal recommendations students received from parents, relatives, friends, and gatekeepers. The third factor related to financial issues, including fees and living and travel expenses, along with social costs, such as crime, safety, and racial discrimination. The presence of other students from home nations and the option for part-time work were important attributes of this factor. Additional factors included: the environment, as related to perceptions about the climate in the host country; the geographic and time difference between home and host nations; and social links, defined as family or friends residing in the destination country.

The utility of the push-pull framework is apparent in this identification of factors that affect mobility patterns and trends of university international students from developing nations. Yet in some respects, the push-pull framework compromises attention to the complexities associated with the international-student experience. There are, however, limitations in terms of the exclusion of international students from developed countries who pursue higher education in either developing or other developed nations. The design of the push-pull framework, moreover, locates the national identity of international students as a reference for commonality; this means all international students have a common notion of being from another country. Thus, international students are defined as a homogenized group rather than as clusters of individuals who have significant differences among and within their nationalities.

Critics argue that scholarship addressing the complexities of the international student experience remains on the fringe of cross-border education literature due in part to a deficit of concepts to articulate the multidimensional complexities of international students' experiences. In response, a transnational lens is offered to illuminate theoretical and critical interpretations intended to examine the "persistent pull of 'locality' as a social space of identity formation" (Smith and Guarnizo 1998, 22).

The influx of international students is mostly due to the availability of scholarships in Taiwan (Roberts et al. 2010). The MOE, the Ministry of Foreign Affairs (MOFA), the National Science Council (NSC), and the Ministry of Economic Affairs jointly set up the Taiwan Scholarship Program in 2004 to encourage promising international students to pursue undergraduate and graduate degrees in Taiwan. Pursuant to the Employment Service Act, scholarship recipients are entitled to apply for a work permit and work in Taiwan for up to one year after graduation. Furthermore, the MOE has also set up the Huayu (Chinese language) Enrichment Scholarship, which offers qualified students a monthly stipend for one year. It also subsidizes colleges and universities that offer Mandarin courses and grants scholarships to students.

Experiences before and after Coming to Taiwan

A student's choice of a host nation requires high involvement and commitment on the part of the student, due in part to the expanding options for study-abroad destinations around the globe (Cubillo et al. 2006). Today, one of the most promising aspects of Taiwan's system of higher education is the availability of scholarship opportunities for international students, which have been well established as a significant pull factor (Agarwal and Winkler 1985; Cummings 1993). The popularity of scholarships offered by the Taiwan government could in fact be viewed as a factor that has contributed to the increased enrollments of international student. International students' rationale for receiving scholarships from Taiwan has not typically been linked to financial hardship.

In many nations, international students who come there to study represent the chief source for influencing a university to become more international. As a newly emerging competitor host nation, Taiwan envisions its national system of higher education as an international center where people from around the world come to learn from each other. As such, the MOE's government-supported scholarships enhance the cultural composition of Taiwan universities' student bodies and contribute to institutional prestige (Mok and Tan 2004; Lo and Weng 2005). The immersion of international students among the Taiwanese local students represents, therefore, a pivotal objective of universities efforts to gain an international identity.

In a study conducted during the 2009–2010 academic year in Taiwan, a revised survey questionnaire by Roberts, Chou, and Ching (2010) was distributed to all international students in Taiwan through their respective international offices at their colleges and universities. A total of 648 participants who represented twenty countries completed the questionnaire. Data shows that Mandarin Chinese was the predominant first language of participants (39 percent), which would indicate that most of the international students are from countries such as mainland China, Macau, and Hong Kong, which are Chinese Mandarin-speaking regions. This percentage is then followed by students from Vietnam (Vietnamese-speaking, 10 percent), and Indonesia (Indonesian-speaking, 9 percent). Participants' second languages included English (53 percent), Mandarin Chinese (20 percent), and Malaysian (7 percent). Around 76 percent of the sample consisted of international students studying abroad for the first time. In addition, around 80 percent of the respondents are degree-seeking students, with the remaining participants being exchange program students (7 percent) and Mandarin Chinese language students (2 percent).

The study described above identified eight factors as reasons why students choose Taiwan as a host nation. While all of these factors contributed to the decision to study in Taiwan, some were significant to a majority of participants, while others applied to only a small percentage. The availability of established and highly recognized Mandarin-language programs was rated as an important factor. The significance of this factor is not surprising given that nearly all institutions of higher education that have welcomed international students offer intensive courses in the primary languages of the host nation. Nevertheless, the importance of this factor suggests that Taiwan is globally profiled as a viable host destination. The availability of the Mandarin Studies Program provided participants with a foundation in Mandarin for both social and academic mobility in Taiwan.

The survey indicated that 67 percent of participants received scholarships offered by either the Taiwan Scholarship Program (jointly funded by the MOE, the Ministry of Foreign Affairs, the Nation Science Council (NSC), and the Ministry of Economic Affairs) or the MOE Mandarin Enrichment Scholarship Program (funded by the MOE). Students may submit applications for both scholarships to overseas missions located in the students' home nations (see Table 14.1).

The popularity of scholarships sponsored by Taiwan's government could be viewed as a factor contributing to the currently expanding international student enrollments. Studies have shown that approximately 87 percent of

Table 14.1 Reasons for Choosing Taiwan as a Destination (N=648)

Items	N	Weighted scores[a]
Scholarship opportunities	240	575
Learn traditional Chinese characters	170	408
Quality of education	198	389
Future employment opportunity	194	377
Cost of living (including tuition)	163	330
Safety	104	180
Own preference	100	177
Modern city	104	176
Political situation	40	90

Note: [a]The respondents' rankings were given corresponding weights (e.g., first priority – 3, second priority – 2, and third priority – 1) before computing for the individual scores of each item.

scholarship recipients labeled themselves as either middle- or upper class, which supports the assumption that students typically do not apply for support due to financial hardship. Thirty percent of participants labeled their parents as professionals or self-employed business entrepreneurs, and they reported that around 31 percent of their parents had obtained graduate degrees.

The scholarships that Taiwan awards to its international students provide financial support for one to four years of study, and range from NT$25,000 (US$845, exchange rate around US$1 = NT$29.60; March 2011) monthly for undergraduate students to NT$30,000 (US$1,014, exchange rate around US$1 = NT$29.60; March 2011) monthly for graduate students. Thirty-two percent of participants reported that the scholarships were not sufficient for living expenses in Taiwan, and 63 percent reported that the awards provided just enough in terms of financial support. These findings suggest a tremendous discrepancy in living standards, given that newly graduated college students in Taiwan earn from NT$26,000 to NT$28,000 monthly (US$879 to US$946, exchange rate around US$1 = NT$29.60; March 2011) (CENS 2008).

With regards to their educational experiences in Taiwan, students report that the highest difficulty item for them is the application for the Taiwan visa, while the second highest difficulty item is the actual scholarship application. The third highest difficulty item is the lack of sufficient information regarding course programs. These results suggest that Taiwan should invest more efforts in enhancing its visa processing procedures for the international students who come to Taiwan. However, such improvement might be constrained by the political issues surrounding the country.

With regards to the challenges they encounter in their first few months in Taiwan, international students mentioned that the most difficult aspect is memorizing Chinese characters. The second most challenging aspect concerns the students' difficulties with social relationships in Taiwan. The third most challenging aspect is adjusting to the weather. Some international students suggest that they should be given more orientation regarding the cultural and sociopolitical issues surrounding Taiwan even before they travel to the country.

With regards to international students' difficulties with their studies in Taiwan, most students mentioned that their ability to understand professors' lessons/lectures causes them problems. This is then followed by difficulties in expressing their opinions to their professors, and difficulties in expressing or communicating in Chinese. These results suggest that international students are not properly oriented to the educational system of Taiwan. Local faculty and staff should be briefed about the study habits of the international students enrolled at their institutions as well. In this way, they can provide assistance to students.

With regards to how they choose a college or university at which to study in Taiwan, international students indicate that the power of word of mouth exerts the greatest influence. Hence, institutions should give international students who have completed their studies in Taiwan some sort of exit interview in order to gather their impressions, so as to aid in the recruitment of new international students.

Social Norms

In recent years, the concept of social capital has captured the imagination and attention of a broad range of scholars and professionals in various disciplines and practical arenas (Lin 2008). Similarly, the notion of social capital has been used to shed light on the relationship between the microlevel of educational experience and the macrolevel of social forces and structures (Burnheim 2003). Scholars have noted that the idea of social capital has expanded from an individual asset to a feature of communities and even nations (Portes 1998), generating multiple definitions, conceptualizations, and empirical measurements (Dika and Singh 2002). However, the popularity of this concept has been accompanied by increasing controversy about its actual meaning and effects (Portes 2000; Mouw 2006).

Simply put, social capital can be defined as "the investment in social relations with expected returns in the marketplace" (Lin 2002). This general definition is consistent with the works of noted scholars such as Bourdieu (1986), Burt (1992), Coleman (1988, 1990), Flap (1991, 1994), Lin (1982), Portes (1998), and Putnam (1993, 1995, 2000). During the late 1980s, education sociologists Bourdieu (1986) and Coleman (1988) both underlined the functional value of social networks and group membership as resources that can be leveraged by individuals to obtain access to other resources. In addition, both authors placed much emphasis on the role of education and, in particular, the role of the social environment in determining educational outcomes.

In an educational setting, social capital is defined as the "networks, together with norms, values, and understandings that facilitate cooperation with or among groups" (Healy et al. 2001). In a study of Australian universities, Burnheim (2003) noted that it is important to understand (1) the particular role of social capital in networks within universities, which themselves constitute capital, and (2) universities' roles in the creation of the norms, values, and understandings that enable networks to operate.

Similarly, in a mixed-method study regarding international students in Australia, Neri and Ville (2006) noted that students who possess poor social networks in unfamiliar cultural and educational institutions experience an adverse impact on their well-being and academic performance.

To further clarify the issues surrounding the network and the norms of international students in Taiwan, the following two sections shall focus on, namely: the social and the cultural norms that international students encounter in Taiwan. International students were asked about their social interactions in Taiwan, and most replied that they wanted to have more Taiwanese friends. This response is then followed by the expectation that Taiwanese students should have positive feelings towards international students. The third item is that international students try their best to make friends with local students. These top three results reflect that international students are indeed accepting of Taiwanese students as not only their peers or classmates, but their friends as well.

With regards to international students' attitudes about the norms on campus and in the classroom, the highest-ranked item is that teachers encourage interaction. The second highest-ranked item is that teachers make a special effort to help international students, and the third highest-ranked item is that that cultural differences are respected inside the educational institution.

Implications

This chapter contributes to the discourse examining the opportunities and challenges that arise from the enrollment of international students in institutions of higher learning around the globe. In its scope, it details an empirical study exploring the dispositions of international students in terms of their academic and social spheres. Universities committed to the process of internationalizing their institutions are called to address the realities—both positive and negative—of operating as globally competitive institutions. This implies that attracting the right kind of international students and determining standards for their contribution to campus life are more important goals than the total number of international students enrolled. The notion of "diploma disease," as proposed by Dore (1976), signifies this phenomenon. Dore argued that the sheer magnitude of students traveling internationally in the pursuit of advanced degrees, diplomas, or certifications has shifted the purpose and direction of higher education. Education, said Dore, is not a commercial endeavor defined by time or space, but rather the harmonious development of the physical, mental, moral, and social dimensions of life necessary for engaging with opportunities to gain both knowledge and wisdom. This stance suggests that determining the form of higher education best suited for the academic community should remain a pressing issue alongside the engagement with contemporary processes of internationalization.

The Taiwan government's efforts to develop national policies and set targets to attract substantial numbers of international students are impressive. Yet international students entering the country's universities may sometimes experience unhappiness and disorientation on arrival from their home nations. Most are successful in terms of building a circle of friends, and they grow happier over time. However, these friendships are typically with their international student peers from the same nation, which provides fellowship and empathy but limited opportunities for connections with Taiwanese students and to learn about the local culture and institutions.

Taiwan's institutions of higher education are deeply committed to increasing their numbers of international students. However, some issues need to be taken into account, such as the proper orientation for arriving and departing international students. In addition, faculty and staff should also receive proper training or orientation on how to handle issues unique to international students. The majority of international students make little or no use of formal university-sanctioned organizations widely associated with the benefits of social capital, as noted in the literature. Many of these students accept paid employment, often for long hours and with limited social capital benefits besides improving their language skills. These students could derive the benefits of social capital by committing a greater amount of time to university organizations and fewer hours to paid employment. As well, many international students report a high degree of residential instability, which disrupts both their social connections and academic study.

Scholars have argued that because many students are frequently not willing to incur the expense of international education and because the decision to study abroad is an expensive and significant initiative, it is a complex decision that demands a high level of involvement from consumers (Mazzarol 1998). This may not be the case for most participants in the current study. Some factors such as ethnocentrism, country image effect, and city image effect are discussed in the literature, and these are also factors that influence students' decisions about going abroad for to pursue postsecondary education. Several factors that work together to simplify the decision-making process of international students deserve further attention.

The emerging economic power of China has led to the recognition of the importance of learning Chinese for many (prospective) international students. Taiwan, as a democratic society, is also preferred over communist China. Some unique programs offered by Taiwan's universities often make them the only choice for international students who are interested in these fields. These factors commingle and make the decision-making process of international students not as predictable and complex as reported in the literature.

International students' level of dis/satisfaction was also influenced by language barriers, cultural understanding, and the international mentality of both the students themselves and the university (including the administrators, staffs, and faculty). The customer-orientation of the university is also debatable. Given the importance of helping international students to achieve a level of satisfaction by improving the reputation of educational institutions and recruiting high-quality faculty and students worldwide, these factors should be taken into account when building a model of the decision-making process of international students.

The availability of financial support and living expenses appears to be important enough to be singled out as an independent factor that influences the decision-making process of international students in the current study. The weight of this variable as compared to other influencing factors deserves further research in order to determine what positioning strategy Taiwan and other Asian countries should have.

In sum, this chapter examines the growth in the number of international students, and their share of total enrollments is a contributing factor to the higher-education landscape in Taiwan. It has provided an enriched and more diverse cultural experience on Taiwanese campuses, and a range of economic and social benefits for local communities. Hence, social interaction and activities should be encouraged in order to effectively enhance the social capital of all students on university campuses. The ability of international students to form social networks with local Taiwanese students, moreover, is viewed as an important element in the further enhancement of the international dimension of Taiwan's system of higher education.

REFERENCES

Agarwal, Vinod B., and Donald R. Winkler. 1985. "Foreign Demand for United States Higher Education: A Study of Developing Countries in the Eastern Hemisphere." *Economic Development and Cultural Change* 33 (3): 623–644.

Altbach, Philip G. 1997. *Comparative Higher Education: Knowledge, the University and Development.* Chestnut Hill, CT: Center for International Higher Education, Boston College, and Ablex Publishing.

Altbach, Philip G. 2003. "Why the United States Will Not Be a Market for Foreign Higher Education Products: A Case Against GATS." *International Higher Education* 31: 5–7.

Bourdieu, Pierre. 1986. "The Forms of Capital." In *Handbook of Theory and Research for the Sociology of Education*, edited by J. G. Richardson, 241–258. Westport, CT: Greenwood Press.

Burnheim, Catherine. 2003. "Networks and Social Capital in Australian Universities." Paper presented at the Trading Public Good in the Higher Education Market, Enschede, The Netherlands, July 3.

Burt, Ronald S. 1992. *Structural Holes: The Social Structure of Competition*. Cambridge, MA: Harvard University Press.

Chan, David, and Pak Tee Ng. 2008. "Similar Agendas, Diverse Strategies: The Quest for a Regional Hub of Higher Education in Hong Kong and Singapore." Paper presented at the CESHK Annual Conference, University of Hong Kong, February 23.

China Economic News Service (CENS). 2008. "Easy, Low-Paying Jobs Gain Popularity in Taiwan." Taipei: CENS. Available online at: http://www.cens.com.

Coleman, James Samuel. 1988. "Social Capital in the Creation of Human Capital." *The American Journal of Sociology* 94: 95–120.

———. 1990. *Equality and Achievement in Education*. Boulder, CO: Westview Press.

Cubillo, Jose Maria, Joaquin Sanchez, and Julio Cervino. 2006. International Students' Decision-Making Process." *International Journal of Educational Management* 20: 101–115.

Cummings, William K. 1993. "Global Trends in International Study." In *International Investment in Human Capital: Overseas Education for Development*, edited by G. Craufurd, 31–46. New York: Institute of International Education.

Dika, Sandra L., and Kusum Singh. 2002. "Applications of Social Capital in Educational Literature: A Critical Synthesis." *Review of Educational Research* 72 (1): 31–60.

Dore, Ronald P. 1976. *The Diploma Disease*. Berkeley: University of California Press.

Flap, Henk D. 1991. "Social Capital in the Reproduction of Inequality." *Comparative Sociology of Family, Health and Education* 20: 6179–6202.

———. 1994. "No Man Is an Island: The Research Program of a Social Capital Theory." Paper presented at the World Congress of Sociology, Bielefeld, Germany, July 18–23.

Fry, Gerald. 1984. "The Economic and Political Impact of Study Abroad." *Comparative Education Review* 28 (2): 203–220.

Healy, Tom, Sylvain Cote, and John F. Helliwell. 2001. *The Well-Being of Nations: The Role of Human and Social Capital*. Paris: Organisation for Economic Co-Operation and Development.

Kemp, Stephen. 1995. *The Global Market for Foreign Students*. Adelaide, Australia: University of Adelaide.

Kirp, David L. 2003. *Shakespeare, Einstein, and the Bottom Line: The Marketing of Higher Education.* Cambridge, MA: Harvard University Press.

Kishun, Roshen. 2007. "The Internationalisation of Higher Education in South Africa: Progress and Challenges." *Journal of Studies in International Education* 11 (3/4): 455–469.

Ko, Shu-ling. 2008. "International Students in Taiwan at an All-time High." *The Taipei Times*, February 12, 2008. Available online at: http://www.taipeitimes.com.

Lin, Nan. 1982. "Social Resources and Instrumental Action." In *Social Structure and Network Analysis*, edited by P. V. Marsden and N. Lin, 131–145. Beverly Hills, CA: Sage.

———. 2002. *Social Capital: A Theory of Social Structure and Action.* London, UK: Cambridge University Press.

———. 2008. "A Network Theory of Social Capital." In *The Handbook of Social Capital*, edited by D. Castiglione, J. W. van Deth, and G. Wolleb, 50–69. New York: Oxford University Press.

Lo, Y. William, and Fwu Yuan Weng. 2005. "Taiwan's Responses to Globalization: Internationalization of Higher Education." In *Globalization and Higher Education in East Asia*, edited by K. H. Mok and R. James, 137–156. Singapore: Marshall Cavendish Academic.

Mazzarol, Tim. 1998. "Critical Success Factors for International Education Marketing." *International Journal of Educational Management* 12 (4): 163–175.

McCormack, Eugene. 2007. "Worldwide Competition for International Students Heats Up." *The Chronicle of Higher Education*, November 16.

McMahon, Mary. E. 1992. "Higher Education in a World Market: An Historical Look at the Global Context of International Study." *Higher Education Policy* 24 (4): 465–482.

Mok, Ka Ho, and Jason Tan. 2004. *Globalization and Marketization in Education: A Comparative Analysis of Hong Kong and Singapore.* Cheltenham, UK: Edward Elgar Publishers.

Mouw, Ted. 2006. "Estimating the Causal Effect of Social Capital: A Review of Recent Research." *Annual Review of Sociology* 32: 79–102.

Neri, Frank, and Simon Ville. 2006. "The Social Capital Experience of International Students in Australia: The Wollongong Experience." *Economics Working Papers.* Wollongong: School of Economics, University of Wollongong. Available online at: http://ideas.repec.org.

Portes, Alejandro. 1998. "Social Capital: Its Origins and Applications in Modern Sociology." *Annual Review of Sociology* 24: 1–24.

———. 2000. "The Two Meanings of Social Capital." *Sociological Forum* 15 (1): 1–12.

Putnam, Robert D. 1993. "The Prosperous Community: Social Capital and Public Life." *The American Prospect* 13: 35–42.

———. 1995. "Bowling Alone: America's Declining Social Capital." *Journal of Democracy* 6 (1): 65–78.

Putnam, Robert D. 2000. *Bowling Alone: The Collapse and Revival of American Community*. New York: Simon and Schuster.

Roberts, Amy, Chuing Prudence Chou, and Gregory S. Ching. 2010. "Contemporary Trends in East Asian Higher Education: Dispositions of International Students in a Taiwan University." *Higher Education* 59 (2): 149–166.

Sirowy, Larry, and Alex Inkeles. 1985. "University-Level Student Exchanges: The U.S. Role in Global Perspective." In *Foreign Student Flows: Their Significance for American Higher Education*, edited by E. G. Barber, 29–86. New York: Institute of International Education.

Smart, Don, and Grace Ang. 1993. "The Origins and Evolution of the Commonwealth Full-fee Paying Overseas Student Policy 1975–1992." In *Case Studies in Public Policy*, edited by W. J. Peachment and J. Williamson, 111–128. Perth, Australia: Public Sector Research Unit.

Smith, Michael Peter, and Luis Eduardo Guarnizo, eds. 1998. *Transnationalism from Below*. Vol. 6. New Brunswick, NJ: Transaction Publishers.

Teichler, Ulrich, and Volker Jahr. 2001. "Mobility during the Course of Study and after." *European Journal of Education* 36 (4): 443–458.

UNESCO. 2006. *Global Education Digest: Comparing Education Statistics across the World*. Paris: UNESCO. Available online at: http://www.uis.unesco.org.

van der Wende, Marijk C. 2001. "Internationalization Policies: About New Trends and Contrasting Paradigms." *Higher Education Policy* 14 (3): 249–259.

Williams, Peter. 1981. *The Overseas Student Question: Studies for a Policy*. London: Heinemann Educational Books.

Zachrisson, Carl. 2001. "New Study Abroad Destinations: Trends and Emerging Opportunities." In *Study Abroad: A 21st Century Perspective, Volume II, the Changing Landscape*, edited by M. Tillman, 28–30. Stamford, CT: American Institute for Foreign Language.

Chapter 15

Reform Schemes for Students in Need

Education during Global Economic Turmoil

In January 2009, the Taiwan government announced a new initiative to allocate a total amount of NT$13 billion (US$412.4 million) in aid to assist those families hard hit by the worldwide economic downturn, in order to provide a means for students to continue their studies. The subventions plan will identify students from universities, colleges, senior high schools, and vocational high schools who are experiencing financial distress, specifically, those whose parents have been laid off and have remained between jobs for at least one month. From this point on, the Ministry of Education (MOE) will pay some school fees, including costs for lunches, for those elementary and junior high school students whose parents are on an involuntary unpaid leave of absence from work for a month or more.

In addition to the initiative mentioned above, the Ministry of Education Night Angel Illumination Program has been put in place as well to support low-income, single-parent families, orphan students, and those being raised by grandparents. Children in elementary school receive this direct assistance. This measure, which has been in effect since September 2008, focuses on public as well as private elementary schools in cities and counties nationwide, and these funds support children in need, enabling them to obtain assistance with homework after school, participate in group activities, and receive dinner in school classrooms, as well as gain admission to public libraries and other appropriate spaces for studying.

A total of 3,922 schoolchildren in 236 locations received governmental assistance in 2008. The total amount of subvention allocated for the year 2009 was NT$120 million (US$3.8 million), and it targeted a total of 7,571 children in 350 locations who benefited from the program as of June of that year. In total, the estimated number of children in need is more than 99,000, and the original budget is insufficient. Fortunately, private organizations have also recognized this distressing situation and have also offered financial support (Government Information Office 2009).

In 2002, the MOE also implemented a project entitled E-Generation Human Capacity-Building, which was part of a comprehensive six-year national development plan named Embracing the Challenges of 2008. This effort was consistent with the educational reform movements mentioned above, to instigate a shift towards a dynamic and socially responsive education system. In particular, it aimed to foster the creativity and capacity of Taiwan's young citizens so that they can be competitive in a knowledge-based international economy. The highlights of the project included fostering an international environment in schools, enhancing students' ability to master foreign languages, promoting e-learning and education in the fields of culture, arts, sports and civility, and supporting lifelong learning. Such educational reforms in Taiwan have embraced many ideas, theories, actions, experiments, and influences throughout the years.

Another plan to help children from toddler age to five years old was also established in 2008 with the aim of allowing more preschool children to enter daycares at a lower cost, which it was hoped would create more time for parents and raise the general public's willingness to have more children. According to statistics gathered by the MOE, only 32.03 percent of toddlers were enrolled in public preschool institutions in 2008, while 67.97 percent were enrolled in private ones. Establishing more government-funded kindergartens and daycares should make preschool education more accessible for all children. The 2004 and 2006 bans on teachers' authority to use corporal punishment with students, for example, represent a change in educational policies influenced by Western values, especially by the United Nations Educational, Scientific and Cultural Organization (UNICEF), which is an institution that apparently supported that practice on account of the influence of Western values. Through its education reform, Taiwan has begun to look inward, expanding policies that concentrate on Taiwan's heritage and its minority populations, in this way the micro managerial aspect of education reforms.

With the emerging impact of global warming all over the world, natural disasters and sustainable development have also become a major concern as Taiwan has encountered drastic ecological changes. Due to Taiwan's geographic location in the Pacific Rim, it faces major typhoons almost every summer, and consequently, students and schools from those devastated remote areas suffer the most. Moreover, the 921 Earthquake in 1999 also caused severe damage, and many schools faced extensive destruction. In response to these hardships, volunteer groups, nonprofit organizations, and religious organizations, such as the 921 Earthquake Relief Foundation, Tzu Chi, and the Church of Jesus Christ of Latter-day Saints in Taiwan worked together to rebuild the buildings and raise funds for school materials. Contributions from the government, private organizations, and individuals also played a significant role in the rebuilding of damaged areas. Furthermore, many campuses have been renovated and transformed into environmentally friendly sites, which has pioneered a new movement in school construction that aims for sustainable development.

Support for Minority Education

As Taiwan has followed the worldwide trend of globalizing its education system, local responses have also emerged as part of the transformational process in education that the country has experienced in the last decade. One of the unique challenges facing Taiwan is the status of minority populations, such as aboriginal children and children of foreign spouses, who are most vulnerable to unequal educational opportunities, Approximately five hundred thousand aboriginal people live in Taiwan. In school year 2008, their rate of enrollment at the elementary school level was 99.22 percent, the rate at the high school level and below was 85.88 percent, and the rate of enrollment in postsecondary education was 41.46 percent (compared to 84.30 percent in the general population). A 2009 poll of the aboriginal population over fifteen years of age showed that 85.88 percent of all aboriginal people have a level of education at or below high school and vocational school. This significantly lower enrollment rate for aborigines is often linked with family or economic problems, along with difficulty fitting in at school as members of a minority.

Another minority group is foreign spouses, of whom close to 430,000 from all over the world, but mainly from China and Southeast Asia, were living in Taiwan in 2009. Many of these women married into a Taiwanese family for financial reasons, and after their arrival in Taiwan, they frequently face difficulties adjusting to the social environment, understanding the culture, learning the national language, and finding jobs. Children born into families in which one spouse is foreign are often confused about their own nationality and torn between family members, because some families treat foreign spouses poorly and do not see them as an essential part of the family (Zhang 2004). As a result, aboriginal children and those raised by foreign spouses are at a disadvantage, as they face not only discrimination but also other problems, such as a more complicated family structure, a lifestyle different from that of the general public, and economic difficulties. The government has take several steps to respond to their needs, such as setting up aboriginal resource centers, aboriginal education programs, counseling services for foreign spouses, educational counseling programs for the offspring of foreign spouses, and so forth (Zhang 2006). However, the effect of these programs may be limited, and they require further research to determine their efficacy.

Another localization feature of Taiwanese education is the implementation of indigenous-language education. Other than the national language, which is traditional Mandarin, the most widely spoken languages in Taiwan are Min Nan, Hakka, and aboriginal languages, and they have recently been included in the elementary school curriculum. Once banned in schools during the initial Kuomintang (KMT) occupation in order to promote a unified national identity, Min Nan, which is spoken by the largest population in Taiwan, the Hoklo (or Hokkien) people, is still widely used in Taiwan today.

Hakka, spoken by the Hakka people, is relatively less prominent compared to Min Nan, as the Hakka population is much smaller in Taiwan. Other than these two main ethnic groups, Taiwan also has a large variety of aboriginal people (with a population of 458,000 as of 2006), with fourteen tribes that are officially recognized by the Taiwanese government. Of the roughly 23 million Taiwanese people, around 15 million could speak Min Nan as of 1997, and 2.37 million could speak Hakka as of 1993 (Lewis 2009). Since 2003, elementary school students in grades one through six have been required to take language lessons at school in one of the three main indigenous languages: Min Nan, Hakka, or an aboriginal language. Once students enter junior high school, indigenous languages become an elective course. Now, indigenous languages have spread, and there are television programs and broadcasting stations that use indigenous languages, such as Hakka television, the Chinese Television System's Min Nan News, and Taiwan Indigenous Television, which gives students the opportunity to practice these languages they learn at school.

Due to the multiple political, social, and cultural influences in education mentioned above, the country has paid less attention to some of the risks and conflicts related to the process of globalization and localization in the field of education. In the case of the language policy in Taiwan's education system, there has been increasing concern over the declining language proficiency and literacy of Taiwanese primary students in Chinese and Mandarin. The number of teaching hours that were allocated to the Chinese curriculum in the past has been reduced from one-half to one-third across primary and secondary school sectors.

The trend toward localization presents Taiwan with a great predicament, as its case is different from that of developing countries around the globe, whose national identities are mostly filtered through the experience of Western subjugation. Taiwan is confronting a cultural identity problem (Taiwanese versus Chinese) that could split the country into two (Chou 2008). At present, it is most important for Taiwan to participate in the process of globalization and internationalization, and at the same time to reduce the possibility of conflict relating to cultural identity in education as well as other aspects of society.

REFERENCES

Chou, Chuing Prudence. 2008. *Mr. President: How Are You Going to Deal with Education in Taiwan?* Taipei: Psychology.
Government Information Office, 2009. *Mainstream Education*. Taipei: Government Information Office. Available online at: http://www.gio.gov.tw.
Lewis, M. Paul. 2009. *Ethnologue: Languages of the World*. 16th ed. Dallas, TX: SIL International.
Zhang, Bi-Ru. 2006. *Reflection on Issues Related to Foreign Spouses and Multiple Culture Education*. Taipei: Ministry of the Interior. Available online at: http://sowf.moi.gov.tw.
Zhang, Fang. 2004. "Who Cares about Foreign Spouses and Their Children?" *Central Daily News*, Taipei. Available online at: http://cdnews.com.tw

Chapter 16

Cross-Strait Relationships between Taiwan and China

Development of the Cross-Strait Exchanges

The Taiwan cross-strait relationship has been highly politicized since 1949, when the Kuomintang (KMT) government withdrew from China to Taiwan. But the process of educational exchange has made enormous progress as the result of globalization initiatives. The year 1987 played a significant historical role in cross-strait relations, because not only did Taiwan lift martial law in that year, but it also granted permission for her aging soldiers, who had been drafted by the armed military forces from China during the civil war, to visit their families in China. Hence, the cross-strait relationship entered a new era in terms of communication.

Concerning student exchange programs, in November 1987, Taiwan loosened its policy over Chinese visitors, especially for those overseas and distinguished professionals who wished to visit Taiwan. Since 1990, Taiwan has granted more access to Chinese citizens who have made contributions in fields such as academia, culture, sports, mass media communications, and the arts. Moreover, in 1993 Chinese professionals and students were allowed an additional step forward—to pay a visit to Taiwan for educational and cultural purposes. According to statistics, 18,907 Chinese students visited Taiwan officially between January 1, 2002, and October 31, 2009, but statistics are lacking about the reverse visits, and it was expected that many more Taiwan students would be visiting China during their summer and winter vacations. We can therefore see that the data from

Taiwan's side is significantly skewed against the data of its counterpart, China. Furthermore, Chinese graduate students pursuing research who were sponsored by Taiwan were granted a period of from one month to a year to live in the country. The annual quota was less than 200 students per year in the past. Since 1996, Chinese graduate students have been able to apply for a full scholarship of up to three months to conduct research related to a thesis at local universities in Taiwan. Beyond that, more than 235,591 Chinese professionals in the cultural and educational sectors, out of a total of 2,712,572 Chinese visitors in 20 categories, traveled to Taiwan during 1988–2009.

A Leap Forward to University Accreditation and Overseas Schools

In the fall of 2010, Taiwan passed a law that would, under strict regulation, require its institutions of higher education to start recognizing the diplomas from forty-one top Chinese universities and colleges, and to accept Chinese students into the country's postsecondary education system, a step that has generated mixed responses from the public due to political reasons and a fear of competition in the job market (*China Post* 2010).

The Taiwanese government has opened schools in Vietnam's Ho Chi Minh City, Indonesia's Surabaya City and Jakarta City, and Malaysia's Seberang Perai and Kuala Lumpur, as well as China. While Taiwan is opening up to the world, the world is also learning about the culture of Taiwan. As the world begins to pay more attention to Chinese culture and Mandarin, along with the rise of the Chinese economy and its soft power, the Chinese have opened overseas Confucius Institutes that happen to be inspired by the German model of the Goethe Institute and the Alliance Françoise from France. In 2010, China geared up 320 Confucius Institutes with over 337 Confucius Classrooms in over 96 countries, with a vast number of more than 230,000 registered students worldwide. China also aims to open up to one thousand Confucius Institutes by 2020 (Siow 2011). Under the pressure of competing with the Chinese to preserve the Chinese culture and language, the Taiwan government proposed to establish "Taiwan Academies" worldwide, starting with New York, Los Angeles, and Houston (Tsai 2010). The goal of such institutes is to promote the culture of Taiwan with Chinese characteristics by boosting the traditional Chinese language and research and development (R&D) in Taiwan, and, it is hoped, disseminating traditional Chinese language-teaching resources and language tests and examinations, and establishing a Chinese citation database in the future (Shih 2011).

Concerning the Role of Education

According to the Mainland Affairs Council in Taiwan, increasingly liberalized approaches to cultural, educational, and academic exchanges have played a strategic role in facilitating Taiwan's cross-strait interactions and greater understanding between Taiwan and China. Academic exchanges are widely carried out, particularly in the form of conferences and visits by researchers or scholars. Among the important features of Taiwan's and China's reform policy are, first, Taiwan undertook a vigorous approach to regulating visiting scholars and students from China, and a loose approach to encouraging its own scholars and students who wished to travel to the mainland. China, on the other hand, welcomed scholars and students from Taiwan, but set strict regulations on its own scholars and students who visited the island. Both governments' conservative approaches to cross-strait academic exchange limited the frequency and scope of the two countries' interactions to prevent the admission of those groups or individuals whose visits were politically sensitive.

The Taiwan government also conducted a strict check of visiting Chinese scholars' political backgrounds, conference or research themes, periods of stay, and entry process into Taiwan. Chinese scholars were required as well to go through lengthy application processes across different authorities, and comply with strict regulations set by the Taiwan Affairs Office of the State Council. For its part, the Chinese government, although it encouraged academic exchanges, retained power over its own scholars' expression of opinions and required their political discipline during their stay in Taiwan.

Secondly, strict regulations regarding application procedures and special consideration based on political mechanisms, such as preferential treatment from government officials, had been established in Taiwan and the People's Republic of China (PRC) during the late 1980s and early 1990s. In October 2003, however, a new legal mechanism was introduced in Taiwan to enhance cross-strait educational exchanges and academic cooperation between the two countries.

Third, both Taiwan and China undertook approaches to foster and encourage cross-strait academic exchanges, in the form of allowing students and in some cases scholars to pay mutual visits, providing exchange opportunities, and expanding the scope and depth of exchanges. In Taiwan, such exchanges are mainly private and backed with resources and support from a nonprofit fund established by the government. The fund, called the Chinese Development Fund, was established by the Mainland Affairs Council under the Executive Yuan to promote and foster the development of cross-strait relations and civilian exchanges through the allocation of resources from the private sector. Applications are open to university faculty, researchers, graduate students, students affiliated with a special mission group, professional organizations, and so on. Meanwhile, Chinese cross-strait exchanges are carried out primarily within government authorities. It is argued that the rationale behind these different funding sources is due to the politically sensitive nature of Taiwanese affairs in China, coupled with the lack of an autonomous private sector there (Chou and Ho 2007).

Finally, academics in Taiwan and mainland China have played different roles in these cross-strait exchanges. Taiwan regards such exchanges as relatively neutral, with a growing emphasis on academic dialogue and policy debates. In China, however, academia may be viewed as the surrogate through which government authorities implement and promote political agendas and which may affect China's research autonomy (Chou, 2009).

Taiwanese Schools in China

The effect of the process of globalization on the Taiwanese education system can be clearly observed. Since Taiwan joined the World Trade Organization (WTO) in 2001 and signed the Economic Cooperation Free-Trade Agreement (ECFA) with China in 2010, the opening of trade between the two countries has led to the creation of a number of Taiwanese schools in China that cater to the children of Taiwanese businessmen working in Chinese companies, such as the Taiwan Businessmen's Dong-guan School, the Shanghai Taiwanese Children School, and the Hua-Dong Taiwan Businessmen's School. An estimated of seventeen hundred K–12 students were enrolled in these two schools in 2010, which are operated by retired Taiwanese principals, teachers, and local staff. Curricula and textbooks are all imported from Taiwan as well, which represents a breakthrough in relations between Taiwan and China (Cross-Straits Training Web 2009).

Taiwanese Students in China

Students in Taiwan were banned and discouraged from admission to mainland China's higher-education system in the past. Cooperation between Taiwanese and mainland Chinese scholars was also inhibited due to some legislative restrictions. Records show that the first Taiwanese student who went to study at a Chinese university did so in 1979, at which time the Chinese instituted reforms in their economy (Chou 2002). By the mid-1980s, the Chinese government granted more and more universities in the cities of Beijing, Shanghai, and Kwangtung permission to recruit not only students from overseas but also from Hong Kong, Macau, and Taiwan.

During that time, the majority of those students majored in three areas: (1) specializations related to traditional Chinese subjects, such as Chinese literature, history, philosophy, religion, music, archeology, and anthropology; (2) management and business subjects required to work in the field of trade with China: law, finance, trade, and business; and (3) medical sciences related to the practice of medicine: Chinese medicine, and so forth.

It is estimated that nearly twenty thousand Taiwanese students graduated from universities in China and then encountered an accreditation problem at home when Taiwanese institutions would not accredit their Chinese diplomas. Consequently, many of them chose to work in China, moved to other countries, or found jobs in the private sector in Taiwan. In contrast, Chinese authorities, realizing the value of China-educated Taiwanese, started to lift labor restrictions and allow Taiwanese students to work in China permanently.

The Initiative of Educational Exchanges

The MOE announced an act in 1996 that regulated and reviewed the pact that Taiwanese schools had signed with their Chinese counterparts after being approved by the government of Taiwan and China. These regulations apply to approximately 1,420 cases of cross-strait educational and cultural collaboration, and they extend the amount of time that university students from the mainland can remain in Taiwan for research and study purposes.

With respect to academic exchange, according to university law, a university can initiate co-teaching with Chinese professors in Taiwan. Thus more than six hundred Chinese faculty members taught part-time in Taiwan between 2002 and 2009, but Chinese universities also recruited a handful of prestigious Taiwanese faculty members in business with an offer of handsome salaries. Competition between Taiwan and China for professional talent still exists, which has created one of Taiwan's greatest concerns about academic brain drain, and consequently, one of the solutions is the initiation of flexible salaries, as noted in the previous chapter.

Setback Leap of Time for Local Identity

The Taiwan-China cross-strait relationship experienced several ups and downs over the last few decades that would be ascribed to the two countries' different regimes and political ideologies. For instance, in 1997 the MOE intended to grant accreditation to Chinese universities. However, after announcing the legislation that would recognize the diplomas of seventy-three Chinese universities, the MOE immediately corrected itself and the plan was called off by the Control Yuan. Later, influenced by the trend of mutually recognizing the diplomas of most countries, which has been part of the move toward globalization, Taiwan was forced to review the case of Chinese accreditation and passed a law in 2011 to certify forty-one universities in China.

In addition, during 2000–2008, when the Democratic Progressive Party (DDP) administration was in power, President Chen, a pro-Taiwan independent, opposed the one-China policy that mainland China had proposed. During Chen's presidency, there was a lack of legislation that forged cross-strait academic exchanges and cooperation. President Chen, therefore, decided to halt cross-strait relations through the so-called de-Sinization (de-Chinization) policy. First, in 2005, the civil exams were refocused on Taiwanese local history rather than Chinese history, and guidelines for the new high school curriculum were shifted from Chinese history to world history, rather than traditional Chinese history as domestic history. The proportion of Chinese classics in the literature curriculum was decreased and so forth. The attempt to replace Chinese cultural bonds with the local identity of Taiwan was emphasized much more than before. The government highly promoted awareness of local culture and heritage and language in the form of a self-determination initiative.

China University Accreditation

In brief, consultations related to the cross-strait relationship rely on the principle of "easier issues come first, and those are the economic and trade discussions," among which cultural exchanges are in fact the best lubrication in facilitating a constant and stable cross-strait relationship. Such exchanges include the protection of copyright, official visits between the two cultural and educational departments, and academic activities such as conferences and research cooperation.

Unlike President Chen, President Ma (his successor) undertook a pro-China approach, which has helped to facilitate cross-strait academic exchanges and cooperation. For example, in 2010 the Ma government added amendments to the Act Governing the Relations between Peoples of the Taiwan Area and the Mainland Area (兩岸人民關係條例) and the University Act (大學法). These amendments entitled Taiwanese universities to recruit students from mainland China, echoing the Ma government's long-term strategy of developing higher-education institutions (HEIs) in Taiwan into a hub of advanced learning in East Asia (*University World News* 2011). Specifically, in order to ease shortages of university students and enhance mutual communication among the younger generations, after a series of long debates over whether Chinese students should be granted the right to study in Taiwan, the legislature approved a bill in fall 2010 that would admit China's high school graduates and the top university graduates to Taiwan's HEIs. The annual quota of Chinese students admitted to Taiwan can only account for less than 1 percent of the total university student population in Taiwan (approximately two thousand) the first year, which is 2011.

There are forty-one universities in China, including Peking University, Tsinghua University, Renmin University, and Beijing Normal University (MOE 2009), and they are all on the list to be accredited by Taiwan in 2011. Furthermore, according to the MOE, sixty-seven universities will be granted the right to enroll 1,123 Chinese students, while sixty-five technology colleges can admit 877, in the first year, in accordance with an annual quota of 2,000 set by the government. Students from coastal high schools and forty-one prestigious universities are the targeted population for Taiwan's universities and graduate schools (*University World News* 2011). According to a research survey of one hundred Chinese students who visited Taiwan, most students express a positive opinion about their stay, and the longer they remain in the country, the better the impression they have of Taiwan. It is hoped that this educational exchange will eventually be open to more primary and secondary students and that universities in Taiwan will accredit mainland China's universities as well.

In sum, Taiwan has approved the accreditation of Chinese universities with some limited conditions. Meanwhile, since China's population base is sixty times larger than that of Taiwan, China's Ministry of Education has recognized Taiwan's university diplomas.

The Cross-Straitization of Education: The Global and the Local Complex

Taiwan has been faced with identity conflicts, whether during the period when it was under Japanese colonization (1895–1945), followed by the re-Sinicization after World War II, or during the de-Sinicization era under the Lee and Chen regime (1988–2008). Taiwan's constant striving for national identity goes beyond the conflicts it has encountered due to troublesome cross-strait relations and the tensions of globalization and localization, however. Unlike its counterparts with different policies, such as the former East and West Germany, North and South Korea, Israel and the Arab world, and even the United States and the Soviet Union during the Cold War, Taiwan and China have developed an unprecedented relationship via ongoing cultural and educational exchanges coupled with economic cooperation over the last two decades. In this process, Taiwan as a whole, drawing on traditional Chinese culture and with the power of its intellectuals behind it has begun to shape a national identity that is not only multifaceted and dynamic but also is emerging with some uncertainty in Taiwan. It will be worthwhile to see how education in general plays a role in defining Taiwan's identity, especially through civic education (Wilde 2005).

Civic Education and Self-Identity

A 1999 study, the International Association for the Evaluation of Educational Achievement (IEA), sponsored by the Civic Education Study (CES), assessed German eighth graders to evaluate the importance of conventional citizenship participation among teenagers: 1) democracy, democratic institutions, citizenship; 2) national identity and international relations; and 3) social cohesion and diversity. The participants ranked poorly in the IEA Civic Education Study, which included samples of students in the modal grade for fourteen-year-olds (a total of about ninety thousand students from twenty-eight countries). Though, in contrast to another less satisfactory result of PISA (Program for International Student Assessment) in 2000 which aroused many social controversies as "the German PISA-Shock" and it turned out to note great reviews of the German educational policies, CES abides with a low profile in Germany, as its society remains in a transitional stage of building cohesive national identity upon reunification between the East and West Germany since 1990 (Gruber 2006).

In the case of Taiwan, there have also been instances of a struggle to define its identity that has occurred along with the processes of globalization and localization. In 2009, Taiwan (also referred as Chinese Taipei) participated in an IEA study of civic and citizenship education (International Civic and Citizenship Education Study) with other thirty-seven countries around the world, and the results showed the overall scores of Taiwanese teenagers (fourteen years old) ranked fourth out of thirty-seven countries. On several questions regarding "trust in national government, political parties, media, schools, and people in general" the participants scored much lower than the average, however. In particular, almost three-quarters of Taiwan secondary students stated that they did not believe in political parties or their message or their system overall (Schulz et al. 2010). Clearly, there is an obvious sense of distrust among fourteen-year-olds for political institutions in Taiwan. These relatively low scores suggest that Taiwan's teenagers deserve a more detailed analysis to understand this situation

The Confucianism Lineament

While Taiwan and China deal with the cross-strait relationship, some questions remain, including "Is the Confucian social hierarchy really capable of *contributing* to the economic balance in China?" and "Does Confucian civility affect Chinese hyper competitiveness, including education?" (Bell 2008). Many Chinese visitors to Taiwan, including high-ranking officials and scholars, have come to the conclusion that the island has made a greater effort and accomplished more than their Chinese counterparts in preserving the Chinese culture and Confucian heritage in the field of education. Therefore, the Chinese leadership began to promote ancient Confucian values in contemporary China, which is currently undergoing a dramatic socioeconomic transformation. In addition to economic incentives, can commonly shared Confucian values bring Taiwan and China closer, especially when increasing numbers of the younger generation from both countries are now allowed to attend the same schools or to visit each other? In terms of Confucian belief, singing and having fun with friends fosters "social trust," which consequently carries over to social harmony (Bell 2008).

Can the ongoing relationship between Taiwan and China go beyond the existing framework of globalization and localization and develop into a unique model of "cross-straitization," which prioritizes cultural and educational exchange and then creates more acceptable forms of communication based on mutual respect and understanding? "Friendly manners to all with steady principles and believes always in mind" would this serve as a standing ground to any rival parties? Another important belief to take into account is: "The counterpart empathizes and cooperates as needs be, but does not jeopardize its principles and beliefs to any extent" (Confucian principle).

A Bettor or a Foe?

According to a popular poll (National Policy Foundation 2010), the Taiwanese people currently believe that in the cross-strait relationship: (1) it is very unlikely that any immediate war will break out; (2) a state of "moderation" still exists in "social, political, economic and trade" endeavors; and (3) there is still "tension or competition" in military and foreign affairs. It is clear that relations between the cross-strait partners still have room for improvement. Both Taiwan and China cannot deny the political reality of separation over the last five decades, though they share a common history, culture, and language.

The sharing of the Confucian belief in the "inclusive and diverse: civilization of coexistence" might be a good place to start for citizens in the Taiwan and China, especially since the signing of the ECFA, through which Taiwan can reach out to the world officially via China, and, in reverse, China can learn from the Taiwanese about the soft power of freedom and democracy (National Policy Foundation 2010). As Hao (2010) indicated in his book entitled *Whither Taiwan and Mainland China: National Identity, the State, and Intellectuals*, people in mainland China and Taiwan have throughout time been able to control the image of their national identities, and this phenomenon is still apparent today. Thus, among the uncertainties that remain between these two countries regarding education include: Will education eventually bring China and Taiwan into closer communication and exchanges between faculty members, students, and visitors? Is the education system in Taiwan likely to be a key element in this process? Will the transformation of China not only influence the shaping of Taiwan's self-identity, but also enhance the growth of the new Chinese identity in the era of globalization?

Since 2009, the word *Chiwan*, created by the Korean media, has become popular due to increasingly frequent business communication and cultural cooperation between the two countries on either side of the Taiwan Strait. This new trend of close ties represents the formation of two complementary communities. Long before the creation of this term, citizens and the various parties in Taiwan seemed to accept the fact that it was inevitable that economic and educational interaction between China and Taiwan would come first, before any political issue (Liu 2010). The future of Taiwan-China relations still cannot be predicted, but an ongoing and improved relationship between the two nations in the field of education will definitely be advantageous to both sides and the region overall (Kuo 2009).

In brief, in the process of globalization and localization, "Taiwan and China have always been in charge of maneuvering their own identities"

(Hao 2010). As the younger generations of future leaders from the cross-strait countries are anticipated to have more common interests as a result of their educational and economic contacts, they are likely to compromise on their political differences and devise solutions to promote peace between both sides.

REFERENCES

Bell, D. A. 2008. *China's New Confucianism: Politics and Everyday Life in a Changing Society*. Princeton, NJ: Princeton University Press.
China Post. 2010. "Taiwan Will Not Recognize Chinese Diplomas Retroactively." *The China Post*, Taipei 2010. Available online at: http://www.chinapost.com.tw.
Chou, Chuing Prudence. 2002. *The Tips for Studying in Mainland China: Taiwan students in the PRC*. Taipei: Cheng Chung.
———. 2009. "Academic Exchange between Taiwan and China: A Preliminary Result of National Taiwan University." Paper presented at the Cross-Taiwan Strait Talk on Education Conference, National Cheng-Chi University, Taiwan, October 24.
Chou, Chuing Prudence, and Ai-Hsin Ho. 2007. "Schooling in Taiwan." In *Going to School in East Asia*, edited by G. Postiglione and J. Tan, 344–377. New York: Greenwood.
Cross-Straits Training Web. 2009. *More and More Children of Taiwanese Businessmen Studying in China*. Yun Cheng Consulting, Taipei 2009. Available online at: http://ilearning.tw.
Gruber, Karl-Heinz. 2006. "The German 'PISA-Shock': Some Aspects of the Extraordinary Impact of the OECD's PISA Study on the German Education System." *Oxford Studies in Comparative Education* 16 (1): 195–208.
Hao, Zhidong. 2010. *Whiter Taiwan and Mainland China: National Identity, the State, and Intellectuals*. Hong Kong: Hong Kong University Press.
Kuo, Yi-Hsiung. 2009. *The Prospective of Cross-strait Cultural and Educational Exchange*. National Cheng-Chi University, Taipei 2009. Available online at: http://www.ppf.nccu.edu.tw.
Liu, Frank. 2010. *Taiwan Foundation for Democracy*. Taiwan Foundation for Democracy, Taipei 2010. Available online at: http://www.tfd.org.tw.
Ministry of Education (MOE). 2009. *MOE towards the Opening of Schools to Mainland Chinese Students*. Taipei: MOE. Available online at: http://www.edu.tw.
National Policy Foundation. 2010. *Using Educators as a Way to Opened up Cross-Straits Interactions*. National Policy Foundation, Taipei 2010. Available online at: http://www.npf.org.tw.
Schulz, Wolfram, John Ainley, Julian Fraillon, David Kerr, and Bruno Losito. 2010. *Initial Findings from the IEA International Civic and Citizenship Education*

Study. International Association for the Evaluation of Educational Achievement, The Netherlands 2010. Available online at: http://www.iea.nl.

Siow, Maria Wey-Shen. 2011. *China's Confucius Institutes: Crossing the River by Feeling the Stones*. East West Center, Washington, DC. Available online at: http://www.eastwestcenter.org.

Shih, Hsiu-chuan. 2011. "Taiwan Academies to Open First in the US." *Taipei Times*, August 5. Available online at: http://www.taipeitimes.com.

University World News. 2011. "Taiwan: New plan to boost foreign student numbers." *University World News*, May 29. Available online at: http://www.universityworldnews.com.

Tsai, Xin-Hua. 2010. "Competition between Cultures: Taiwan Academy to Enter America. Webs-TV, Taipei, 2010. Available online at: http://n.yam.com.

University World News. 2011. *Taiwan: Recruitment of Chinese Students Begins*. Higher Education Web Publishing, London 2011. Available online at: http://www.universityworldnews.com.

Wilde, Stephanie. 2005. *Political and Citizenship Education*. Oxford: Symposium Books.

Chapter 17

Conclusion

When the seventh, and last, National Education Conference was held in 1994, an atmosphere of change was developing in Taiwan society, which was due to the liberation of both the political and the economic environment. The whole society was demanding the deregulation, democratization, liberalization, and diversification of education.

Almost two decades later, the status of the education system both in Taiwan and abroad has changed in many ways. A global society has arrived earlier than expected due to the rapid development of information technology. Higher-education authorities worldwide have begun to focus on nurturing international personnel and are concerned with the flow of and the competition for transnational human resources. As *Education at a Glance*, published by the Organisation for Economic Co-operation and Development (OECD) (2009) reveals, most countries tend to pay the greatest amount of attention to the output of students' employability through education. Moreover, they claim that an education system should take responsibility for improving learners' effectiveness and efficiency.

The European Union (EU) has taken also many steps to improve the systems of higher education in their member states, such as reinforcing academic exchanges and strengthening the international vision and employability of students. What is more, innovative proposals, such as the National University Administration Corporatized and University Consolidation, have been approved in Japan. There are also the BK21 project in South Korea, the 211 project and the 985 project in China, and projects like the Program for Promoting Academic Excellence in Universities (PPAE), the Aiming for the Top University and Elite Research Center Development (ATU) and Teaching Excellence plans in Taiwan.

As Thomas Friedman indicated, "The world is flat" and with the effects of global warming, the need for environmental protection, the rule of law, and transnational culture have become common topics in most countries (Friedman 2005). As the influences of globalization reach everyone, major changes are seen throughout society. Taiwanese has faced plenty of problems in the last decade, such as demographic changes (a low birthrate and an aging population), the migration of industries to offshore locations (China in particular), a rising unemployment rate, an excess number of universities and colleges awaiting consolidation or to be closed down, an urgent need for transnational personnel following the upgrade and transformation of industry, a debate on national identity and ideology in education, problems related to educational opportunities and cultural inheritance for social vulnerable groups, the distribution of educational resources, a plan for twelve-year compulsory education, an imbalance of supply and demand of qualified teachers in primary and secondary schools, and so forth (Chou 2008).

In the effort to respond to Taiwan society's eagerness for education reform and to implement the government's innovations in education policy, the Ministry of Education (MOE) convened the eighth National Education Conference in August 2010 to gather the wisdom and experience of citizens in order to make a blueprint for Taiwan's education system for the next ten years (2011–2020). During 2011, Taiwan (ROC) entered its centenary, in which nine-year popularity education has been in existence for more than 40 years, enrollment rate of school-age children goes beyond 99.9 percent, postsecondary education opportunity rate goes to 100 percent, higher education's expansion tends to popularity, illiteracy rate of students over fifteen-years-old drops down to 2.09 percent, and education budget to GDP ratio reaches 6.51 percent by 2010 (MOE 2010a).

Education policy aims to no longer focus on quantity but quality in Taiwan. While Europe and the United States have suffered from the global financial downturn since 2008, Taiwan, which regards education as the foundation of the country, has announced, in contrast, a substantial increase in its education budget, revealed a new vision of the national infrastructure called the Golden Decade, and formulated six directions for development in the future, that is, innovation, culture, environmental protection, constitutional politics, welfare, and peace ("Building Up Taiwan" 2011).

Social Transition and Challenges in Education

Taiwan is still encountering the following social changes that create challenges in the area of education (MOE 2010b).

The Rise of the Internet Age

With the rapid development of the Internet, it has become cheaper and more convenient to get information. The Internet has not only expanded people's visions but also altered the traditional school system. The rise of the Internet offers adults a great opportunity to study for life, while on the other hand, it helps schools to offer courses designed according to individualized requirements and multiple intelligences. Therefore, with the rapid transition to a global society, the Internet has become an important medium to reinforce e-learning and interconnections of many kinds (especially relating to social and informative connections), and improving information flow and social agendas among students.

The arrival of the virtual world and cloud networks have not only provided more accessible information via the Internet, but have also resulted in various problems, such as a network subculture that has appeared among teenagers and that deviates from the mainstream. Moreover, the addiction to the Internet, which is a serious digital indulgence among students, has divided parents, teachers, and students. In particular, moral education is more important than ever. The challenge of how to educate the next generation in such a complex environment deserves more creative and unconventional policies in the field of education.

The Emergence of a Low Birthrate and an Aging Society

In recent years, Taiwan's population structure has changed into a heterogeneous one with a low birthrate and an aging population, factors that will eventually have a great impact on the country's economic, social, and educational development. The birthrate has dropped, from 410,000 newborn babies in 1981, to 270,000 in 1998, to 191,000 in 2009, which is the lowest level in the last fifty years. Many schools (especially in the remote areas) have found themselves confronted with serious problems related to the need to lay off teachers and shut down schools. Universities will face a series of institutional closures or mergers in 2016, when the first wave of members of a declining population reaches college age (Hu 2010). In addition, among this younger generation, according to statistics of the MOE (2010a), children of foreign nationality and those who have one Chinese parent account for nearly 10 percent of the total student population, and 3 percent at the lower secondary level in Taiwan (MOE 2011).

Furthermore, in 1993, the population ratio of the elderly, those over sixty-five years old, surpassed 7 percent for the first time. Since then, the percentage has grown gradually each year, and it will reach 20 percent in 2026. It is clear that the aging of the population will be related to a rising rate of dependency and will place a burden on society. Under such circumstances, the Taiwan school system and its educational resources need to be adjusted and reconfigured so that they are more suited to a changing society.

Impact of the M-Shape of Education Development

With the transition of Taiwan's domestic economic and social structure, phenomena such as an uneven distribution of regional resources, varied teaching quality in various schools, and differences in students' ability to learn in urban versus rural areas have been found to exist in the educational sector, too. Moreover, those vulnerable social groups that are influenced by economic factors or family status (for example, single parents and grandparents) have become important reasons for the M-shape of educational distribution, according to the Japanese writer Ōmae Ken'ichi (1990). Children who have grown up in such environments are usually subjected to poverty and crime due to the lack of cultural capital and role models. As the family structure declines and is transformed in Taiwan, an integrated task force will be needed that can collaborates with various government departments, such as those in education, social welfare, healthcare, and the police, to provide support to these at-risk children.

Challenges Related to Climate Change and Environmental Sustainability

Over the last ten years, Taiwan has been hit by a series of natural disasters, such as the devastating 921 Earthquake of 2000 and an unexpected typhoon, and the 88 Wind Hazard in 2009, which caused serious destruction to educational facilities, especially in the most remote and disadvantaged regions (MOE 2009). According to the World Bank's Natural Disaster Hotspots—A Global Risk Analysis (Arnold 2005), Taiwan is one of the areas of the world where natural disasters occur most frequently. Thus, more educational awareness is required to enhance citizens' understanding of global climate change and the balanced coexistence of economic development and environmental protection.

In particular, sustainable development is the focus of the United Nation's plans for (UN) educational development in 2005–2014 (United

Nations 2011). Therefore, authorities at all school levels have to consider how to integrate the concept of "sustainable development" into the existing school curriculum and instruction as one of the core competencies to raise students' level of literacy in this area.

Critical Issues Confronting Taiwan's Education Development

The general public in Taiwan has many concerns related to education. Heavy pressure associated with high school and university entrance exams still exists on school campuses, and students suffer from the double pressure of academics and finances (supplementary education). With gang members invading campuses, incidents of bullying, drug abuse, and the violation of rules arise more frequently. Though Taiwan's students at the primary and secondary levels continually win prizes in international academic contests, including the Programme for International Student Assessment (PISA) and the Third International Mathematics and Science Study (TIMSS) and Olympia, most students study without much curiosity and show little interest in outside reading.

As result of Taiwan's declining birthrate and the oversupply of teachers, the teaching profession can now recruit only a very limited number of professionals, a practice that will eventually impair the circulation of fresh blood from the younger generation. Since the textbooks were privatized, curriculum design now lacks pilot studies or experiments, and textbooks contain more pictures than text and content with opposing ideas. As increasing numbers of students come from diverse backgrounds, ethnically and economically, more in-service training and awareness programs based on a multicultural context are needed.

As Taiwan's birthrate declines, public and private universities have been encountering a shortage in student enrollment. Universities' self-positioning and institutional classification should be taken into consideration, as well as an action plan for university consolidation or merging. Furthermore, with the coming of an aging society, the establishment of a lifelong learning society is needed. Schools at all levels should reinforce the establishment of a lifelong learning network and incorporate it into their programs, especially in universities and adult continuing educational institutions. In accordance with the MOE's organizational restructuring in 2012, it will be necessary to revise laws and regulations, as well as staff training in order to adapt to the new challenges facing this department.

Prospective Education Policies for the Next Generation

According to the MOE, the prospective policies, based on four core values, will be incorporated into the education system and blueprinted as the major action plan for future generations in Taiwan (MOE n.d.). The four core values include: delicacy, innovation, justice, and sustainability. The education policies linked to these values are as follows:

1. The Twelve-Year Basic Education and Public Subsidy for Preschool Education

A plan to implement twelve-year basic education has long been a topic of discussion and the expectation of many citizens in Taiwan. Based on the principles of "exemption from entrance exams, free tuition, and noncompulsory," this policy, expected to launch in 2014, will serve as the locomotive of a new age of education reform in Taiwan. In addition, addressing the trend of the low birthrate, the government has determined, after a long and heated discussion about integrating kindergarten and nursery schools, that they will remain intact and gradually be replaced by free tuition for five-year-old children and an education allowance for those under four years old. By the government providing this, children can enjoy an affordable, diverse, nearby, and high-quality preschool education.

2. Promotion of National Literacy and Health

Due to the social transition resulting from networking and the forces of globalization, modern citizens must possess much more literacy. For example, for students, except for the basic skills and core competency necessary in this new age, should be educated in school about morals, law and regulations, human rights, gender equity, ecology and the environment, safety and disaster prevention, and become literate in technology and media, and art and aesthetics.

3. Respect and Care for Diverse and Vulnerable Groups

The population in Taiwan is composed of diverse groups. The aboriginal culture, the local Taiwanese culture, traditional Chinese culture, and the culture of new immigrants must all coexist with each other. Thus, more effort is required on the part of the education system to integrate people of different cultures and backgrounds into a new Taiwanese identity.

4. Restructuring the Education System and Resources

Along with the governmental restructuring process, new relationships between the MOE and other related government agencies are emerging in this new era. There is a demand for a more responsive and dynamic educational and school administration. As for educational resources, a more transparent and accountable budget allocation scheme is expected in order to narrow the gap between public and private, and urban and rural schools.

5. Cross-Strait and International Exchanges and Overseas Chinese Education

More international resources will be channeled into and more overseas students introduced to local campuses across all levels of education in the near future. In particular, with the moderation and improvement in cross-strait relations, cultural and educational exchanges will also gain in popularity. As for education overseas in China, the Taiwan government's policies will continue to encourage more recruitment of Chinese students by providing work opportunities for them.

6. Teacher Education and Professional Development

To ensure teacher quality, a teacher evaluation system will be implemented to optimize the quality of teachers at the primary and secondary levels.

7. Lifelong Study and a Learning Society

Promoting lifelong study and establishing a learning society will be a crucial policy for the coming new era. Issues such as upgrading the lifelong study network and establishing a lifelong study support system are also essential to this policy.

Above all, the implementation of twelve-year basic education in 2014—a step toward a new milestone—will become the most important education policy since nine-year popular education was put into effect in 1968. Education for the "cultivation of the whole person, the value of life, respect for diversity, and a focus on international and lifelong learning" will be the core policy that will be promoted in the future (Mo 2012, 416). This blueprint of the future development of the system of education (as shown in Figure 17.1) not only outlines the direction of Taiwanese education but also shows the world how Taiwan is dealing with the issues of globalization and localization through cross-stratization policies in the coming new age.

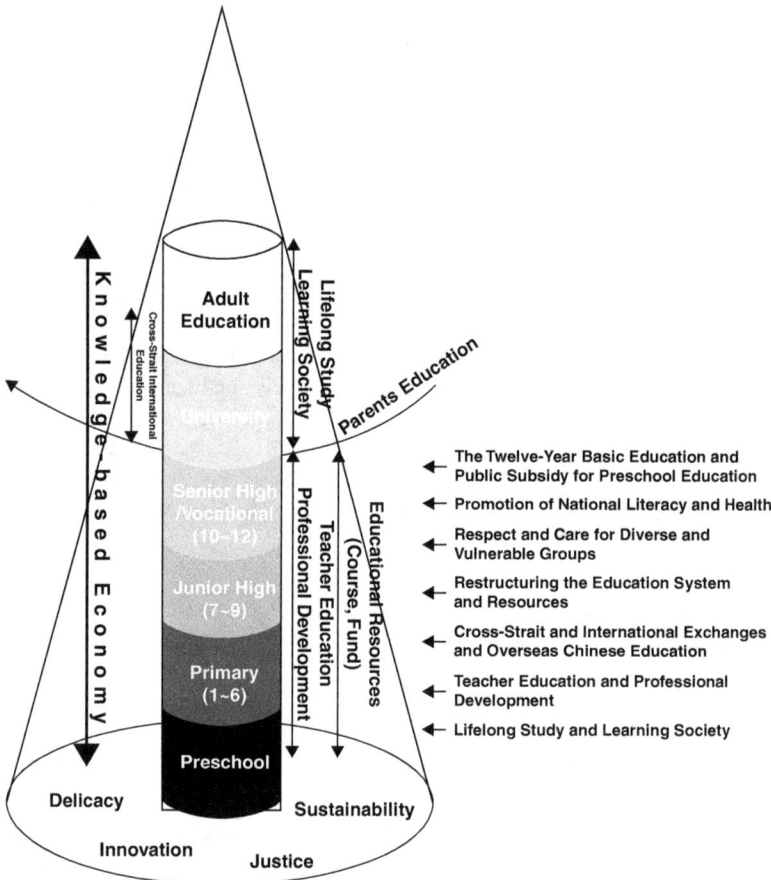

Figure 17.1 Blueprint of Future Education Development.

Wobbling between the Old and New

Taiwan's education system represents an integration of Confucian culture, capitalism, and state authoritarianism. As members of a Confucian society, Taiwan's parents highly value the education of their children as the key to their future success and personal fulfillment. Influenced by Western capitalist ideology, especially the neoliberal principles in practice since the 1980s, the market mechanism as well as deregulation and competition have been embedded in education reform policies over the last two decades.

The modern education system also retains vestiges of Japanese colonial influence in the form of state authoritarianism and education value. The current Taiwanese education system supports a period of twenty-two years of formal education. In particular, nine-year compulsory education, introduced in 1968, requires students to compete in order to proceed to the next higher level in the education system. A twelve-year basic education plan will be put into action in 2014. The education system has undergone a number of controversial reform programs and experienced some unexpected policy consequences, and it is in the process of becoming diversified, democratized, pluralized, and liberalized as Taiwan transforms in the ongoing process of globalization and internationalization.

The education system has been successful in terms of key indicators such as student enrollment rates, percentages of graduates admitted to the next higher level of education, and students' high scores on international mathematics and science tests (such as the Third International Mathematics and Science Study (TIMSS) (Fang 2004; International Association for the Evaluation of Educational Achievement (IEA) 2008; Lin 2004) and the Programme for International Student Assessment (PISA) (Taiwan PISA National Center 2010). However, achievement in quantitative terms is insufficient in determining the overall effectiveness of Taiwan's education system. Education in Taiwan has been criticized by some for placing too much stress on students' test scores which are in favor of rote memorization (Chou and Ho 2007). Furthermore, Pan and Yu (1999) pointed out that "the normal development of individuals has been distorted, and schools have become preparation institutions for high schools and colleges" (76). In order to address these issues, citizens in Taiwan began to engage civic organizations to facilitate educational reform activities, as did academic scholars and the Ministry of Education (MOE). Change and transformation have thus become the main characteristics of educational development in Taiwan.

Educational reform in Taiwan encompasses a mixture of ideas and multidimensional demands for a robust education system. As the literature suggests, reform activities in the field of education have mainly dealt with deregulation, equality of educational opportunity, the opening of teacher-education programs, reform of the school system, reduction in school and class size, multiple ways of recruiting students, and the privatization of textbook markets. Other education-reform areas include curriculum reforms related to economic and cultural globalization, and emphasis on information and communication technology and English as transnational skills (Law 2004). Reformers are also struggling to strike a balance between enabling institutions to become more international in scope and outlook and honoring local customs and traditions (Yang 2001).

When Globalization Meets Localization

Ideological conflicts that result from these processes of globalization and localization are also inevitably to be found behind education reforms in Taiwan. The country has strived to look beyond the Japanese colonial influence and the alienation it once felt due to the influence of a China-oriented nationalism over the past few decades in order to build up its own national and cultural identity. The recent nine-year integrated curriculum reform attempts to increase the number of materials that contain local history, geography, culture, and the arts at every level of schooling. In addition, as more and more calls to respect social pluralism and the cultural diversity of all the ethnic groups in Taiwan have been heard, a variety of Taiwanese dialects (and possibly the inclusion of foreign-spouses' mother tongues in the future) have become part of the required courses at the primary level, as compared to the former favoring and monopolization of Mandarin in the school curriculum before 1987. It is obvious that local or indigenous forms of knowledge and values are much more recognized in the recent education reform (Yang 2002).

Overall, the current shortfalls in Taiwan's education system include the government's tight education budget and its ineffectiveness in making educational investments. Since the budget for each school is difficult to obtain from regional governments, schools must follow the national government's policies in order to compete for budgets, severely hindering public schools' ability to develop in terms of their individual uniqueness. There is also a shortage of educational supplies and skilled teachers due to the low budgets, and the extreme variations in income that exist among members of the Taiwanese public mean that education also faces such extremes: the rich and more developed districts gain more money in their budgets to improve their schools, but the poor districts have no chance in competing for funds. This situation is the same for students: families with a better financial background have the power to send their children to cram schools, raising their grades and improving their chances of being admitted to a better school, but families with less financial power do not have the ability to compete with the well-off families.

The Unfinished Business in Education

From a global perspective, many questions remain unanswered. What have Taiwan schools accomplished after more than a decade of educational reform? Has students' examination stress lessened? Has the quality of education improved? Are students healthier and happier? Has parents' faith in schools increased? Do we need to reevaluate some controversial educational policies, such as the Basic Competence Test (for junior high school students), college entrance examinations, nine-year compulsory education, designated textbooks, and an excessive number of universities?

Without a doubt, education in Taiwan has its advantages. The recent education reform may still need further evaluation, but it has triggered public attention to education, which has in turn made schools and teachers more enthusiastic. Moreover, the high value that Taiwan has traditionally placed on education means that parents are more than willing to invest in their children's education, and that education is very accessible, resulting in a society with very low illiteracy and drop-out rates. Taiwan also has a beautiful, diverse natural landscape and a highly developed transportation system, creating many opportunities for outdoor lessons and field trips. Last, there has been a wave of immigrants to Taiwan recently, which has not only made the society more diverse, but also raised the general public's awareness of minority populations and human rights (Chou 2008).

The Global Mindset for the New Generation

Just as tensions and conflicts between globalization and localization have arisen in many countries, education reform in Taiwan also faces new challenges. The fundamental issue in the course of this worldwide trend in education is how to find a balance between these two, sometimes conflicting principles. Education should not only be limited to the construction of knowledge, but the forging of the transformation of values and attitudes in students' and teachers' outlooks should also play a key role.

The country has taken the initiative in this by offering English in primary schools, initiating systems of credit transfer between universities at home and abroad, creating interuniversity and international programs, increasing the budget for academic exchanges, raising the quality of its universities to world-class status, and so forth. All of these efforts will eventually facilitate students in broadening their mind-set and acquiring new knowledge as well preparing them to become global citizens.

Taiwanese Culture with Chinese Characteristics

Efforts to localize the education system cannot be separated from the global trend of education reform, especially in terms of the process of forming a self-identity and increasing the national prosperity of Taiwan. It is important for Taiwan to embrace the world with an open-arms attitude while maintaining its own traditions and national identity, and especially to educate future generations in this regard. In the present decade, probably the only solution to resolving the ideological conflicts in the reforming of Taiwan's education system is to help the Taiwanese people to appreciate their own cultural roots while enabling them to position themselves in the global village. A clear cultural self-identity can serve as a milestone in the process of achieving global understanding and respect for different world cultures and civilizations.

Nevertheless, there are currently conflicts that have the potential to entrap education reformers and that need special attention in order to lead to the successful achievement of such a harmonious integration. Today, the issues that Taiwan is experiencing in terms of administration and exploratory research are still in a very early stage of development.

Also, moving to a paradigm shift towards internationalization through a restructuring mindset strategy, or by immediate changes tackled directly in the roots of the aforesaid issues, heritage, culture, and system of beliefs that archaically encompass and withhold the key for independent development, are all barriers that Taiwan needs to go through. It is also believed that the Taiwanese education system needs to break through its current "inward" approach in delivering curriculum and instruction, its alienation in the global diplomatic relationships, coupled with the impact of its often over-emphasis on domestic news coverage, which may inadvertently lead to an isolationist mindset. The challenge of overcoming the personal inner mind-set dilemma on dealing with heritage and historical beliefs, relies heavily on education reforms that help restructure bureaucratic barriers that are often inevitable in the global era. In order to keep up with modern globalizing trends, much change is needed in education. Hence, the current education system and the results of its reforms in the last decade are clear evidence of this need and ability to meet the challenges of the future.

The Next Move for Cross-Straitization

Another key factor for the forthcoming changes that the nation aims to achieve in the following decade is to enhance education exchanges and economic collaboration opportunities with neighboring countries, especially by strengthening the ongoing cross-straitization process with China. Succinctly, the cross-strait relations in education and cultural exchanges should be used as a threshold or doorway for Taiwan to start reaching the acceptance and respect it desires in the world. This effort by Taiwan to achieve global recognition takes place in a variety of aspects, including the economy, technology, diplomatic relations, and self-identity. Education is the key to future development that will facilitate Taiwan's sustainable coexistence with China and the rest of the world.

References

Arnold, Margaret, Maxx Dilley, Uwe Deichmann, Robert S. Chen, and Arthur L. Lerner-Lam. 2005. *Natural Disaster Hotspots: A Global Risk Analysis.* Washington, DC: World Bank. Available online at: http://www.worldbank.org.

"Building up Taiwan, Invigorating Chinese Heritage." 2011. *China Times*, February 5. Available online at: http://www.wantchinatimes.com.

Chou, Chuing Prudence, and Ai-Hsin Ho. 2007. "Schooling in Taiwan." In *Going to School in East Asia*, ed. G. Postinglione. New York: Greenwood.

Chou, Chuing Prudence. 2008. *Mr. President: How Are You Going to Deal with Education in Taiwan?* Taipei: Psychology.

Fang, Tai-Shan. 2004, Sept. 26. Current Youth Science Education Activities in Taiwan. Paper presented at the **3rd Beijing APEC Youth Science Fair, Teacher's Forum, September 26**. Available online at: http://icho.chem.ntnu.edu.tw.

Friedman, Thomas, 2005. *The World Is Flat.* New York: Farrar, Straus & Giroux.

Hu, Chin-Huei. 2010. "Consolidation of Universities Will Reach a Peak in 5 Years." *Liberty Times*, December 12. Available online at: http://www.libertytimes.com.tw

International Association for the Evaluation of Educational Achievement (IEA) 2008. *TIMSS Advanced 2008*. Herengracht, The Netherlands: IEA. Available online at: http://www.iea.nl.

Law, Wing-Wah. 2004. "Translating Globalization and Democratization into Local Policy: Educational Reform in Hong Kong and Taiwan." *International Review of Education* 50 (5-6): 497–524.

Lin, Pi-Jen. 2004. *The Mathematical Achievement of Fourth Graders of Taiwan in the TIMSS 2003 Field Test.* The National Science Council Grant Report. Hsinchu, Taiwan: National Hsin-Chu Teachers College. Available online at: http://www.iea.nl.

Ministry of Education (MOE). 2009. *MOE to Subsidize More Than 5,000 NT Dollars to Sudents Injured during Typhoon Morakot.* Taipei: MOE. http://english.moe.gov.tw

―――. 2010a. *Education in Taiwan 2010–2011.* Taipei: MOE.
―――. 2010b. *Report Addressed at the Legislation Yuan.* Taipei: MOE. Available online at: http://www.edu.tw
―――. 2011. *Statistics of Foreign Spouses Offspring in Compulsory Education.* Taipei: MOE. Available online at: http://www.edu.tw
―――. n.d. *Chart of Educational White Paper.* Taipei: MOE. Available online at: http://140.111.34.34
Mo, Yan-chih. 2012. Ma unveils education plan aimed protests. *Taipei Times*, April 26. Available online at: http://www.taipeitimes.com.
Ōmae Ken'ichi. 1990. *The Borderless World: Power and Strategy in the Interlinked World Economy.* New York: Harper Business.
Organization for Economic Co-operation and Development (OECD). 2009. *Education at a Glance.* Paris: OECD.
Pan, Hui-Ling, and Chien Yu. 1999. "Educational Reforms with Their Impacts on School Effectiveness and School Improvement in Taiwan, R.O.C." *School Effectiveness and School Improvement* 10 (1): 72–85.
Taiwan PISA National Center. 2012. *Rankings.* Tainan, Taiwan: Taiwan PISA National Center. Available online at: http://pisa.nutn.edu.tw.
Yang, Shen-Keng. 2001. "Dilemmas of Education Reform in Taiwan: Internationalization or Localization?" Paper presented at the Annual Meeting of the Comparative and International Education Society, Washington, DC, March 14–17.
―――. 2002. *Theories of Science and the Development of Education Science.* Taipei: Psychology.
United Nations. 2011. *Education for Sustainable Development (ESD).* New York: United Nations. Available online at: http://www.unesco.org/en/esd/

Index

Academia Sinica, 69, 71–73, 190
Ad-hoc Council on Education
  Reform, 40
Adult Education, 80, 282
Alternative Education, 30, 79, 125
American "six-three-three-four"
  system, 3, 24, 55, 56, 73
Association of Southeast Asian
  Nations (ASEAN), 51

Buxiban, 164–166, 168

Children's Reading Movement, 70
Citation index, 72, 191, 197, 199–200,
  221–225, 233–234
Civil education reform, 28
Civil Society, 52–53
Cold War, 48, 270
Commission for Promoting Education
  Reform, 41
Confucian Culture, 55, 282
Confucian Tradition, 4, 44, 60
Control Yuan, 16, 18, 268
Cram School, 62, 79, 125, 127, 134,
  142, 150–152, 164–168, 284
Credential, 44, 55–56, 59, 60, 69, 83,
  134, 137, 164, 167
Cross-straitization, 269, 271,
  286–287

Democratic Progressive Party, 13,
  61, 268

Deregulation, 5, 6, 29–30, 34–35,
  39–41, 50, 63, 95, 100, 199, 200,
  275, 282–283
Discrimination, 169, 246, 360
Diversity, 30, 34, 39, 51, 144, 183,
  232, 270, 281, 284

Economic Framework Agreement
  (ECFA), 14, 51, 266, 272
Education Basic Law, 26, 32, 35, 39,
  43, 70–71, 99, 101
Education Evaluation, 38, 186, 206,
  227–228
Education Reform, 4–5, 28, 30–33,
  40–44, 47–50, 55–58, 60, 63,
  69–70, 72, 81, 94, 104, 110, 139,
  141–143, 155, 167, 183, 230, 258,
  276, 280, 282–286
Educational Opportunity, 61–62, 283
Empowerment, 30, 39, 41
Equity, 33, 37, 43–44, 50, 53, 60–62,
  123, 226, 229, 280
Examination system, 21, 44, 55,
  58–60, 62, 115, 137
Examination Yuan, 16–18, 95
Excellence, 21, 30–32, 34, 38–39,
  42, 44, 107, 112, 152, 184–185,
  190–191, 196–197, 203, 214,
  222, 231, 238, 275
Executive Yuan, 16, 18, 31, 37, 41,
  67–68, 109, 153, 265
Extension Education, 82–83

Family Background, 62, 125, 141, 178–179
Family Value, 42, 51, 53, 118
Five-year Fifty Billion–Aiming for the Top University and Elite Research Center Development Plan, 38–39, 197
Formosa, 11–12, 22–23
410 Education Reform Movement, 70

Gender Equity, 33, 37, 43, 60–61, 280
General Consultation Report for Education Reform, 40, 42
Global Westernization, 1
Globalization and Localization, 2, 4, 56, 67, 92–93, 148, 174, 258, 260, 270–272, 281, 284–285
Government Structure, 15, 164
Grading competition, 63

Higher Education Expansion, 174–175
Higher education institutions (HEIs), 2, 6–7, 27, 29–30, 62, 77, 81–82, 91, 106–107, 111–112, 145, 169–172, 174–178, 183–184, 190–193, 195–196, 199, 202, 205–207, 209–211, 213–215, 221, 230, 269

Indigenous, 3, 13, 33, 37, 43, 62, 81, 89, 92, 94–95, 148, 235, 260, 284
International Education, 83, 209, 252, 282
Internationalization, 27, 34, 41, 45, 57–58, 67, 83, 91, 93, 186, 195, 197, 205–215, 252, 261, 283, 286

Judicial Yuan, 16–18
Junior Colleges and Institutes of Technology, 77

Keju Examinations (Imperial Examination System), 21–22, 25, 36
Knowledge-based Economy, 2, 154, 176, 185
Korea's BK21 Program, 49, 275
Kuomingtang (KMT), 3, 12–15, 26, 28, 57, 59, 69, 96, 124, 260, 263

Lee Yuan-Tze, 40
Legislative Yuan, 16, 18, 32
Lifelong Learning, 30–31, 38–39, 41–43, 70, 75, 81–82, 89, 93, 174, 258, 279, 281–282
Local Government, 15, 18–19, 35, 49–50, 63, 99–100, 108–110, 158

Market Economy, 5, 48
Martial Law, 5, 7, 13, 15–16, 27, 29–30, 40, 57, 70, 171, 195, 229, 263
Massification of Higher Education, 2, 51
Ministry of Education Organization Act, 68
Modernization, 40–41, 47, 52, 54
Multiculturalism, 57, 94, 125, 135
Multiple entrance programs, 32, 34, 36
Multiple Ways, 30, 35, 283

National Education Reform Review Conference, 31
National Identity, 3, 26, 56, 93, 94, 96, 206, 212, 246, 247, 260, 270, 272, 276, 286
National Science Council, 16, 72, 191, 199, 229, 246
National University of Administrative Corporation, 49
NGO, 52, 75, 198
Nine-year compulsory education, 26, 55, 75, 85, 90, 101, 125, 131, 145, 283, 285
Nine-year Integrated Curriculum, 34, 38, 146, 284

INDEX 291

Patriotization, 56
Politics, 15, 24, 27, 28, 132, 276
Postcolonial, 25, 229
Postmodern, 48
Provincial Government, 18

Republic of China, 3, 11, 12, 15, 19, 26, 28, 33, 43, 52, 57, 95, 265
Resource Allocation, 49, 123

School Day, 115, 117, 121, 126–127, 129, 132, 134, 140, 148
Schooling in Taiwan, 136
Science Citation Index (SCI), 72–73, 188, 191, 197, 199–202, 221–223, 225, 227–233, 235, 237–238
Shadow Education, 130, 164, 179
Sino-Japanese War, 12
Social Education, 18, 67, 68, 80, 81, 119
Social Science Citation Index (SSCI), 72–73, 188, 191, 197, 199–202, 221–223, 225–233, 236–238
Social transformation, 40, 54, 192
Special Education, 68, 71, 74, 78, 99

Taiwan Educational System, 28, 34, 36, 38, 41, 55, 59, 92, 117, 119, 120, 145, 146, 148, 169, 249
Taiwan Social Science Citation Index (TSSCI), 199
Taiwan Strait, 11, 14, 52, 272
Taiwanization, 3, 57, 95
Teacher Act, 35, 37, 39
Teacher Education Law, 35, 39, 163
Teacher-student ratio, 86, 103
Teaching Excellent Project, 39
Textbooks, 3, 4, 28, 32, 34, 35, 37–40, 42, 57, 63, 68, 89, 91, 94–96, 135, 142, 167, 266, 279, 283, 285
Treaty of Shimonoseki, 12
Twelve-year, 32, 39, 55, 105, 155, 276, 280–283
211 Project and 985 Project, 49, 275
228 Incident, 26, 57, 228

University Act, 35, 39, 171, 185, 186, 188, 205, 269
University Education Reform, 28

GPSR Compliance

The European Union's (EU) General Product Safety Regulation (GPSR) is a set of rules that requires consumer products to be safe and our obligations to ensure this.

If you have any concerns about our products, you can contact us on

ProductSafety@springernature.com

In case Publisher is established outside the EU, the EU authorized representative is:

Springer Nature Customer Service Center GmbH
Europaplatz 3
69115 Heidelberg, Germany